TRANSNATIONAL REPRESSION AND EXPLOITATION OF NORTH KOREAN WORKERS IN RUSSIA

REVISITING CONDITIONS AMID SANCTIONS AND GEOPOLITICAL TENSIONS

UNIQUE KIM

Transnational Repression and Exploitation of North Korean Workers in Russia: Revisiting Conditions Amid Sanctions and Geopolitical Tensions

Author: Unique Kim

Publisher: Database Center for North Korean Human Rights

Phone: +82-2-723-6045

Fax: +82-2-723-6046

E-mail: info@nkdb.org

Website: en.nkdb.org

Copyright © 2025 by Database Center for North Korean Human Rights.

All rights reserved.

No part of this book may be reproduced in any form or by any electronic or mechanical means, including information storage and retrieval systems, without prior permission from the author and publisher.

ISBN 979-11-90000-57-4

ACKNOWLEDGEMENTS

This report would not have been possible without the invaluable contributions of fifteen North Korean escapees who entrusted us with their stories of working in Russia. Their testimonies shed light on the human rights realities of North Korea's labor export program, giving voice to the tens of thousands who remain subject to systematic exploitation and transnational repression. Their courage in coming forward inspires our continued efforts to pursue accountability for the injustices endured by the North Korean people, both within and beyond the country's borders.

We extend our deepest gratitude to Valerie Gabard and Nurul Azmi of UpRights; Svetlana Gannushkina of the Civic Assistance Centre; Nataliya Sekretareva of the Memorial Human Rights Defense Centre; Anton Sokolin of NK News; and five other experts who have chosen to remain unnamed. Their insights—as human rights lawyers, investigative journalists, and former North Korean officials—have been instrumental in grounding this report in international human rights and labor law, contextualizing it within the current geopolitical landscape, and unpacking the command structure of the North Korean state apparatus.

We are also proud to acknowledge the contributions of our interns—Jungheun Yang, Laura Demeulnaere, and Megan Van Stensel—who joined us from Turkey, France, and the United States to support our work, including this research. Their dedication reflects the spirit of a growing global movement for North Korean human rights.

Finally, we express our sincerest appreciation to the Embassy of the Netherlands in the Republic of Korea for funding this project. The

Embassy's support has been vital at every stage—from our research implementation to our efforts to raise awareness and advocate for accountability for the abuses documented herein.

CONTENTS

EXECUTIVE SUMMARY	7
1. INTRODUCTION	15
1.1 Subject and Rationale of Investigation	15
1.2 Geopolitical Context of Investigation	17
1.3 Methodology and Scope of Investigation	21
2. HISTORY OF NORTH KOREA'S LABOR EXPORT TO RUSSIA	29
3. CONTEMPORARY ARCHITECTURE OF NORTH KOREA'S LABOR EXPORT PROGRAM	35
3.1 Role of the Labor Export Program in North Korea's Court Economy	35
3.2 Strategic Drivers of the Military-Economic Complex	37
3.3 Workers' Party of Korea as the Apex of Command	41
3.4 Cabinet as the Formal Economic Apparatus	44
3.5 Military as an Ad Hoc Economic Apparatus	48
3.6 Front Lines: Aliases and Operations in Russia	51
4. PROCEDURAL ASPECTS OF NORTH KOREA'S LABOR EXPORT TO RUSSIA	57
4.1 North Korea's Recruitment and Selection of Workers	59
4.2 Russia's Admission and Documentation of Workers	67
5. ONSITE MANAGEMENT AND WORKING CONDITIONS	81
5.1 Onsite Management: A North Korea Outside the North Korean State	82
5.2 Exploitative Working Conditions	85
5.3 Use of Violence at Workplace	90
6. LIFE OUTSIDE OF WORKPLACE	95
6.1 Housing and Privacy	95
6.2 Access to Food and Basic Necessities	97
6.3 Movement, Information, and Communication	97
6.4 Ideological Indoctrination	100
7. PROCESS OF REPATRIATION AND REINTEGRATION INTO NORTH KOREA	105
7.1 Standard Reentry and Reintegration Process	105
7.2 Forced Repatriation	107

7.3 Repatriation of the Injured and Deceased	108
7.4 Impact of the COVID-19 Pandemic on Ability to Return	109
8. APPLICATION OF INTERNATIONAL HUMAN RIGHTS AND LABOR LAWS	113
8.1 Hierarchy of Domestic and International Obligations	113
8.2 Escalation From Forced Labor to Servitude and Enslavement	118
8.3 Web of Accountability: State and Corporate Responsibility	127
9. CONCLUSION	137
9.1 Synthesis of Findings on the Post-Sanctions Context	137
9.2 Policy Recommendations	139
Bibliography	155
Appendix 1a. Treaty on Comprehensive Strategic Partnership (Russian Original)	165
Appendix 1b. Treaty on Comprehensive Strategic Partnership (English Translation)	177
Appendix 2a. Agreement on the Temporary Labor Activities of Citizens of One State in the Territory of the Other State (Russian Original)	187
Appendix 2b. Agreement on the Temporary Labor Activities of Citizens of One State in the Territory of the Other State (English Translation)	197
Appendix 3a. Agreement on the Transfer and Receipt of Illegal Entrants and Residents (Russian Original)	205
Appendix 3b. Agreement on the Transfer and Receipt of Illegal Entrants and Residents (English Translation)	219
Appendix 4a. Regulations on External Economic Projects (Korean Original)	231
Appendix 4b. Regulations on External Economic Projects (English Translation)	237

EXECUTIVE SUMMARY

North Korea's deepening military alliance with Russia—cemented by the 2024 Treaty on Comprehensive Strategic Partnership and the unprecedented deployment of North Korean troops to Ukraine—has transformed its long-standing labor export program into a militarized apparatus serving the state's geopolitical and strategic objectives. What began as a scheme to generate hard currency has evolved into a system of state-sponsored exploitation with global security implications. This report investigates the contemporary conditions of North Korean workers in Russia, arguing that the program represents one of the world's most severe and institutionalized forms of transnational repression.

In late 2017, United Nations Security Council (UNSC) Resolutions 2375 and 2397 were adopted to dismantle this program by prohibiting new work authorizations and mandating the repatriation of all workers by December 2019. The sanctions were intended to sever a key financial lifeline for North Korea's illicit weapons of mass destruction (WMD) program. However, this report finds that the North Korean and Russian states, in a deliberate effort to circumvent UN sanctions, engineered a new, more opaque system of labor trafficking. This state-led evasion strategy has perversely exacerbated the human rights crisis for the tens of thousands of North Korean workers who remain in Russia.

Based on in-depth interviews with fifteen North Korean escapees who worked in Russia post-2017, expert consultations, and an extensive review of legal and public records, this report documents how North Korea and Russia have institutionalized a sanctions-evasion scheme primarily through the fraudulent use of student and tourist visas. As of mid-2025, an estimated 15,000 North Koreans continue to work in Russia under these illicit arrangements. This shift into informal and clandestine channels has been codified by Russian domestic law, notably a 2020 amendment allowing foreign students to work without separate permits, and is facilitated by a network of corrupt officials, quasi-private intermediaries, and complicit Russian educational institutions.

The main findings of this investigation are as follows:

- **Systematic Sanctions Evasion**: The shift from work visas to student visas has created a new ecosystem of corruption. North Korean companies now strike deals with Russian universities, paying tuition and bribes to secure visa sponsorships and fabricate attendance records. In cases where these partnerships cannot be arranged, workers are instructed to use photocopies of student visas issued to others, leaving them entirely undocumented. These undocumented workers are particularly vulnerable to extortion by Russian police, who solicit bribes to overlook their visa irregularities. Meanwhile, companies that do secure university partnerships pass the costs of tuition and bribes down to the workers through inflated wage deductions. This scheme has been further institutionalized through quasi-private intermediaries like the Intergovernmental Migration Center, which connects the North Korean embassy, local universities, and Russian employers while extracting commission fees. The widespread use of fraudulent or duplicated documents renders official visa data unreliable and obscures the true scale of North Korea's labor presence in Russia.

- **Impact of Sanctions on Human Rights**: The informal and opaque student visa scheme has made workers significantly more vulnerable to abuse. First, they bear the financial burden of tuition and broker fees, while their irregular status discourages them from reporting abuse or seeking essential aid, including emergency medical care, for fear of being classified as immigration offenders. Moreover, with North Korean firms barred from formal subcontracting under sanctions, workers are pressured to secure informal employment to meet strict remittance quotas. In navigating this shadow economy, they become exposed to harassment and exploitation by local police and labor brokers.

- **From Forced Labor to Servitude and Enslavement**: The conditions endured by North Korean workers comprehensively meet all eleven of the International Labour Organization's (ILO) indicators of forced labor, including deception (e.g., no employment contracts), retention of identity documents, withholding of wages (e.g., up to 90% of earnings seized), abusive living and working conditions, and restriction of movement. Under international legal frameworks, this systematic exploitation escalates beyond forced labor. Jurisprudence from bodies like the European Court of Human Rights (ECtHR) defines servitude as an aggravated form of forced labor characterized by a profound loss of personal autonomy and the inability to change one's condition—a precise description of the workers' situation. While Russia withdrew from the ECtHR in September 2022, the Court retains jurisdiction over violations that occurred on Russian territory prior to this date. Moreover, because the North Korean state exercises "powers attaching to the right of ownership" over its workers, as defined by Article 7 of the Rome Statute of the

International Criminal Court, these practices meet the legal threshold for the "crime against humanity" of enslavement. These abuses amount to violations of *jus cogens* norms, including the prohibitions against slavery and forced labor, and implicate both North Korea and Russia under binding international law.

- **The Military-Economic Complex**: Under Kim Jong Un, the labor export program has become deeply integrated into a military-economic complex. The pursuit of nuclear development has justified the diversion of conventional military resources into economic operations. Military units, including those linked to the WMD program through the Workers' Party of Korea's Second Economic Commission, are dispatched as workers to self-fund their operations, blurring the lines between civilian and military personnel and directly linking their labor to the state's strategic objectives.

- **Russia's Breach of Positive Human Rights Obligation**: Under international law, Russia bears a positive obligation to protect all individuals within its jurisdiction from human rights abuses. This report finds that Russia's conduct goes beyond negligence and amounts to active complicity in North Korea's abuses against its overseas workers. By facilitating the student visa scheme, dismissing credible allegations of abuse, and formalizing the transfer of defectors through a 2016 bilateral agreement, Russian authorities have entrenched their role in North Korea's architecture of transnational repression and exploitation. They have even permitted abductions of North Korean defectors by North Korean authorities on Russian soil. Thus, Russia may be regarded as complicit under customary international law, as reflected in the International Law Commission's Articles on the Responsibility of States for Internationally Wrongful Acts.

Thus, this report concludes not only that the sanctions narrowly focused on security have failed to dismantle North Korea's labor export system but also that the sanctions evasion tactics employed by Russia and North Korea have entrenched its most exploitative features. The evidence demonstrates that human rights cannot be treated as peripheral to security concerns. On the contrary, protecting the rights of North Korean workers—ensuring control over earnings, possession of identity documents, and freedom of movement—can undermine the state's ability to extract foreign currency, weaken the apparatus of coercion that sustains the regime, and reduce the incentives for illicit networks that facilitate sanctions evasion. In this sense, the fulfillment of human rights is not only a moral obligation but also a pathway to diminishing the structural conditions that threaten global peace and security.

Building on this understanding, the report offers policy recommendations to address the intertwined human rights and security challenges posed by North Korea's labor export program. These recommendations are directed to the Russian state, the North Korean state, Russian companies, and the international community. Taken together, they outline a framework of principled engagement in which the employment of North Korean workers is conditioned on the protection of their rights and individual agency, with each group of stakeholders bearing responsibility for ensuring that the framework succeeds.

The policy recommendations proposed in the report include, but are not limited to the following:

To the Government of Russia:

- End the misuse of student visas and cooperate with the international community to establish a lawful channel for employing North Korean workers, conditioned on wage protection mechanisms and safeguards against diversion of funds to prohibited weapons programs.

- Enact mandatory corporate human rights due diligence legislation across all sectors, supported by credible enforcement mechanisms and penalties for non-compliance.

To the Government of North Korea:

- Prevent abuse of workers by requiring written contracts that guarantee pay and working conditions, prohibiting arbitrary deductions and wage theft, and ensuring workers have direct access to their compensation.

- Cease the diversion of overseas labor revenues to prohibited activities, including weapons development, and commit to channeling these funds toward healthcare, education, and social welfare, with verification through third-party financial audits.

To the Other Governments & Multilateral Bodies:

- Replace blanket bans on the employment of North Korean nationals with a structured framework for principled engagement, incorporating wage protections such as third-party–managed escrow accounts and in-kind compensation in the form of humanitarian resources.

- Expand asylum pathways for North Korean defectors in Russia, including the adoption of a Safe Harbor Protocol and the creation of emergency transit facilities in neighboring states.

To the Corporations:

- Implement enhanced human rights due diligence in line with international standards such as the UN Guiding Principles on Business and Human Rights (UNGPs) and the EU Corporate Sustainability Due Diligence Directive (CS3D), ensuring direct wage payments to workers and independent monitoring of worksites.

- Guarantee comprehensive workplace protections, including mandatory insurance coverage, enforceable safety standards, and transparent public reporting on labor conditions throughout supply chains.

CHAPTER 1
INTRODUCTION

1.1 SUBJECT AND RATIONALE OF INVESTIGATION

The crucible of the Russo-Ukrainian War has reforged the partnership between the Democratic People's Republic of Korea (DPRK; North Korea) and the Russian Federation (Russia) into an overt military alliance, culminating in the deployment of North Korean troops to the battlefield.[1] While the security dimensions of this move have sent shockwaves across the international community, its place within North Korea's broader human rights landscape has received comparatively little attention. The dispatch of soldiers represents a chilling militarization of North Korea's pre-existing practice of exporting its citizens as commodities: where it once sent workers abroad to generate hard currency, it now also deploys troops to cement its military alliance with Russia.[2]

---

1. See *Section 1.2: Geopolitical Context of Investigation*.
2. Kim, Unique. "Introducing a Human Rights Paradigm: The Human Cost of North Korea's Support of the Russo-Ukrainian War." *Database Center for North Korean Human Rights,* 23 Dec. 2024.

For decades, North Korea has sent workers to Russia, first formalizing the practice with a bilateral agreement in 1967 during the Soviet era.[3] This program largely escaped international scrutiny until the mid-2010s, when evidence emerged that North Korea was diverting the wages of its overseas workers to finance its weapons of mass destruction (WMD) program. In response, the UN Security Council adopted Resolutions 2375 and 2397 in late 2017, immediately banning new work authorizations for North Korean nationals and mandating repatriation of all existing workers within two years.[4] Rather than ending the scheme, however, these sanctions inadvertently drove it underground: today, an estimated 15,000 North Koreans continue working in Russia on non-work visas.[5]

As this labor export program endures, it demands renewed scrutiny as one of the world's most institutionalized systems of transnational repression (TNR). Far more than a simple revenue-raising enterprise, it is structurally designed to project Pyongyang's control apparatus beyond its borders, ensuring its workers' compliance and loyalty even while they live overseas. In addition to seizing their wages, the state employs a range of TNR tactics: confiscating passports after customs clearance, planting state security agents onsite, and requiring official approval for any travel beyond designated worksites and residences. These tactics, constituting severe violations of basic freedoms and rights, have been consistently documented by the Database Center for North Korean Human Rights (NKDB) through interviews with North Korean workers from more than ten host countries.[6]

---

3. See *Chapter 2: History of North Korea's Labor Export to Russia.*
4. "North Korea: UN imposes fresh sanctions over missile tests." *BBC News*, 23 Dec. 2017, https://www.bbc.com/news/world-asia-42459670.
5. Luxmoore, Matthew, Dasl Yoon, and Kate Vtorygina. "North Korean Leader Kim Jong Un's Latest Gift to Russia Is Migrant Workers." *The Wall Street Journal*, 5 May 2025, www.wsj.com/world/asia/kim-jong-uns-latest-gift-to-russia-is-migrant-workers-916693a4
6. NKDB has long documented the human rights abuses endured by North Korean overseas workers, having released three reports on its prior findings: *North Korean Overseas Laborers in Russia* (2016); *The North Korea Outside the North Korean State* (2016); and *Human Rights and North Korea's Overseas Laborers: Dilemmas and Policy Challenges* (2015). In particular, the first of these three reports covers the conditions of North Koreans who worked in Russia between the 1970s and 2015.

This report transcends the conventional focus of TNR studies on political dissidents to examine a population of workers dispatched from the world's most reclusive nation. It finds that North Korea's labor export program is unique, functioning pre-emptively to neutralize any potential for defection or "ideological contamination." The report reveals how North Korea embeds these TNR mechanisms within its global economic strategy, making sociopolitical control a prerequisite for exploiting the workers it sends abroad. Building upon NKDB's earlier research, this analysis primarily focuses on developments since 2018 to demonstrate how the shift to informal labor—an adverse effect of the 2017 UN sanctions—has heightened the vulnerability of North Korean workers to abuse in Russia. This dangerous trend is situated within the context of North Korea's deepening strategic alliance with Russia, which has cultivated an unusually permissive environment for this system of exploitation and transnational repression.

1.2 GEOPOLITICAL CONTEXT OF INVESTIGATION

In January 2025, a video filmed at a Kyiv detention center went viral, as it put a human face on the grim realities of the North Korea-Russia alliance.[7] The footage showed two North Korean soldiers who were captured among the 11,000 troops deployed by North Korea to bolster Russian forces in the invasion of Ukraine. Their appearance, disoriented and youthful, immediately cast doubt on prior speculations that the North Korean troops belonged to a highly skilled infantry.[8] Subsequent interviews with the two soldiers, identified as Ri (age of 26) and Baek (21), quickly revealed a harrowing truth: they had been deployed without knowing they were heading into combat, and

---

7. Pourahmadi, Adam and Audry Jeong. "Zelensky offers to release captured North Korean soldiers in exchange for Ukrainian soldiers held in Russia." *CNN*, 13 Jan. 2025, https://edition.cnn.com/2025/01/12/europe/north-korean-soldiers-interrogation-video-ukraine-intl-latam
8. Ng, Kelly. "What we know about North Korean troops fighting Russia's war." *BBC News*. 24 Dec. 2024, https://www.bbc.com/news/articles/cm2796pdm1lo

their families were uninformed of their whereabouts.⁹ One of the soldiers also explicitly expressed a desire to defect to South Korea, fearing execution if repatriated to the North.

The capture of these two prisoners-of-war occurred amid months of official silence from Pyongyang and Moscow regarding the presence of North Korean troops first discovered in October 2024.¹⁰ Only in April 2025 did North Korea and Russia publicly acknowledge the participation of these troops in the Russo-Ukrainian War.¹¹ The deployment of these troops to the Kursk region marked a significant escalation of North Korea's engagement in the war, which had previously been limited to the provision of munitions. Between August 2023 and March 2025, North Korea also shipped an estimated 4.2 to 5.8 million munitions.¹² Now, North Korea is showing a growing willingness not only to provide weapons but to sacrifice its own people to fight for Russia's war, an act of aggression in clear violation of international law. As recently as June 2025, it pledged to send an additional 5,000 military workers and 1,000 sappers to demine and rebuild the war-torn Kursk region.¹³

Through its alliance with Russia, North Korea has received a significant transfer of advanced military hardware and technical support. An investigation published in May 2025 by the Multilateral Sanctions Monitoring Team indicates that Russia has delivered at least one Pantsir-S1 air defense system, anti-aircraft missiles, and electronic

---

9. Jung, Chul-hwan. "Exclusive: Captured North Korean soldiers speak out on deployment to Russia." *The Chosun Daily*. 20 Feb. 2025, https://www.chosun.com/english/north-korea-en/2025/02/19/2TUJ44HQBVGJNJFEA6XD2A4IPU/

10. Garamone, Jim. "Pentagon Says 10K North Korean Troops in Kursk Oblast." *U.S. Department of Defense*, 4 Nov. 2024, https://www.defense.gov/News/News-Stories/Article/Article/3955757/pentagon-says-10k-north-korean-troops-in-kursk-oblast/

11. Guinto, Joel, and Jean Mackenzie. "N Korea confirms it sent troops to fight for Russia in Ukraine war." *BBC News*. 28 Apr. 2025, https://www.bbc.com/news/articles/ckg25wxvpy2o

12. Armenzoni, Alessio, et al. "Brothers in Arms: Estimating North Korean Munitions Deliveries to Russia." *Open Source Centre*, 15 Apr. 2025, https://www.opensourcecentre.org/research/brothers-in-arms

13. Troianovski, Anton. "North Korea Will Send 5,000 Workers to Russia, Kremlin Says." *The New York Times*, 17 June 2025, https://www.nytimes.com/2025/06/17/world/europe/north-korea-workers-russia.html

warfare systems to North Korea.[14] In addition, Ukrainian intelligence reports that Russia has helped North Korean engineers resolve an accuracy flaw with their KN-23 ballistic missiles upon combat testing in late 2024.[15] Moreover, this military exchange appears to encompass training, as suggested by reports of 25,000 North Korean workers slated for a Russian drone factory.[16]

However, while the transfer of sensitive military technology falls under North Korea's long-term strategic interests, the country's alliance with Russia, on a more fundamental level, secures an immediate economic lifeline as sanctions have increasingly estranged it from the global economy. Even the North Korean troops—much like their laborer counterparts—are estimated to earn USD 2,000 a month, the majority of which is remitted directly to the North Korean state as hard currency.[17] Though not excluded from the possibility of funding the very WMD program targeted by sanctions, these remittances offer the cash-strapped regime financial relief at large. Russia's economic support also includes the direct provision of flour to North Korea, which has persistently faced food shortages.[18]

This military and economic cooperation is formalized in the Treaty on Comprehensive Strategic Partnership, which was drafted in June and ratified in November 2024.[19] This treaty effectively revives the spirit of

---

14. Multilateral Sanctions Monitoring Team. *Unlawful Military Cooperation including Arms Transfers between North Korea and Russia*. Ministry of Foreign Affairs of Japan, 29 May 2025, https://www.mofa.go.jp/press/release/pressite_000001_01321.html
15. Balmforth, Thom. "Exclusive: Ukraine sees marked improvement in accuracy of Russia's North Korean missiles." *Reuters*. 6 Feb. 2025, https://www.reuters.com/business/aerospace-defense/ukraine-sees-marked-improvement-accuracy-russias-north-korean-missiles-2025-02-06/
16. "N.Korea to send workers to Russian drone factory to gain expertise." *NHK WORLD-JAPAN News*, 19 June 2025, https://www3.nhk.or.jp/nhkworld/en/news/20250619_05/
17. Kang, Taejun. "Russia pays North Korean soldiers about $2,000 a month: South's spy agency." *Radio Free Asia*, 23 Oct. 2024, https://www.rfa.org/english/korea/2024/10/23/north-korea-troop-kursk/
18. Kim, Jieun. "North Korean authorities begin to distribute Russian flour rations." *Radio Free Asia*, 20 Nov. 2024, https://www.rfa.org/english/korea/2024/11/20/north-korea-russian-flour-rations/
19. Viner, Katharine. "Ukraine war briefing: North Korea ratifies landmark mutual defence pact with Russia." *The Guardian*, 12 Nov. 2024, https://www.theguardian.com/

the 1961 Treaty of Friendship, Cooperation, and Mutual Assistance from the Cold War era, most notably through the incorporation of a mutual defense clause. Article 4 of the new treaty compels either country to provide immediate military assistance if the other is attacked, echoing Article 1 of its Cold War predecessor.[20] While the 1961 treaty had been left to expire in the immediate aftermath of the Soviet Union's collapse, and the 2000 follow-up agreement omitted any military assistance clause, the 2024 treaty signals a formidable resurgence in the military ties between North Korea and Russia under the latest leadership of Kim Jong Un and Vladimir Putin.

In the grand scheme of things, the alliance between North Korea and Russia dates further back to 1948, when Russia—then the Soviet Union—became the first major power to recognize the newly founded Democratic People's Republic of Korea. However, throughout the 1990s and early 2000s, post-Soviet Russia sought a partnership with the West, drifting away from North Korea and even contributing to efforts to curb its nascent nuclear ambitions.[21] When Vladimir Putin took office in 2000, the relationship between the two states grew warmer, yet remained conflicted, as Russia still opposed North Korea's nuclear program at the time. The past decade gradually set the stage for the recent resurgence in their alliance, with both states facing escalating pressure from multilateral sanctions like those responding to Russia's annexation of Crimea and North Korea's continued ballistic missile tests.

The decisive push toward the current state of bilateral relations was arguably Russia's launch of a full-scale invasion of Ukraine in February 2022. In March of that year, North Korea was one of only five

---

world/2024/nov/12/ukraine-war-briefing-north-korea-ratifies-landmark-mutual-defence-pact-with-russia
20. Cha, Du Hyeogn. "Implications of the DPRK-Russia 'Treaty on Comprehensive Strategic Partnership'." *The Asan Institute for Policy Studies*, 8 Oct. 2024, https://en.asaninst.org/contents/implications-of-the-dprk-russia-treaty-on-comprehensive-strategic-partnership/
21. Kim, Tong-Hyung. "A Timeline of the Complicated Relations between Russia and North Korea." *AP News*, 13 Sep. 2024, https://apnews.com/article/north-korea-russia-kim-jong-un-putin-timeline-336b51634fab28a34ec210a78866f4d9

UN member states to vote against a resolution demanding Russia's withdrawal of forces.[22] A few months later, Russia, along with China, vetoed a Security Council resolution to impose additional sanctions against North Korea for its ballistic missile tests—the first such obstruction since 2006, signaling a new era of diplomatic impunity for Pyongyang.[23] Thus, this latest chapter of the partnership between North Korea and Russia was born from a newfound realization: the mutual condemnation they faced could be repurposed into a mutual defiance of international norms on peace, security, and human rights.

1.3 METHODOLOGY AND SCOPE OF INVESTIGATION

This report employs a comprehensive research methodology to analyze the conditions of North Korean workers in Russia following the adoption of United Nations Security Council Resolutions (UNSC) 2375 and 2397. The research incorporates information from three primary sources: (1) in-depth interviews with North Korean escapees who worked in Russia after the adoption of sanctions, (2) publicly available data, laws, and literature, and (3) in-depth consultations with experts from relevant fields. This multi-faceted approach allows for a robust analysis by comparing and contrasting publicly disclosed information from the Russian and North Korean governments with investigative findings from independent experts and the firsthand testimonies of those directly affected.

A cornerstone of this research is a set of in-depth interviews conducted with fifteen former North Korean workers who defected to South Korea from their posts in Russia.[24] These interviewees either were

---

22. "General Assembly Overwhelmingly Adopts Resolution Demanding Russian Federation Immediately End Illegal Use of Force in Ukraine, Withdraw All Troops." *Meetings Coverage and Press Releases*, United Nations, 2 Mar. 2022, https://press.un.org/en/2022/ga12407.doc.htm
23. Beech, Samantha. "China and Russia veto new UN sanctions on North Korea for first time since 2006." *CNN*, 27 May 2022, https://edition.cnn.com/2022/05/26/asia/us-north-korea-united-nations-intl-hnk
24. All interviews were conducted only after participants provided written informed consent. Prior to any questions, they were briefed on the study's objectives and how their

newly dispatched to Russia after the passage of UNSC Resolution 2375 in September 2017 or continued to work there past the repatriation deadline mandated by Resolution 2397 (December 22, 2019). The regions where these interviewees worked were Primorsky Krai, Amur Oblast, Irkutsk Oblast, and Moscow. Among these fifteen interviewees, the earliest departure from Russia was in the spring of 2018, and the latest departure was in the fall of 2023.[25] Fourteen interviewees worked in construction, and one interviewee worked in forestry. However, some of these interviewees performed duties not directly related to their industry, serving as an interpreter, chef, medic, or driver. Lastly, eleven interviewees were civilian workers, two of whom were civilian specialists at a construction company normally reserved for military workers. The remaining four interviewees were soldiers who worked in Russia as part of their mandatory military service.

Table 1. Interviews with Former North Korean Workers from Russia

No.	Year of Departure from Work Post	Type of Worker	Industry	Region of Residence (Military Service) in North Korea
1	2021	Military	Construction	Jagang (Pyongyang)
2	2022	Civilian	Construction	Pyongyang
3	2020	Military	Construction	South Pyongan (Pyongyang)
4	2022	Civilian	Construction	South Pyongan
5	2023	Military	Construction	South Pyongan (Pyongyang)
6	2021	Civilian	Construction	Pyongyang
7	2021	Civilian	Construction	Pyongyang

responses would be used, and were clearly informed of their right to decline participation or to skip any question at any time without penalty.
25. Even interviewees who defected in 2018—within a year of the sanctions' adoption—were able to attest to changes in their documentation status in Russia.

8	2018	Civilian	Construction	South Pyongan
9	2018	Civilian	Construction	Pyongyang
10	2020	Military	Construction	North Pyongan (Pyongyang)
11	2018	Civilian	Construction	Pyongyang
12	2018	Civilian	Construction	Pyongyang
13	2019	Civilian	Logging	Pyongyang
14	2019	Civilian	Construction	Pyongyang
15	2023	Civilian	Construction	Pyongyang

The in-depth interviews covered the following categories of information:

1. **Pre-Dispatch Procedure:** This category addresses the role of various North Korean government agencies in selecting and dispatching workers abroad. It also examines the fairness of the process of selecting workers, the presence of employment contracts, and the extent of the workers' informed consent.

2. **Exit and Entry Procedure:** This category addresses the logistical and legal aspects of the workers' emigration from North Korea to Russia, including the method of travel, the type of documentation (e.g., visa) used for entry into Russia, and security checks upon exit from North Korea and entry into Russia.

3. **Control of Personal Documents and Finances:** This category addresses the extent of these workers' ability to retain personal documents (e.g., passport) and access a personal bank account for independent management of finances.

4. **On-site Management and Working Conditions:** This category addresses the management system implemented at the workplace, including the reporting hierarchy. It also examines core aspects of the working conditions, such as compensation, workload, rest, workplace safety, and access to medical care for on-site injuries.

5. **Living Conditions:** This category addresses the workers' quality of life outside of work, focusing on residential autonomy, adequacy of housing, and access to food, hygiene, and other necessities. It also examines the degree of privacy afforded to workers outside the workplace.

6. **Movement, Information, and Communication:** This category addresses the workers' ability to move freely outside their workplace and residence, as well as their access to information and various methods of communication with families remaining in North Korea.

7. **Other Human Rights Concerns:** This final category covers the mechanisms of ideological indoctrination of workers, the incidence of physical or psychological violence, and other forms of oppression and abuse. It also examines the process of returning to North Korea and the availability of vaccines and other health measures for those who experienced the COVID-19 pandemic while working in Russia.

The literature review includes but is not limited to publicly available data on Russia's issuance of work permits and visas; bilateral agreements between Russia and North Korea; Russia's Labor Code and other domestic laws related to migrant workers; North Korea's regulations on external (or transnational) economic affairs; news articles from various outlets; and investigative reports from the UN Panel of Experts and the Multilateral Sanctions Monitoring Team. To achieve a better understanding of the context, the research is further enriched by consultations with ten different experts, including former high-ranking North Korean officials, former North Korean workers from host countries besides Russia, international human rights lawyers, investigative journalists, and lawyers experienced in assisting North Korean or other migrant workers in Russia.

Table 2. Consultations with Experts from Various Backgrounds

No.	Background/Expertise
1	North Korean escapee with experience working for the Central Committee of the Workers' Party of Korea
2	North Korean escapee with experience working in Russia prior to the adoption of UNSCR 2375 and 2397
3	North Korean escapee with experience working for North Korea's economic consular representative in the Middle East
4	Investigative journalist covering North Korea's relations with Russia
5	Investigative journalist covering North Korea's relations with Russia
6	Lawyer specialized in international labor standards (e.g., International Labor Organization conventions, UN Guiding Principles on Business and Human Rights)
7	Lawyer specialized in international human rights treaties
8	Lawyer from *F.M. and Others v. Russia* (case adjudicated under the European Court of Human Rights in 2024)
9	Lawyer with experience assisting North Korean defectors in Russia
10	Investigative journalist covering North Korean overseas workers

Based on this research, this report compares the labor and human rights realities of North Korean workers with the domestic laws and international legal obligations of Russia, giving precedence to peremptory norms (*jus cogens*). The table below shows the main legal and regulatory frameworks that are discussed throughout this report.

The report then concludes with policy recommendations to counter North Korea's mechanisms of exploitation and transnational repression. These recommendations offer innovative approaches that address the security concerns underpinning sanctions while preserving the opportunity for North Koreans to safely engage with the outside world.

Table 3. Key Legal Frameworks Used in Analysis

Domestic Laws & Regulations	**Russia:** Constitution (Adopted 1993); Labor Code (Adopted 2001); Federal Law No. 109-FZ on the Migration Registration of Foreign Citizens and Stateless Persons (Adopted 2006); Federal Law No. 110-FZ on Amendments to the Federal Law on Legal Status of Foreign Citizens in the Russian Federation (Adopted 2006) **North Korea:** Regulations on External Economic Projects (Adopted 2020)
Bilateral Agreements Between Russia & North Korea	Agreement on the Temporary Labor Activities of Citizens of One State in the Territory of the Other State (Signed by Russia & North Korea 2007); Agreement on the Transfer and Receipt of Illegal Entrants and Residents (Signed by Russia & North Korea 2016); Treaty on Comprehensive Strategic Partnership (Signed by Russia & North Korea 2024)
Multilateral Treaties	**United Nations:** United Nations Charter (Ratified by USSR 1945; Acceded by North Korea 1991); Vienna Convention on the Law of Treaties (Ratified by USSR 1986);

International Covenant on Civil and Political Rights (ICCPR; Ratified by USSR 1973 & Acceded by North Korea 1981);

International Covenant on Economic, Social, and Cultural Rights (ICESCR; Ratified by USSR 1973 & Acceded by North Korea 1981);

Convention against Torture and Other Cruel, Inhuman or Degrading Treatment (CAT; Ratified by USSR 1987);

International Convention on the Elimination of All Forms of Racial Discrimination (ICERD; Ratified by USSR 1969);

Convention against Transnational Organized Crime and its Palermo Protocol (Ratified by Russia 2004);

Convention against Corruption (Ratified by Russia 2006)

International Labor Organization:

Forced Labour Convention (No. 29; Ratified by USSR 1956) & Protocol of 2014 (Ratified by Russia 2019);

Freedom of Association and Protection of the Right to Organise Convention (No. 87; Ratified by USSR 1956);

Right to Organise and Collective Bargaining Convention (No. 98; Ratified by USSR 1956);

Abolition of Forced Labour Convention (No. 105; Ratified by Russia 1998);

Discrimination (Employment and Occupation) Convention (No. 111; Ratified by USSR 1961);

Occupational Safety and Health Convention (No. 155; Ratified by Russia 1998);

Promotional Framework for Occupational Safety and Health Convention (No. 187; Ratified by Russia 2011);

Equal Remuneration Convention (No. 100; Ratified by USSR 1956);

Forty-Hour Week Convention (No. 47; Ratified by USSR 1956);

	Weekly Rest (Industry) Convention (No. 14; Ratified by USSR 1967); Weekly Rest (Commerce and Offices) Convention (No. 106; Ratified by USSR 1967) **Other:** European Convention on Human Rights (ECHR; Acceded by Russia 1996 & Withdrew 2022)

CHAPTER 2
HISTORY OF NORTH KOREA'S LABOR EXPORT TO RUSSIA

For over seventy-five years, the export of North Korean labor to Russia has constituted a remarkably resilient and strategic enterprise, adapting to profound political and economic shifts. The origins of this program lie in the immediate aftermath of World War II, as the Soviet Union (USSR) faced acute manpower shortages in its Far Eastern territories and northern Korea grappled with high unemployment.[26] In response, the Soviet administration initiated a system of *orgnabor*, or "organized recruitment," to bring Korean workers to its fisheries, forests, and farms.[27] The scale of this initial wave was substantial: between 1946 and 1949 alone, over 26,000 North Koreans arrived in the Sakhalin Oblast.[28] In this early phase, workers signed voluntary contracts, were paid directly, and enjoyed a degree of autonomy.[29]

---

26. Bezik, Igor V. "Участие граждан КНДР в хозяйственном освоении советского Дальнего Востока (1950-е начало 1960-х гг.)" [The Participation of the Citizens of the DPRK, in the Economic Development of the Soviet Far East (early 1950s - early 1960s)]. *Известия Восточного Института [Oriental Journal Institute]*, vol. 17, no. 1, 2011.
27. Lankov, Andrei. "North Korean Labor Export to the USSR/Russia: Why the Project Has Survived Against All Odds." *Russia in Global Affairs*, vol. 18, no. 3, 2020.
28. Bezik, *supra* note 26, at pp. 29.
29. Lankov, *supra* note 27, at pp. 29.

While the program began as a Soviet-managed initiative, it saw a move toward a state-to-state regulation, as the newly established state of North Korea consolidated more authority in the late 1950s. In 1957, the Soviet Union and North Korea signed a convention to settle border issues, such as the illegal crossing of North Koreans without official employment in Russia. In the same year, the two states also signed a treaty to determine the legal status of North Koreans in the USSR under various situations, such as marriage or the formation of family with Russian nationals.[30] These agreements were early steps toward the centralized control that would define the program's next era.

A turning point came with the 1967 bilateral logging agreement, which shifted control of the labor program from Moscow to Pyongyang. The program was repurposed into an engine for generating hard currency for the North Korean state. This new arrangement institutionalized a "closed system of wage distribution" that allowed Pyongyang to capture the vast majority of revenue—often in the form of raw materials like timber that it could resell on the international market.[31] Consequently, workers' conditions deteriorated dramatically. They were dispatched in highly disciplined teams to remote, heavily monitored logging camps, and their freedoms were sharply curtailed.

The dissolution of the USSR in 1991 dealt a severe blow to this established system, as the "near breakdown of trade" between Moscow and Pyongyang disrupted the reliable flow of payments and materials.[32] The collapse created parallel crises. North Korea, having lost its main patron and facing a devastating famine, became desperate for hard currency. Russia, meanwhile, experienced a significant need for cheap foreign labor as it grappled with industrial restructuring, population decline, and a skills mismatch in its workforce. This chaotic period was defined by legal and political flux, as Russia relied on

---

30. Troyakova, Tamara G. "Рабочая сила из КНДР на российском Дальнем Востоке: история и современное состояние" [Workers from DPRK in the Russian Far East: history and current situation]. *Ойкумена [Ojkumena: Regional Researches]*, no. 2, 2017; Bezik, *supra* note 26, at pp. 29.
31. Lankov, *supra* note 27, at pp. 29; Troyakova, *supra* note 30, at pp. 30.
32. Lankov, *supra* note 27, at pp. 29.

outdated Soviet laws before slowly developing a permit-based migration framework in the 1990s.[33] Despite this turmoil, the labor export program survived precisely because the economic needs of both sides had become more acute than ever: Russia for cheap labor, and North Korea for cash.[34]

In the post-Soviet era, the program's focus shifted to the construction industry.[35] This period is defined by a central paradox: while working conditions remained exceptionally harsh, competition among North Koreans for a position abroad became fiercer than ever.[36] The motivation was overwhelmingly financial. A worker could save a few thousand dollars over a couple years—a sum that, while inadequate for the labor performed, was transformative for a North Korean family, often serving as startup capital for a small business.[37]

To formalize this exchange in Russia's restructured legal framework, the two states signed the "Agreement on the Temporary Labor Activities of Citizens of One State in the Territory of the Other State" on August 31, 2007.[38] Entering into force on December 29, 2009, the agreement integrated North Koreans into Russia's official, permit-based system (Article 4). However, it also legally enshrined Pyongyang's control by stipulating that pay and other terms be regulated by contracts with the North Korean state companies that serve as their direct employers (Article 6).[39] Furthermore, the agreement offloaded most social welfare costs, making insurance and

---

33. Chudinovskikh, Olga, and Oxana Kharaeva. "Migration policy towards skilled labor in the Russian Federation." BRICS Journal of Economics, vol. 1, no. 2, 2020.
34. Lankov, *supra* note 27, at pp. 29.
35. Troyakova, *supra* note 30, at pp. 30.
36. Lankov, Andrei. "Северокорейские рабочие в России: критерии отбора и мотивация работников" [North Korean workers in Russia: Selection criteria and motivation of workers]. Вестник Санкт-Петербургского университета Международные отношения [Vestnik of Saint Petersburg University International Relations], vol. 13, no. 2, 2020.
37. Ibid.
38. See Appendix 2a/2b for the full text in Russian/English.
39. The three entities identified in the agreement are: (1) Russian "customers" (who subcontract North Korean companies), (2) North Korean "employers" (who represent the North Korean workers), and (3) North Korean "workers" (who belong to the North Korean companies that get subcontracted by the Russian "customers").

compensation for worksite accidents a responsibility to be handled by the North Korean employers under their own country's laws (Article 8).[40]

By the mid-2010s, North Korea's labor export program had come under intense international scrutiny amid mounting evidence that its revenues were underwriting Pyongyang's illicit WMD efforts. Investigations by human rights organizations, including NKDB, documented conditions tantamount to modern-day slavery, in which workers were systematically exploited for state profit.[41] In response, the United Nations, the European Union and numerous national governments imposed sanctions designed to sever this financial lifeline by barring North Koreans from overseas employment altogether. Notably, these sanctions include:

- **UN Security Council Resolution 2371** (August 2017), which capped the total number of DPRK workers permitted abroad;

- **Resolution 2375** (September 2017), which prohibited UN member states from issuing any new work permits to North Korean nationals;

- **Resolution 2397** (December 2017), which mandated the repatriation of all existing North Korean workers by December 22, 2019.[42]

---

40. The agreement stipulates that Russia will only provide emergency medical services free of charge.
41. Park, Chan Hong. *Conditions of Labor and Human Rights: North Korean Overseas Laborers in Russia*. Database Center for North Korean Human Rights, 2016;

Higgins, Andrew. "North Koreans in Russia Work 'Basically in the Situation of Slaves'." *The New York Times*, 11 Jul. 2017, https://www.nytimes.com/2017/07/11/world/europe/north-korea-russia-migrants.html.
42. United Nations, Security Council. Resolution 2371 (2017). 5 Aug. 2017, S/RES/2371(2017);

United Nations, Security Council. Resolution 2375 (2017). 11 Sept. 2017, S/RES/2375(2017);

United Nations, Security Council. Resolution 2397 (2017). 22 Dec. 2017, S/RES/2397(2017).

Although well-intentioned, this security-centric approach proved too narrow to address the program's core economic and human rights dimensions. As formal channels closed, persistent labor demand in host countries fueled a shift into informal—and largely opaque—networks. Thus, this policy incentivized the illegal employment of North Koreans while also overlooking the imperative to safeguard their fundamental right to explore the outside world. Evidence from the UN Panel of Experts, intelligence reports, and on-the-ground footage confirms their continued presence in the country well past the deadline imposed by sanctions.[43] Under Russia's feigned compliance, many North Korean workers are now registered under non-work visas or undocumented altogether. This shift into the informal economy has substantially heightened their vulnerability to abuse.

While North Korean workers have long faced systematic exploitation under bilateral agreements that gave Pyongyang direct oversight, their situation has become even more precarious due to the adverse effects of sanctions. Now, they are subject to the same control from Pyongyang while also dealing with Russian firms that hire their services off the books and operate outside international scrutiny. This lack of transparency, which facilitates sanctions evasion, makes it extremely difficult to identify and hold these firms accountable for their role in enabling North Korea's exploitative labor practices. Russia's recent veto of the renewal of the mandate for the UN Panel of Experts, the very body tasked with monitoring sanctions compliance, further exacerbates this opacity.[44] Moreover, the misclassification of these workers as "non-working foreigners" creates a legal loophole

---

43. United Nations Security Council, Panel of Experts established pursuant to resolution 1874. *Final report of the Panel of Experts submitted pursuant to resolution 2680 (2023)*. 7 Mar. 2024, UN doc. S/2024/215;
"Video shows North Korean workers working in Russia in violation of UN sanctions." *Korea JoongAng Daily*, 15 Apr. 2025, https://koreajoongangdaily.joins.com/news/2025-04-15/national/northKorea/Video-shows-North-Korean-laborers-working-in-Russia-in-violation-of-UN-sanctions/2285289
44. Gordon, Michael R. "Russia Blocks Extension of North Korea Sanctions Monitoring." *Wall Street Journal*, 28 Mar. 2024, https://www.wsj.com/world/russia/russia-blocks-extension-of-north-korea-sanctions-monitoring-51ada1f3

that nullifies the applicability of Russia's labor laws, limiting potential domestic recourse for rights violations.

CHAPTER 3
CONTEMPORARY ARCHITECTURE OF NORTH KOREA'S LABOR EXPORT PROGRAM

3.1 ROLE OF THE LABOR EXPORT PROGRAM IN NORTH KOREA'S COURT ECONOMY

North Korea operates a two-tiered economic system that can be broadly divided into the "people's economy" (인민경제) and the "second economy" (제2경제).[45] While the former is the official, Cabinet-led planned economy, the latter functions as a parallel, prioritized system dedicated to sustaining the regime and its strategic projects, such as the WMD program. The core of this second economy is what former North Korean banker Kim Kwang-jin has termed the "royal court economy."[46] This two-tiered structure creates a constant demand for foreign currency, as the local North Korean won (KPW) is non-convertible and effectively valueless beyond the state's borders. The remittances from the labor export program serve as one of the primary engines to meet this demand.

---

45. Lim, Soo-ho. 북한 경제전략 변화의 정치동학 [*Political Dynamics of Changes in North Korea's Economic Strategy*]. Institute for National Security Strategy, 2021.
46. Kim, Kwang Jin. "The Defector's Tale: Inside North Korea's Secret Economy." *World Affairs*, vol. 174, no. 3, 2011, pp. 71–80.

The income from these activities, often called "ruling funds" (통치자금), is kept separate from the official state budget and invisible in public reports.[47] Instead of being managed by the Cabinet-led Ministry of Finance, these funds are collected and controlled by entities under the direct command of the Workers' Party of Korea (WPK), such as the infamous Office 39. The second economy, including its vast network of military-run factories and enterprises, operates with priority over the people's economy, enjoying preferential access to resources, labor, and electricity, effectively functioning as a "second cabinet" outside the formal state economic plan.

Serving as an engine for this second economy, the labor export program operationally relies on a complex web of institutions within the WPK, the state, and the military. Under the national ideology of *Juche* (self-reliance), public agencies and the enterprises they control are pressured to fund their core projects by running profitable ventures and meeting centrally assigned quotas for foreign currency (Interview 14).[48] As the domestic economy offers limited opportunities to acquire hard currency, the exportation of labor has surfaced as one of the most effective ventures to achieve this objective. Lacking capital, state agencies often partner with North Korea's entrepreneurial class (*donju*) that invest in and manage ventures under the protection and legitimacy of a state-owned enterprise. In return, they must remit a

---

47. Fifield, Anna. "He ran North Korea's secret moneymaking operation. Now he lives in Virginia." *The Washington Post*. 13 Jul. 2017, https://www.washingtonpost.com/world/asia_pacific/he-ran-north-koreas-secret-money-making-operation-now-he-lives-in-virginia/2017/07/12/4cb9a590-6584-11e7-94ab-5b1f0ff459df_story.html.

Kim, Dae-hoon. "북한 노동당 39호실 '김정은 통치자금' 총괄하는 곳 [Room 39 of North Korea's Workers' Party: The Organization Managing Kim Jong-un's Slush Fund]." *Hankyung*, 14 Feb. 2016, www.hankyung.com/article/2016021474691

48. The application of the *Juche* principle of self-reliance to the domestic economic system was announced by the Supreme Leader Kim Jong Un as the "Socialist Enterprise Responsibility Management System" (사회주의기업책임관리제) in his "5.30 Measures" speech on May 30, 2014 and later codified through the amendment of the Enterprise Act in November of that same year. The characteristics of this system is explained in-depth in a publication released in North Korea: Ri, Chang-ha. "사회주의기업책임관리제는 우리 식의 독특한 기업관리방법" [Our Unique Method of Enterprise Management: The Socialist Enterprise Responsibility Management System]. *Journal of Philosophy and Economics*, no. 2, 2018, Kim Il-sung University Press, Pyongyang, DPRK. Periodical Registration No. 19923.

large share of their profits, ensuring that the state entity meets its revenue targets.[49] This symbiotic relationship creates a hybrid model that combines elements of both command and market economies.

The foreign currency generated through these schemes, estimated to be between several hundred million and over two billion dollars annually, is funneled back to Pyongyang through a network of front companies and illicit financial channels. These "ruling funds" are not used for public welfare, but rather for supporting the Kim family's lavish lifestyle, rewarding elites to maintain their loyalty, and facilitating strategic programs like the development of nuclear weapons and ballistic missiles. In essence, the two-tiered economy insulates the funds most critical to the regime's survival from the formal state budget.

3.2 STRATEGIC DRIVERS OF THE MILITARY-ECONOMIC COMPLEX

North Korea's labor export program has undergone significant shifts since Kim Jong Un took power in late 2011, characterized by two primary trends: a re-centralization of authority and an expansion of the military's economic role. The re-centralization of authority over both economic and military institutions provided the necessary groundwork for the expansion of the military's economic role. While the balance between military and economic imperatives has been dynamically adjusted over time—from the dual-focus "Byungjin Line Policy of Economic Construction and Nuclear Force Development" (경제건설과 핵무력건설 병진노선) (2013), to the economy-focused "All-out Concentration Policy for Economic Building" (사회주의경제건설 총력집중노선) (2018), and back toward a re-emphasis on military development in recent years—these tactical recalibrations have consistently contributed to the core strategy of utilizing a portion of the

---

49. Chung, Young Chul. "북한 경제의 변화—시장, '돈주', 그리고 국가의 재등장" [Changes in North Korea's Economy: Markets, 'Donju,' and the Reemergence of the State]. 역사비평 [Critical Review of History], no. 126, 2019, pp. 134–159.

conventional military forces for economic activities.[50] Both the re-centralization of authority and the expansion of the role of the military are evident in the contemporary infrastructure of North Korea's labor export program.

The process of re-centralizing authority began with the purge of Jang Song-thaek in December 2013. Prior to his execution, Jang operated a semi-independent economic network through the Workers' Party of Korea (WPK) Administration Department (행정부) and its subordinate External Construction General Bureau (대외건설지도국), controlling major ventures outside the Cabinet's authority. Following his removal, this network was dismantled, and its responsibilities were transferred to the Cabinet and its ministries. Although publicly presented as a move to empower the Cabinet, the restructuring in fact served to eliminate rival power centers and centralize foreign currency operations within a more manageable state framework. This trend extended to the military, with the dismissals of Chief of the General Staff Ri Yong-ho (2012) and Minister of the People's Armed Forces Hyon Yong-chol (2015).[51]

The second trend, the expanded economic function of the military, began with the "Byungjin Line Policy of Economic Construction and Nuclear Force Development." This policy posited that a credible nuclear deterrent could provide the ultimate security guarantee, thereby reducing the need for significant investment in conventional forces.[52] To facilitate this initiative, the military's structure was

---

50. An, Kyeong-mo. "새로운 전략적 노선' 이후 북한의 국가전략: 균형전략으로의 재전환과 그 함의" [North Korea's National Strategy After the 'New Strategic Line': Reconversion to a Balancing Strategy and Its Implications]. 한국정치연구 [Korean Political Research], vol. 32, no. 1, 2023, pp. 8.
51. Byeon, Woisuk, and Heo, Jeongpil. "김정은 시기 북한군의 주요 활동 변화 연구: 비군사활동을 중심으로" [A Study on the Major Changes in North Korean Military Activities during the Kim Jong Un Era: Focusing on Non-Military Activities]. 보훈학술논총 [Journal of Patriots and Veterans Affairs in the Republic of Korea], vol. 24, no. 1, 2025.
52. The summary of North Korea's definition of the "Byungjin Line Policy of Economic Construction and Nuclear Force Development" adopted at the Plenary Meeting in March 2013 is as follows: ① It is the succession, deepening, and development of the "Byungjin Line Policy of Economy and National Defense" thoroughly implemented by Kim Il Sung and Kim Jong Il. ② Nuclear weapons are not objects of political or economic bargaining,

differentiated in 2014 with the establishment of the Strategic Force under the Korean People's Army as a fourth branch singularly responsible for the nuclear arsenal. This organizational division isolated the nuclear mission, freeing some of the conventional army, navy, and air forces to serve as instruments of economic policy by supplying labor for domestic construction, international contracts, and other revenue-generating activities.

After the declaration of a "completed national nuclear force" in 2017, the state adopted the "All-Out Concentration Policy for Economic Building" in 2018.[53] This policy placed a clearer emphasis on the economy, leading to a restructuring of the military to better support economic goals, such as downsizing infantry units to expand construction brigades.[54] The recent re-emphasis on strengthening defense capabilities since April 2022, represented by the resumption of intercontinental ballistic missiles tests after four years, does not negate this trend. Instead, it shows that even when military development is prioritized, it is done selectively, with conventional military forces supporting economic operations. Thus, despite shifts in rhetoric, the underlying paradigm of mobilizing military resources to generate

---

but a lifeline that cannot be abandoned for any reason. ③ The nuclear force will be qualitatively and quantitatively expanded and strengthened until the denuclearization of the world is realized. ④ Combat readiness of the nuclear force as the linchpin of military power and operations will be perfected. ⑤ It is a way to decisively increase the effectiveness of war deterrence and defense capabilities without additionally increasing defense expenditures, thereby allowing concentration on economic construction and improving the people's lives. ⑥ It is a rational line that can strengthen nuclear power based on the Juche-oriented atomic energy industry while also solving electricity problems.

See "경애하는 김정은동지께서 조선로동당 중앙위원회 2013년 3월전원회의에서 하신 보고" [Report by Respected Comrade Kim Jong Un at the March 2013 Plenary Meeting of the Workers' Party of Korea Central Committee] *Rodong Sinmun*, 2 Apr. 2013.

53. "김정은 동지의 지도밑에 조선로동당 중앙위원회 제7기 제3차전원회의 진행" [7th Plenary Meeting of the 3rd Central Committee of the Workers' Party of Korea Held under the Guidance of Comrade Kim Jong Un]. *조선중앙통신* [*Korean Central News Agency*], 21 Apr. 2018.

54. Lee, Seungwon. "김정은 시대 북한의 군민관계 변화에 관한 연구: 조선인민군 사회적 역할의 변화양상과 특성을 중심으로" [A study on the changes in the military-civil relations of North Korea, in the era of Kim Jong Un: A focus on the changing patterns in the social-role and characteristics of the KPA]. University of North Korean Studies, PhD dissertation, 2022.

economic support for defense objectives, particularly the nuclear program, has been consistently maintained.

These dynamics have created a self-reinforcing cycle. The development of nuclear weapons requires hard currency, which the state labor export program helps generate. This income funds the WMD program, which, in turn, provides the security guarantee that justifies the mobilization of conventional military forces as a state workforce for economic development, thus perpetuating the cycle toward building a "socialist civilized country."

The remainder of this chapter will dissect the institutional architecture of this system. The analysis will examine the Workers' Party of Korea as the central nervous system, setting the strategic vision, with its Munitions Industry Department (군수공업부) and its executive arm, the Second Economic Commission (제2경제위원회), overseeing the financing of the WMD enterprise. It will then analyze how the State Affairs Commission (SAC; 국무위원회)—the state's supreme policy-making body—operationalizes this vision. Explicitly designed to supersede the old military-first power structure, the SAC functions as the command hub, coordinating the Cabinet's economic apparatus with the defense and security ministries that operate outside its direct control: the Ministry of National Defense (국방성), the Ministry of Social Security (사회안전성), and the Ministry of State Security (국가보위성).

Figure 1. Organizational Chart of Key North Korean Agencies Involved in Labor Export

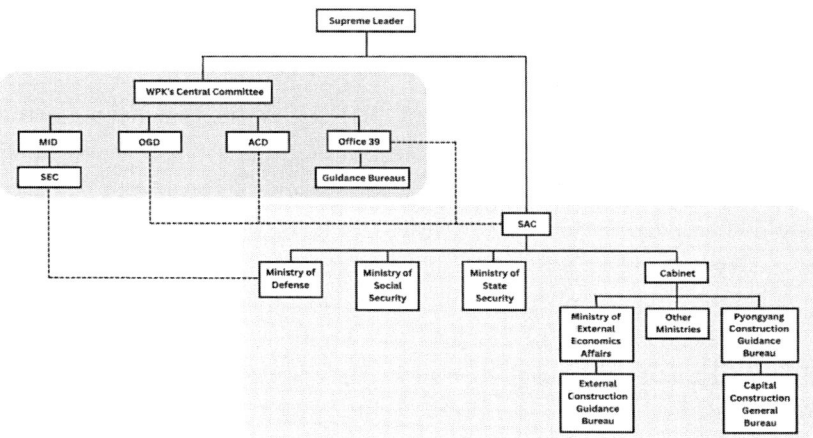

3.3 WORKERS' PARTY OF KOREA AS THE APEX OF COMMAND

At the apex of this command structure is Supreme Leader Kim Jong Un, who is concurrently the General Secretary of the Workers' Party of Korea (WPK) and the Chairman of the State Affairs Commission (SAC). The institutional vehicle for his command is the WPK's Central Committee. As the country's highest political body, its directives override all state laws and constitutional provisions, advising all government policies and overseeing the ideological compliance of citizens. The top-down nature of this system is illustrated by the case of an interviewee whose dispatch in the mid-2010s stemmed from a directive issued by the Central Committee to his military unit, at the behest of Kim Jong Un (Interview 1).

Within the WPK's Central Committee are key departments that provide the parameters of the labor export program: the Administrative Cadres Department (ACD; 간부부), the Organization and Guidance Department (OGD; 조직지도부), the Munitions Industry Department (MID; 군수공업부), and Office 39 (39호실). Together, these departments vet and select the dispatched workforce, appoint the management of overseas enterprises, and control the revenue generated from their labor.

3.3.1 Administrative Cadres Department and Organization and Guidance Department

In all cases, the Central Committee of the WPK is the final arbiter in the selection of the dispatched workforce, as its authority spans across all Party, state, and military agencies. The selection of North Korea's dispatched civilian workers begins with a recommendation from a cadre officer at their state-owned enterprise (SOE) (Interviews 2, 7, 8, 9, 12). This initiates a rigorous approval process that involves documentation from officials like the regional security officer and requires consent from each layer of the institutional hierarchy that commands the SOE. As a result of this multilayered system, many workers do not know the specific unit within the Central Committee that provides the final sign-off, but they consistently identify the Committee as the ultimate authority.

However, a few interviewees were able to pinpoint two departments within the Central Committee as the specific units responsible for this vetting: Administrative Cadres Department (ACD; 간부부 or 행정간부부) and Organization and Guidance Department (OGD; 조직지도부) (Interviews 2, 11, 12, 14). According to an analysis of their testimonies, the ACD is most directly involved in selecting the dispatched workforce and appointing the general management personnel for each North Korean company stationed overseas. However, the OGD, which functions as the Party's ultimate human resources authority, is also routinely engaged in the vetting process because many dispatched workers are Party members and their departure may require more sensitive attention.[55]

---

55. One example is the selection of local party secretaries, who routinely accompany dispatched workers to enforce ideological indoctrination through group lectures and self-criticism sessions known as *saenghwal chonghwa*.

3.3.2 Munitions Industry Department and Second Economic Commission

The Munitions Industry Department (MID; 군수공업부) and its executive arm, the Second Economic Commission (제2경제위원회), are the core of North Korea's nuclear and missile weapon programs. The MID oversees the production of nuclear weapons and ballistic missiles and directs its own revenue-generating operations, including labor dispatch, to self-fund development and procure sanctioned materials (Interviews 3, 4, 10).

In addition to dispatching workers from its own bureaus, the Ministry of National Defense uses its sub-entity, the Second Economic Commission (제2경제위원회), to mobilize soldiers from the Korean People's Army (KPA; 조선인민군). This commission facilitates a dual command structure over military units involved in labor operations. For example, the 131st Guidance Bureau (131원자력지도국), which is involved in nuclear facility construction, falls under the Second Economic Commission's jurisdiction when deployed for overseas industrial work. However, when not engaged in such operations, the same bureau typically receives guidance from the KPA's General Staff Department (총참모부) (Interviews 3, 10). One interview clarified that the Second Economic Commission handles dispatches differently, as it functions as a semi-autonomous body (Interview 14).

3.3.3 Office 39

Office 39 (39호실) serves as the executive body managing the off-the-book funds North Korea earns from its overseas labor operations. Office 39's control ensures that revenues from labor exports are directed toward strategic projects—including the procurement of sanctioned goods and luxury items for the elite—rather than the civilian economy. In essence, it acts as the financial hub of the "royal court economy," channeling illicit and quasi-licit earnings into Kim Jong Un's discretionary funds. In addition to handling funds from other Party, state, and military agencies, it dispatches workers directly through its own bureaus. Some of these bureaus manage construction and goods manufacturing, whereas others are suspected of involvement in illicit activities such as arms trafficking, drug production, and counterfeiting.

Among the bureaus identified by interviewees are the Neungra (능라), Daeseong (대성), Ragwon (락원), Kyoung-heung (경흥), Moran (모란), Unha (은하), Ryukyoung (류경), and Yeohyang (여향) Guidance Bureaus, along with the Daeheung (대흥) and Geumgang (금강) Management Bureaus (Interviews 11, 12).[56] While each bureau can request permission to engage in various businesses, they have traditional specializations; for instance, Moran is associated with department stores and Neungra with textiles and shipping (Interview 11).

3.4 CABINET AS THE FORMAL ECONOMIC APPARATUS

As the country's official administrative body, the Cabinet (내각) is responsible for the "people's economy" and implementing the national economic plan. This role was recently reaffirmed by Kim Jong Un in a policy speech at the 12th Session of the 14th Supreme People's Assembly on January 22-23, 2024, where he demanded that all sectors unconditionally obey the Cabinet's instructions.[57] However, the Cabinet's authority is technically limited to this civilian economy and does not extend to the military economy. This institutional divide is bridged by the State Affairs Commission (SAC), the country's supreme policy-making body. Because the SAC holds command over both the Cabinet and the military ministries (like the Ministry of National Defense and the Ministry of Social Security), it can direct the mobilization of the military for economic operations.

---

56. These guidance bureaus are named after regions in North Korea. As a result, their names may overlap with other institutions, regardless of whether or not they are affiliated with each other.
57. Lee, Sang-sook. "북한 최고인민회의 제14기 12차 회의 결과와 그 함의" [The Results and Implications of the 12th Session of the 14th Supreme People's Assembly of North Korea]. 주요국제문제분석 [Analysis of Major International Issues], edited by Jeong, Jong-hyeok, Institute of Foreign Affairs & National Security, 28 Feb. 2025, pp. 4.

While the involvement of the Ministry of External Economic Relations (대외경제성) and the Ministry of Foreign Affairs (외무성) in labor exports is expected given their global purview, the participation of other ministries and committees is less straightforward. The primary mandate for most ministries is to carry out domestic economic projects. However, the *Juche* principle of self-reliance compels nearly all of them to dispatch workers abroad. Dispatching workers allows these agencies to generate the hard currency required to both fund their core domestic projects and satisfy revenue quotas assigned from above.

3.4.1 Ministry of External Economic Relations and Ministry of Foreign Affairs

A key dispatching entity within the Cabinet's Ministry of External Economic Relations (대외경제성) is the External Construction Guidance Bureau (대외건설지도국), which was formerly under the WPK's Administrative Department during the Jang Song-thaek era (Interviews 7, 10, 11). This bureau sends construction workers to major enterprises that double as training centers, such as the Neungra External Construction Training Center (능라대외건설양성소). These centers are notorious for their exploitative conditions; as a test of loyalty and discipline, "trainees" are forced to work for two to three years without compensation before being dispatched overseas (Interviews 4, 7).

Once abroad, the operations of North Korean workers and companies are governed by a strict framework laid out in the Regulations on the Foreign Economic Activities of the Economic and Trade Counselor's Office, Economic Cooperation Delegations, and Economic Working-level Delegations (경제무역참사부와 경제협조단, 경제실무대표단의 대외경제사업규정), adopted by the Cabinet in July 2020.[58] This regulation formally defines the different entities and their roles:

---

58. Moon, Dong-hui. "북, '김정은 비자금' 39호실 돈줄인 대흥총국 평양종합무역회사 인사 교체" [North Korea Replaces Personnel at Daehung General Bureau's Pyongyang General Trading Company, a Key Cash Source for Kim Jong-un's Slush Fund, Office 39]. *Daily NK*, 2 May 2025, https://www.dailynk.com/20250502-1/.

1. **"Representative" - Economic and Trade Counselor's Office (경제무역참사부):** This entity is the official "trade representative." Expert insights identify its role as acting as a state-sanctioned broker and providing a "legal face" for dispatching companies (Expert 3). This aligns with its official duties as the diplomatic mission's "economic diplomacy department" (Article 2), which connects North Korean entities with foreign partners (Article 13) and supervises all other North Korean economic entities in the host country (Article 18). For successfully brokering deals, this office is authorized to collect a commission (e.g., 2-5% of an export's value) (Article 15).

2. **"Company" - Economic Cooperation Delegation (경제협조단):** This term refers to the actual North Korean business entities residing in a foreign country to generate profit (Article 2). This category includes the branches of trading companies, overseas construction firms, and other investment enterprises (Article 2). These are the organizations that employ the dispatched workers and operate under the direct guidance of the Counselor's Office (Article 20).

3. **"Temporary Delegations" - Economic Working-level Delegation (경제실무대표단):** This is a temporary group dispatched for a specific, short-term purpose, such as signing a contract, participating in an exhibition, or attending a training session (Article 2). They also fall under the supervision of the Counselor's Office during their stay.

The 2020 regulations establish a dual chain of command in which the Ministry of External Economic Relations (MoEER) ultimately directs all overseas economic activities in line with the state's central economic plan, while the Ministry of Foreign Affairs (MFA) manages local operations. The MFA holds on-site operational authority, as all economic personnel and activities in a host country are formally under the "unified command" of the head of the diplomatic mission (Article

6). It also provides supporting services such as processing passports and visas (Interviews 3, 7, 11), and oversees the day-to-day management of personnel in the field. The MoEER, however, retains functional command over economic strategy and is designated in the regulations as the "central foreign economic guidance organ" (Article 27), with ultimate authority over the purpose and direction of economic work. Although the Counselor's Office operates within the diplomatic mission, it reports its economic findings, market analysis, and performance evaluations directly to the MoEER in Pyongyang (Article 9). This arrangement ensures that, despite the MFA's operational role, all overseas economic activities remain subordinated to the state's central economic plan.

It is important to note the possibility that sanctions have affected this official diplomatic formal structure in Russia, given the push into informal channels. However, expert insights indicate that the Counselor's Office and other economic divisions of North Korean diplomatic missions still facilitate business with local firms in Russia, as they have been observed advertising contacts for North Korean companies (Expert 4). Testimony from the workers themselves on these official representatives is limited, as workers are far more likely to engage with their direct company head (the leader of their Economic Cooperation Delegation) than with officials at the embassy or consulate (Expert 3).

3.4.2 Industry-Specific Ministries

Besides the external economic and foreign affairs ministries, other Cabinet ministries are also involved in labor export, including the Ministry of Forestry (임업성), Ministry of Agriculture (농업성), and Ministry of Light Industry (경공업성) (Interviews 3, 4, 7, 9, 12, 13; Expert 1). However, unlike well-staffed entities such as the External Construction Guidance Bureau (대외건설지도국) under the Ministry of External Economic Relations, these ministries often lack enough internal personnel to dispatch for overseas labor operations. Consequently, they conduct separate recruitment drives, coordinating with the Pyongyang City Party Committee to find workers (Interviews 12, 13). In some cases, workers are assigned to support North Korean construction companies as drivers or in other auxiliary roles, rather than being placed in jobs that match their professional backgrounds (Interview 12). This practice strongly suggests that construction has become the dominant form of labor demanded from overseas. The demand for construction workers supersedes each ministry's specific area of expertise.

3.4.3 Special Committees and Bureaus

In addition to ministries, various committees and bureaus also dispatch workers. For instance, workers can apply for overseas assignments through the Pyongyang Construction Committee (평양건설위원회), formerly known as the Capital City Construction Committee (수도건설위원회) (Interviews 7, 14). This committee contains divisions that manage labor exports at a more granular level, such as the Capital City Construction General Bureau (수도건설총국) (Interview 9).

Testimonies also pointed to bureaus like the External Service Division (대외봉사국), which operates under the Service General Bureau for the People (인민봉사국). The External Service Division is responsible for managing overseas North Korean restaurants and dispatching workers to them (Interview 14).

3.5 MILITARY AS AN AD HOC ECONOMIC APPARATUS

Despite the Cabinet's role as the formal economic apparatus, the military has increasingly functioned as an ad hoc economic apparatus under the strengthened military-economy complex, dispatching military workers abroad to generate revenue. This places military units under a dual command structure: they may report to a non-military agency (within the Party or Cabinet) for their overseas economic operations, while maintaining their primary affiliation with their military agency back home.

3.5.1 Ministry of National Defense and Korean People's Army

The Ministry of National Defense (국방성), which oversees the Korean People's Army (KPA), is a key military agency for dispatching workers. It utilizes subordinate bodies like the General Staff Department (총참모부), the Rear Services General Bureau (후방총국), and the 7th General Bureau (7총국) for these operations (Interviews 3, 6, 9, 11). Within the military, the General Political Bureau (총정치국) was identified as having the greatest authority for approving the roster of soldiers to be dispatched (Interview 6).

According to one testimony, even the most elite military units are involved in the labor export program (Interview 3). The Guard Command (호위사령부), responsible for the Kim family's personal security, and the Capital Defense Command (수도방위사령부), which protects Pyongyang, both dispatch personnel on overseas labor assignments to generate independent funds for their specialized operations. This suggests a pervasive system where nearly every powerful institution is expected to be economically self-sufficient and contribute to the central "loyalty fund."

The involvement of the Second Economic Commission establishes a direct link between the labor conducted by designated military units and the financing of North Korea's WMD program (Interviews 3, 10). A prime example of these special military units is the 131st Guidance Bureau (131원자력지도국), which is involved in constructing nuclear facilities and procuring materials used to harness atomic energy. The dispatch of military workers from this bureau shows how the labor export program is used to generate revenue for the development of the WMD program. This bureau operates under a dual command structure: responding to the Second Economic Commission under the WPK's Munitions Industry Department when involved in overseas labor operations, while maintaining ties to the General Staff Department under the Ministry of National Defense. To obscure these sensitive military and nuclear connections, the 131st Guidance Bureau operates abroad under the civilian alias "Daedong River Overseas Construction Site" (대동강 대외건설장) (Interview 3).

3.5.2 Ministry of Social Security and Social Security Forces

The Ministry of Social Security (사회안전성) also dispatches workers to Russia, recruiting them from its internal armed forces, the Social Security Forces (사회안전군). While these forces are tasked with maintaining internal order and patrolling the border as essential police officers, they are also heavily involved in industrial operations both at home and abroad. Domestically, these soldiers provide manpower for various industrial projects. A specific example of a dispatching entity is the ministry's Subway Railway Operations Bureau (지하철도 운영국), which normally manages the Pyongyang Metro system but was also identified as sending military workers to Russia (Interview 1; Expert 1).

3.5.3 Ministry of State Security

The Ministry of State Security (국가보위성) has a fundamentally different role from the Ministry of National Defense (국방성) and the Ministry of Social Security (사회안전성) in overseas labor operations, reflecting its unique mandate to investigate political treason. Consequently, the Ministry of State Security takes primary responsibility for monitoring the movement and behavior of personnel dispatched abroad. All interviewees reported that when they were sent to Russia, they were accompanied by an official from the Ministry of State Security who retained all workers' personal documents and disciplined any behavior deemed anti-socialist, such as watching South Korean dramas. Importantly, this scrutiny extends even to the highest levels of management, including the company head.

Moreover, according to one testimony, the Ministry of State Security oversees the transfer of earnings from the labor export program in Russia back to North Korea; units of officers called *gitongsu* from its 3rd Bureau are periodically dispatched to collect these funds, often in cash (Interview 9). In addition to these support functions, interviewees believe that the Ministry of State Security also sends its own personnel as workers (Interviews 6 and 11).

3.6 FRONT LINES: ALIASES AND OPERATIONS IN RUSSIA

The directives issued from Pyongyang are executed on the ground through a sprawling network of government agencies, state-owned enterprises, trading corporations, and construction companies. These entities serve as the corporate face of the government, enabling it to secure international contracts, manage workers, and navigate the global financial system. A key feature of this operational layer is the pervasive use of aliases and the deliberate blurring of lines between military and civilian enterprises, a strategy designed to obscure ownership, evade sanctions, and maintain operational flexibility. Companies that have been targeted individually by sanctions have reportedly continued operations by dispatching small teams for projects, such as interior design or small-scale construction, that can be arranged without formal company-to-company contracts (Expert 10).

Table 4 lists companies identified in interviews with former North Korean workers and corroborated by other sources. Multiple interviews suggest that a company may employ a mix of civilian and military workers, depending on the availability of open positions, the supply of deployable personnel from its parent organization (i.e., the body that typically recruits and dispatches workers to the company), and the skills required (Interviews 1, 4, 6).

Table 4. North Korean Front Companies Identified in Interviews

North Korean Companies in Russia	Known Details
Jeonseong Construction Company (전성건설회사)	Mainly associated with paramilitary workers from the Ministry of Social Security. Newly formed in the mid-2010s. Not sanctioned.
Namgang Construction Company (남강건설회사)	Mainly associated with military workers from the Ministry of National Defense. Sanctioned by the U.S. Department of Treasury pursuant to Executive Order 13722 (2016).
Korea General Corporation for External Construction (GENCO; 젠코건설회사)	Mainly associated with civilian workers. Sanctioned by the U.S. Department of Treasury pursuant to Executive Order 13722 (2016). Sanctioned by the U.S. North Korea Sanctions and Policy Enhancement Act of 2016, as amended by the Countering America's Adversaries Through Sanctions Act (2020). Sanctioned by the European Union Council Implementing Regulation 2022/659 (2022), 2022/1331 (2022), and 2023/2576 (2023). Sanctioned by the Japan Ministry of Finance (2013).
Mokran LLC (목란 LLC)	Mainly associated with civilian workers. Sanctioned by the U.S. Department of Treasury pursuant to Executive Order 13722 (2020). Sanctioned by the U.S. North Korea Sanctions and Policy Enhancement Act of 2016 (NKSPEA), as amended by the Otto Warmbier Banking Restrictions Involving North Korea (BRINK) Act within the FY 2020 National Defense Authorization Act (NDAA).

Korea Cholsan Trading Corporation (철산무역회사)	Mainly associated with civilian workers. Sanctioned by the U.S. Department of Treasury pursuant to Executive Order 13722 (2020). Sanctioned by the U.S. North Korea Sanctions and Policy Enhancement Act of 2016 (NKSPEA), as amended by the Otto Warmbier Banking Restrictions Involving North Korea (BRINK) Act within the FY 2020 National Defense Authorization Act (NDAA).
Hyangryun Joint Venture Company (향련합작회사)	Mainly associated with civilian workers. Not sanctioned.
Korea Rungrado General Trading Corporation (능라도무역회사)	Mainly associated with civilian workers. Sanctioned by the U.S. Department of Treasury pursuant to Executive Order 13722 (2016). Sanctioned by the European Union Council Implementing Regulation 2022/1331 (2022). Sanctioned by the U.K. Commonwealth & Development Office (2020).

Testimonies indicate that, beyond the officially listed enterprises, the government routinely assigns front-company names by combining the host city in Russia with a numerical designation—e.g., "Moscow Third Company" (모스크바 3회사). These entities, however, exist entirely off the books, with no formal registration in Russia; their aliases merely serve to distinguish one North Korean labor detachment from another.

This strategic use of civilian-front organizations for military-linked operations reflects a deliberate feature of North Korea's military-economy complex. In practice, the distinction between "military" and "civilian" personnel is largely nominal: all workers are state assets mobilized by government organs to generate revenue in support of the Kim family's lavish lifestyle, the elite reward system, and the state's dual objectives of economic development and nuclear-based security. These labels serve primarily as bureaucratic devices, allowing the government to obscure its core aims on the international stage while pursuing the integrated goal of mobilizing the military as an economic instrument for military ends.

Excerpts from Interviews with Workers

> Our dispatch was under the Party's affiliation. The fact that the affiliation was transferred from the Organization and Guidance Department to the Munitions Industry Department can be interpreted to mean that the funds earned abroad became more necessary for the munitions sector, such as for nuclear and missile development. The Party's funds are the national defense funds, and the national defense funds are the Party's funds. (Interview 4)

> My dispatching agency was the Second Economic Commission. It's the department that handles war preparations. For example, the money goes into making airplane wheels or producing artillery shells. All of our (the workers') income is used for that purpose. (Interview 5)

> The Neungra Guidance Bureau is one of the representative organizations under Office 39. You should assume that all the money earned there goes into the Party's funds, which is to say, the Supreme Leader's ruling funds. (Interview 11)

> From what I've heard recently, even the 131st Guidance Bureau, the unit for the nuclear power plant, is dispatching workers overseas…The 131st Guidance Bureau was so thoroughly controlled within North Korea that even after the soldiers' discharge from the bureau,

the Party couldn't let these people roam freely because of the secrecy of their work. I was surprised to hear that even they were going abroad. (Interview 14)

> We belong to a military organization, but it's a different organization from the Social Security Forces under the Ministry of Social Security. Ours was under the Rear Services General Bureau of the Korean People's Army. The Rear Services General Bureau is a place that guarantees everything related to the welfare of soldiers, such as their clothing and medical equipment, but they also send people for overseas construction. (Interview 6)

> During the Jang Song-thaek era, the process was consolidated into the External Construction Guidance Bureau, but now it seems they have returned to dispatching individually by ministry (省), such as the Ministry of External Economic Relations. In effect, dispatch through the Cabinet is centered on the Ministry of External Economic Relations. (Interview 11)

CHAPTER 4
PROCEDURAL ASPECTS OF NORTH KOREA'S LABOR EXPORT TO RUSSIA

The employment of North Korean workers in Russia is a distinct phenomenon in global labor migration, orchestrated not by individual agency but by the strategic objectives of the state. Unlike other foreign nationals who might seek employment independently, North Korean workers are dispatched as part of a state-run enterprise from start to finish—from the negotiation of contracts between governments to the management of on-site conditions. This system is not designed to recognize a citizen's freedom to work abroad, but rather serves as a state initiative to earn hard currency, a process underscored by the inclusion of state actors at every stage.

Instead of direct communication between a worker and an employer, the process is mediated by North Korean state representatives. Prior to the adoption of the 2017 UN sanctions, Russian authorities would allocate annual quotas for North Korean workers under the 2007 bilateral agreement.[59] North Korean state representatives, such as those stationed at consular offices, would then be notified of the available work permits and coordinate with the North Korean Ministry

---

59. See Appendix 2a/2b for the full text in Russian/English.

of External Economic Relations.[60] In response to communications on the labor demand, North Korea would dispatch workers recruited from various Party, state, and military apparatuses, effectively eliminating any direct engagement between the individual worker and the employing entity.

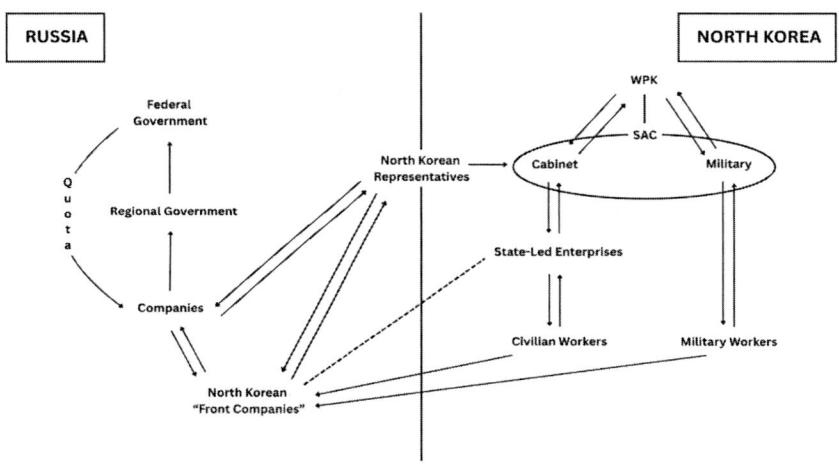

Figure 2. Intrastate and Interstate Connections Underlying Labor Export Program Before Sanctions

Following the adoption of UN sanctions in late 2017, the system evolved to feign compliance. To circumvent the prohibition on work authorization, Russia began issuing thousands of student visas to North Korean workers, altering their documented status. With the shift to student visas, the labor export program remains state-controlled, but North Korean representatives now secure the required entry documents by cooperating with Russian educational institutions and intermediaries other than companies. In 2020, Russia amended its laws to allow foreign students to work without separate permits,

---

60. See *Section 3.4.1 Ministry of External Economic Relations and Ministry of Foreign Affairs* for more information on the role of North Korean representatives and the broader diplomatic structure behind the labor export program.

formalizing this sanctions-evasion tactic in its domestic legal framework.

On the supply side, the selection process is managed by the state, not by market demand. North Korea often maintains a long waiting list of prospective workers, a result of both the high desirability of overseas posts and the lengthy, meticulous internal vetting process required for approval. This dynamic creates an unusual system where the dispatching state (North Korea), rather than the receiving entity (Russian client firm), dictates personnel selection. Workers are dispatched under the banner of North Korean state-owned enterprises subcontracted by Russian firms, yet they are rarely provided with employment contracts of any kind. The ultimate authority for their dispatch is the Workers' Party of Korea (WPK), which signs off on each individual only after a rigorous screening process.

This chapter will outline the architecture of this system, from the initial selection and dispatch procedures in North Korea to the adapted documentation methods used for their entry and residence in Russia. It will begin by examining North Korea's coercive internal procedures that ensure its command over the workforce even before departure.

4.1 NORTH KOREA'S RECRUITMENT AND SELECTION OF WORKERS

North Korea's selection of overseas workers is a meticulously engineered system of control designed to ensure their ideological reliability. The process unfolds on two tracks: an arduous civilian application and quasi-compulsory military conscription. All candidates undergo invasive ideological screening based on their *songbun* (state-assigned social class), *todae* (extended family background), and a series of "loyalty stress tests."[61] While ideological reliability remains the

---

61. *Songbun*, which literally translates to "ingredient," effectively refers to an individual's background. It is the system North Korea uses to categorize its citizens into classes based on their perceived political allegiance to the regime. This allegiance is determined by an individual's family history and the actions of their relatives. Based on this assessment, citizens are placed into one of three broad classes: "core," "wavering," and "hostile."

decisive factor, the process is deeply compromised by institutionalized corruption, with bribery functioning as an essential, unspoken requirement for a candidate to advance. This creates a profoundly unfair dynamic: while candidates endure invasive personal and ideological vetting, they are granted no corresponding agency over their own employment. The process ultimately deprives them of any say in their assignment, leaving them uninformed about the specifics of their placement, working conditions, or compensation until they arrive at the worksite. The entire selection process thus serves as a preparatory stage for mechanisms of transnational repression and exploitation, shaping a workforce deliberately conditioned for obedience and control far from home.

4.1.1 Dual Recruitment Tracks: Civilian and Military

The recruitment process begins on two distinct tracks: civilian and military. Under the civilian track, an aspiring worker must first gain a recommendation from their enterprise's party secretary or cadre officer (Interview 7, 12). This initial endorsement often requires a period of unpaid pre-qualification labor, where candidates must toil for up to three years at their state enterprise or special "training centers" to prove their work ethic (Interview 8, 12). This practice amounts to forced labor as an entry fee into the formal selection process (Interview 8, 12). Once recommended, the candidate embarks on a highly centralized and lengthy application process, which can take an additional one to two years to complete as they navigate a labyrinth of bureaucratic approvals (Interview 6).

Conversely, the pathway for military personnel mostly precludes personal volition in overseas labor deployment. Young men, who are typically performing their mandatory military service in their 20s, are subject to direct conscription for these overseas assignments upon the directive of their superiors (Interview 1, 3, 5, 10). A salient example occurred in 2014, when a list of 100 soldiers designated as

---

See United Nations, Human Rights Council. *Report of the Detailed Findings of the Commission of Inquiry on Human Rights in the Democratic People's Republic of Korea.* 7 Feb. 2014, A/HRC/25/CRP.1.

"outstanding," reportedly at the behest of Kim Jong Un, was repurposed as a roster for compulsory work abroad (Interview 1). Consequently, while these deployments are officially presented as "opportunities," they are functionally understood by the conscripts as unassailable commands.

4.1.2 Family Background and Ideological Screening

All candidates in the pipeline undergo a profound and invasive ideological and background investigation based on *songbun* (North Korea's hereditary social classification system) and *todae* (family lineage). A clear preference is given to candidates with a high *songbun*, evidenced by the fact that 82% of interviewees approved under the civilian track were residents of Pyongyang. While the regions of residence for military personnel were more varied, all were serving in Pyongyang at the time of their dispatch. This favoritism reflects the political leverage of the capital's residents, whose proximity to the Central Committee of the Workers' Party of Korea (WPK) can facilitate the approval process.

The vetting process involves meticulous genealogical reviews that can extend to a candidate's sixth cousin in order to uncover any family history of political offenses or hostile associations. Rooted in the principle of collective punishment, this system automatically disqualifies anyone with a relative imprisoned in a labor or political prison camp (Interviews 2, 7). At the same time, having family members in high-ranking Party or military posts (major or above) is also grounds for rejection, as such individuals are deemed security risks due to their potential access to sensitive information (Interview 2). Scrutiny further extends into personal life: unmarried or divorced individuals are often rejected for their weaker ties to the homeland, while married workers with children are explicitly preferred. This preference serves a deliberate purpose, as their immediate families remain in North Korea as effective collateral against defection (Interviews 7, 12).

Finally, candidates must endure multiple "loyalty stress tests," a series of intensive ideological interrogations designed to assess their allegiance and psychological fitness (Interview 1, 3, 6). This multi-stage process involves up to five separate interviews with a hierarchy of officials, including enterprise cadres, Party secretaries, and state security officers (Interview 3, 6). Conducted both individually and in group settings, these sessions probe a candidate's motivations, beliefs, and commitment to the state. Officials look for any possibility of wavering or political unreliability that might be triggered by exposure to foreign influences (Interview 1, 3, 4, 6).

4.1.3 Corruption and Bias

Layered atop the formal criteria is a system of institutionalized corruption, making bribery an unofficial but mandatory prerequisite for virtually all civilian applicants (Interview 2, 7, 8, 9, 11, 12, 14). Payments are distributed through a extensive chain of command, with each bureaucratic gatekeeper—from local enterprises to provincial Party committees—demanding a share (Interviews 2, 8, 14). A first-time applicant might pay approximately USD 150, while a returning worker could be required to pay up to USD 800 (Interview 7, 12). The costs escalate for managerial roles, reaching roughly USD 5,000 for a workplace manager (직장장) and USD 20,000 for a company president (사장) (Interview 14). The system even accommodates downward mobility for a fee: one cadre officer, unable to afford the bribe for a managerial post befitting his status, paid USD 200 to be officially demoted and dispatched as an ordinary laborer (Interview 14).

In the final stage of vetting, candidates undergo medical and technical screenings that serve both practical and discriminatory purposes. The comprehensive medical exam assesses fitness for labor and ensures compliance with host-country entry requirements, such as Russia's screening for infectious diseases like tuberculosis (Interviews 1, 2, 3, 6, 8, 14). At the same time, the process is discriminatory: individuals with visible disabilities or physical "imperfections" (e.g., a missing finger) are barred, as the state deems them unfit to represent the nation abroad (Interviews 8, 14). Depending on the position, applicants may also be required to pass technical or language examinations (Interviews 2, 3, 9, 14).

Nonetheless, these final evaluations are also deeply compromised by corruption. While severe conditions or visible disabilities are difficult to conceal, other disqualifying medical issues can be overlooked for a bribe of USD 20 to 50 to secure a "clean" report (Interview 6, 8). Similarly, technical and language exams often become mere formalities that can be circumvented through bribery rather than demonstrated merit. This practice cements a system where financial capacity, not fitness or skill, is often the ultimate qualifier for dispatch (Interview 3, 6, 9, 12, 14).

These bribes constitute a significant financial burden, often requiring families to pool resources or take on debt (Interview 2, 12). Many borrow from informal lenders at usurious interest rates exceeding 20%, which places immense pressure on workers to maximize their earnings immediately upon arrival and increases their susceptibility to exploitation (Interview 14).

4.1.4 Information Asymmetry and Lack of Agency

Despite enduring a rigorous selection process, North Korean workers have virtually no agency over the final terms of their deployment. Once approved, placements are determined unilaterally by state authorities, with no guarantee that a worker will be assigned to their desired location (Interviews 1-15). For instance, one interviewee who had paid a bribe for a posting in the Middle East was instead sent to Russia when a position became available there sooner (Interview 14).

Furthermore, labor recruits are systematically kept uninformed about the specifics of their assignments. All interviewees confirmed that they were not issued employment contracts. Before departure, they reported knowing at most their general destination (e.g., a province in Russia) but receiving no details about their specific worksite, hours, or compensation (Interviews 1–15). This lack of transparency effectively pre-conditions them for exploitation.

This information asymmetry facilitates direct financial exploitation, as exemplified by a scheme involving state incentives for new companies. To encourage the formation of overseas enterprises, the state grants them a one-year exemption from remitting mandatory "loyalty payments" and typically covers the initial travel costs for their workers (Interview 14). This policy is designed to give new operations a temporary window to accumulate capital.

However, managers exploit this grace period by fraudulently charging workers for travel costs that the state has already covered. One interviewee, for instance, was charged USD 1,500 for his flight to Russia—a sum deducted from his earnings—even though his company was in its first year and therefore exempt from reimbursing the state for such expenses (Interview 14). This scheme, reportedly common, allows company presidents to pocket the funds directly. Such internal fraud is implicitly tolerated, as it remains largely invisible to the central government so long as the company begins remitting its required payments after the one-year exemption ends. This illustrates how the state's objectives are often met through a system that not only permits but depends on corruption at the operational level (Interview 14).

Excerpts from Interviews with Workers

In North Korea, we build apartments with human labor. Due to electricity shortages, we can't use cranes. Even for a four-story building, all materials are carried by hand. Instead of ready-mix concrete, we mix cement ourselves, and carry the heavy concrete in buckets up the stairs to the fourth floor. It was to escape such harsh labor that I dreamed of being dispatched overseas, but the reality here was just another form of hell. (Interview 7)

To be dispatched overseas, you need the approval of a total of twenty-four people. You have to get stamps from six people, from the head of your local people's unit to security and state security agents, and your family background is investigated up to the sixth degree of kinship, including the deeds of your grandfather. None of this process moves forward without money. Even in the medical check-up, doctors will intentionally fail you to get a bribe. And in the interview, which tests your political loyalty, you have to answer that you are 'going to earn foreign currency for the Party' to pass. It took me nine months to get through this entire process. (Interview 5)

> You can't even get started without money and connections. In the past, people went abroad because they had no money, but now the structure is such that you can't go if you don't have money. First-timers usually spend about 750 dollars, and this money is passed up through various levels of cadres. In my case, because I was a university graduate, I wasn't allowed to be dispatched as a laborer. To get my cadre position rescinded, I had to pay an additional 200 dollars. In North Korea, there's a saying that regulations are made to be broken. The cadres create unnecessary procedures to make money, and the workers have no choice but to pay bribes to get through them. It's a vicious cycle. (Interview 14)

> You have to work for three years at the training center. For three years, you have to work diligently without pay. Only then can you even start the paperwork. In my case, the Party secretary changed, and the new one said, 'You have to be at the enterprise for three years, and your brother is already abroad, so you can't go.' I had no choice but to work there for three years. It's a system where you have to prove yourself through unpaid labor before you're even considered for dispatch. (Interview 8)

> I was a translator, but there's no work for translators in North Korea. So, I just did construction work. Without

pay. It was a review... a test. They test you to see, 'Can this person go overseas and work like a worm, or will they rebel?' It wasn't an interview; they make you work for a year. Without pay. So, for a year, if you do all the work they tell you to without complaint, like a servant, then they'll sign your recommendation letter, saying, 'This person can work.' But if you miss even one day out of 365, if you don't show up for the unpaid work, they won't sign it. That means your unpaid work period gets extended for another year. That's how it is. You have to do that to get the recommendation. (Interview 6)

There was no employment contract. No documents. The part about receiving 200 euros a month was just a verbal report. The information I received before dispatch was that I was going to Moscow to do construction work, and that the dispatch period was three years. There was nothing about working hours or salary.(Interview 3)

4.2 RUSSIA'S ADMISSION AND DOCUMENTATION OF WORKERS

The legal and administrative framework governing North Korean labor in Russia offers a compelling case study in the weaponization of domestic law for geopolitical purposes. The system has transitioned from a phase of formal regulation to one of clandestine sanctions evasion and, more recently, to an era of open defiance of the international legal order. This trajectory demonstrates that Russia's domestic legal framework has functioned not as a passive backdrop but as an adaptable instrument of state policy, repurposed to navigate and ultimately subvert its international obligations. The scheme of registering workers as "students" is not a mere loophole but a parallel, state-sanctioned immigration system operating under a veneer of legitimacy. Its complexity—implicating North Korean state representatives, Russian government agencies, educational institutions, and quasi-private intermediaries—reveals a fully developed system that depends on the complicity of Russian authorities at multiple levels.

4.2.1 Standard Work Authorization Process

To understand the illegality of the current system, it is first necessary to outline the legitimate framework for foreign labor that Russia employed before the imposition of UN sanctions in 2017. This multi-stage process, which in theory still applies to other foreign nationals, is entirely contingent on sponsorship from a Russian employer and grants the North Korean state significant control. Two key documents govern the work authorization of foreigners in Russia: a work permit, which confers the legal right to be employed, and a work visa, which authorizes entry and residence for that purpose. Importantly, a work visa cannot be obtained unless a work permit has already been secured.

Between 2007 and 2017, this process of employing North Korean workers was governed by the domestic permit framework established by Federal Law No. 115-FZ ("On the Legal Status of Foreign Citizens in the Russian Federation"), as significantly amended by the 2006 reforms of Federal Law No. 110-FZ.[62] The 2007 North Korea-Russia bilateral agreement on labor activities explicitly linked the employment of North Korean workers to this amended system.[63] The process unfolds in four sequential steps:

---

62. Federal Law No. 115-FZ of 25 July 2002 established the rights and obligations of foreign nationals in the Russian Federation but imposed such extensive administrative requirements that a substantial portion of migrant labor migrated into the informal economy. To remedy these shortcomings, the Russian legislature enacted two interrelated statutes on July 18, 2006: ① Federal Law No. 110-FZ, which amended 115-FZ by abolishing the separate "Permit to Attract and Use Foreign Workers" and consolidating all authorization procedures into a single, employer-driven application for individual work permits. This reform significantly reduced pre-employment administrative barriers. ② Federal Law No. 109-FZ, which instituted a compulsory migration registration system. Under this law, the "receiving parties" (such as employers or landlords) must notify authorities of each foreign national's residential address, thereby strengthening state oversight of migrant whereabouts. Together, these measures streamlined the legal employment process while reinforcing mechanisms for state control. The bilateral labor agreement with North Korea, signed in August 2007, subsequently integrated the employment of North Korean nationals into this streamlined Russian framework, facilitating direct intergovernmental channels for migrant employment.

See Russian Federation. *Federal Law No. 115-FZ, On the Legal Status of Foreign Citizens in the Russian Federation.* 25 July 2002, amended 23 May 2025. *Garant Legal Information System,* https://base.garant.ru/184755/.

Russian Federation. *Federal Law No. 110-FZ, On Amendments to the Federal Law "On the Legal Status of Foreign Citizens in the Russian Federation" and on Repealing Certain Provisions of the Federal Law "On Amendments and Additions to Certain Legislative Acts of the Russian Federation."* 18 July 2006, amended 24 November 2014. *Garant Legal Information System,* https://base.garant.ru/12148410/.

Russian Federation. *Federal Law No. 109-FZ, On Migration Registration of Foreign Citizens and Stateless Persons in the Russian Federation.* 18 July 2006, amended 23 May 2025. *Garant Legal Information System,* https://constitution.garant.ru/act/right/12148419/.

63. See Appendix 2a/2b for the full text in Russian/English.

1. **Work Permit:** The process is initiated by the Russian employer, who must apply to the local branch of the Russian Ministry of Internal Affairs (MVD) to secure a work permit for the foreign employee.[64] This permit, typically a plastic card, authorizes the holder to work for a specific company within a designated region. The Ministry of Internal Affairs compares the work permit application with the annual quota determined by the Ministry of Labour and Social Protection.

2. **Work Invitation:** With the work permit secured, the employer applies for an official Letter of Invitation from the local office of the Russian Ministry of Internal Affairs (MVD). This government-issued invitation is the foundational document for the foreign national's visa application.

3. **Single-Entry Work Visa:** The foreign national presents the MVD's invitation at a Russian consulate in their home country to obtain an initial single-entry work visa. Typically valid for up to 90 days, this visa allows the worker to legally enter Russia and formalize their employment.

---

64. Before it was dissolved on April 5, 2016, the Federal Migration Service (FMS) managed the issuance of work permits and work visa invitations. Following its dissolution, its functions, powers and personnel were transferred to the Main Directorate for Migration Affairs within the Ministry of Internal Affairs (MVD).

   See Russian Federation, President. *Presidential Decree No. 156 of April 5, 2016, "About Enhancement of Public Administration in the Sphere of Control of Drug Trafficking, Psychotropic Substances and Their Precursors and in the Sphere of Migration."* 5 Apr. 2016, amended 2 Apr. 2025. CIS Legislation Database, https://cis-legislation.com/document.fwx?rgn=84320.

4. **Multiple-Entry Work Visa and Registration:** Upon arriving in Russia, the employer must register the worker with local MVD authorities, as required by Federal Law No. 109-FZ ("On the Migration Registration of Foreign Citizens and Stateless Persons in the Russian Federation"). Registration is a mandatory step to convert the initial single-entry visa into a renewable, multiple-entry work visa whose validity is linked to the work permit. The criticality of this final step was underscored by a worker who arrived in 2017 but could not complete the conversion after sanctions were imposed, rendering his status illegal (Interview 2).

Under this permit-based migration framework, Russia issued large numbers of work permits to North Korean nationals between 2007 and 2017. Official figures show that permit numbers remained steady until 2017 and then fell to zero by the end of 2019. This decline followed UN Security Council Resolution 2375 (September 2017), which barred new authorizations, and Resolution 2397 (December 2017), which required the repatriation of all existing workers by 22 December 2019. The figures, however, created only the illusion of full sanctions compliance and did not reflect the actual number of North Korean workers present.

Table 5. Work Permits Issued to North Korean Nationals in Russia (2007-2019)

Year	Number of North Korean Workers (in thousands)	Year	Number of North Korean Workers (in thousands)
2007	32.6	2014	30.7
2008	34.9	2015	30.4
2009	37.7	2016	29.1
2010	36.5	2017	24.1
2011	19.3	2018	8.0
2012	23.4	2019	0.0
2013	27.2		

Source: Federal State Statistics Service of the Russian Federation

4.2.2 Shift to Alternative Procedure in the Post-Sanctions Context

In practice, Russia's official compliance with UN sanctions masked a systemic effort to continue importing North Korean labor through illicit channels, the most prevalent of which was the fraudulent misregistration of workers as students. This tactic was confirmed by numerous interviewees who either newly entered or left and re-entered Russia on student visas after the sanctions took effect (Interviews 1-15). As part of the procedure, North Korean companies, often through intermediaries, enroll workers in Russian universities and vocational schools. These students enter on legitimate student visas but are immediately dispatched to full-time construction jobs under the guise of "internships" or "practical training" (Interviews 2, 6). This legal fiction allowed Russia to bypass UN sanctions, a reality confirmed by workers who were sent home on an expiring work visa only to return months later with a student visa (Interviews 1, 2, 3, 11). Though not as common, a secondary method involved the use of tourist visas, which required workers to return to North Korea every three months for renewal (Interviews 2, 3).

For those who remained in Russia after their work visas expired, a different predicament arose. Unable to renew their legal status, they became undocumented and resorted to carrying photocopies of valid documents belonging to colleagues whose visas had yet to expire. Of the fifteen individuals interviewed for this report, 80% confirmed they were on student visas, while the remaining 20% relied on using photocopies of other workers' documents. This form of identity fraud was described by several workers who had to rely on these falsified papers to navigate daily life and avoid police scrutiny (Interviews 2, 3, 8). One worker detailed a three-stage process used by his group to remain in Russia: they entered on valid work visas prior to sanctions; once their visas expired, they relied on photocopies of the unexpired visas of other colleagues; and finally, after the repatriation deadline imposed by sanctions, they used photocopies of workers who newly arrived on student visas (Interview 2). This deception was an open secret among the workforce and was often tolerated by Russian police in exchange for bribes (Interview 2).

The student visa scheme was institutionalized by a pivotal legislative amendment passed shortly after the UN's repatriation deadline of December 22, 2019. On June 2, 2020, Russia enacted Federal Law No. 16-FZ, which permits foreign citizens studying full-time at state-accredited institutions to work without a separate permit.[65] By embedding the right to work directly within student status, the Russian state dismantled the last administrative barrier to using "students" as workers, transforming a de facto workaround into a codified policy that signaled a long-term commitment to preserving the flow of North Korean labor.

---

65. Russian Federation. *Federal Law No. 16-FZ, On Amendments to the Federal Law "on the Legal Status of Foreign Citizens in the Russian Federation'" in Part of Simplifying the Employment Procedure for Foreign Citizens and Stateless Persons Studying in Russian Professional and Higher Education Institutions. Official Internet Portal of Legal Information*, 6 Feb. 2020, http://actual.pravo.gov.ru/content/content.html#pnum=0001202002060026

The bureaucratic fingerprints of a coordinated scheme are visible in the official data on the issuance of visas, which reveals a suspicious inversion in the number of work and student visas issued to North Korean nationals. While work permits plummeted after the passage of sanctions, the data reveals an unprecedented surge in student visas issued to North Koreans. Putting aside this small number of work visas, the post-sanctions period has been defined by a high number of student visas, which seems to corroborate testimonies on the systematic reclassification of workers as students. [66]

Moreover, the actual number of North Korean workers in Russia likely far exceeds the official figures for non-work visas, as many workers remain entirely undocumented (e.g., relying on photocopies of others' documents). The uncertainty surrounding the true numbers is further compounded by inconsistent reporting: in early 2020, the Ministry of Internal Affairs recorded 16,613 tourist visas for 2019, whereas the Ministry of Foreign Affairs reported only 14 for the same period.[67]

---

66. A smaller number of work visas (661) were still issued across 2018 and 2019, which Olga Kirillova of the Ministry of Internal Affairs publicly justified as renewals for pre-existing contracts exempt from sanctions.
   See "Ольга Кириллова: более 300 тысяч украинцев получили гражданство РФ с 2014 года [Olga Kirillova: Over 300,000 Ukrainians Obtained Russian Citizenship Since 2014]." *Interfax*, 3 Oct. 2017, https://www.interfax.ru/interview/628692
67. Osborn, Andrew. "Russia Says It Missed U.N. Deadline to Repatriate North Korean Workers." *Reuters*, 24 Jan. 2020, https://www.reuters.com/article/world/russia-says-it-missed-un-deadline-to-repatriate-north-korean-workers-idUSKBN1ZM2FC/

Table 6. Visas Issued to North Korean Nationals in Russia (2015-2024)

Year	Total Visas Issued to North Korean Nationals	Work Visas	Student Visas	Tourist Visas
2015	12,859	12,466	113	10
2016	12,075	11,853	62	9
2017	11,286	10,809	41	7
2018	4,975	232	3,124	2
2019	12,494	429	10,876	14
2020	1,583	0	1,469	0
2021	1	0	0	0
2022	0	0	0	0
2023	20	0	19	0
2024	9,240	0	8,617	6

Source: Ministry of Foreign Affairs of the Russian Federation

4.2.3 Key Institutional Actors in the Sanctions Evasion Scheme

This state-sponsored evasion relies on a network of coordinated institutional actors. At the diplomatic level, the North Korean Embassy in Moscow, Consulate General in Vladivostok, and Consulate in Khabarovsk function as key facilitators in connecting Russian employers and other intermediaries with North Korean workers. For example, the North Korean Embassy in Moscow reportedly accepts applications of requests for North Korean workers while imposing a minimum of 100 workers per order and collecting a fee of approximately USD 1,600, ostensibly for visas and other costs.[68] In addition, the North Korean Consulate General in Vladivostok has been observed to openly advertise North Korean construction crews, serving as a bridge between Russian firms and North Korean subcontractors (Expert 4).

On the ground, quasi-private intermediaries like the Intergovernmental Migration Center (Межгосударственный миграционный центр; MMC) have emerged to manage the logistics of recruitment and placement, making a profit model out of sanctions evasion tactics (Expert 10).[69] The MMC appears to use online messaging platforms like Telegram to receive requests for North Korean workers from Russian firms and even state officials. Notably, Pyotr Popov, a former deputy governor of Zabaikalsky Krai in eastern Siberia, has reportedly directly requested 5,000 workers for a local construction project.[70] Moreover, online forums like Business Russia even provide detailed guides on hiring North Korean workers through both the standard work authorization procedure and the student visa scheme.[71] Rather than relying on intermediaries, some North Korean companies—especially those led by well-connected executives—negotiate directly with Russian universities to secure student-visa sponsorship for incoming workers from North Korea (Interviews 5, 6).

This entire multi-layered system, from official requests to brokered deals, ultimately hinges on the complicity of Russian educational institutions. In exchange for tuition from North Korean companies, institutions like the Far Eastern Federal University (Interviews 1, 5), European Institute Justo (Interviews 3, 10), and an unnamed law school in Moscow (Interview 6) provide the fraudulent enrollments

---

68. Khoroshavin, Kosmos, and Dylan Carter. "Workers of the World: Modern-Day Slave Labor Is Being Imported from North Korea into Russia despite a UN Ban." *The Insider*, 20 June 2025, https://theins.ru/en/inv/282300.
69. Ibid.
70. Ibid.
71. "Как нанять в России рабочих из Северной Кореи в 2025 году: пошаговая инструкция [How to Hire Workers from North Korea in Russia in 2025: A Step-by-Step Guide]." *Business.ru*, n.d., https://www.business.ru/article/5541-kak-nanyat-v-rossii-rabochih-iz-severnoy-korei-v-2025-godu-poshagovaya-instruktsiya

and invitation letters necessary for student visas.[72] To maintain this pretense, these schools then fabricate documents, such as attendance records, creating the false impression that workers are engaged in "practical training" when they are in fact working full-time (Interviews 2, 6).

4.2.4 Construction Sector: Filling Russia's Wartime Labor Gap

Russia's prolonged military mobilization and war-driven emigration have created severe domestic labor shortages, particularly in the construction sector. To fill this gap, Russia has turned to North Korea, whose workers are in high demand for their reputation as disciplined, efficient, and low-cost labor.[73] The scale of this program expanded dramatically in the recent couple years. While an initial estimate cited around 4,000 workers in late 2024, the number surged into the tens of thousands by early 2025.[74] This growth was confirmed by South Korean intelligence, which reported in April 2025 that at least 15,000 North Koreans were working in Russia.[75] By June 2025, the Russian developer Eskadra claimed to have received applications for over 150,000 North Koreans, estimating the workforce would nearly triple to 50,000 by year's end.[76]

---

72. The European Institute Justo has been sanctioned by the U.S. Department of Treasury pursuant to Executive Order 13722 (2021).
   See United States, Department of the Treasury. "Treasury Sanctions Perpetrators of Serious Human Rights Abuse on International Human Rights Day." 1 Dec. 2021, home.treasury.gov/news/press-releases/jy0526
73. The growing perception of North Korean workers in Russia is exemplified by the following article: "Александр Новиков: северокорейские мигранты – идеальные работники [Alexander Novikov: North Korean Migrants—Ideal Workers]." *Аргументы Недели* [*Arguments of the Week*], 4 June 2025, https://argumenti.ru/society/2025/06/953388
74. "$263m a Year, 700,000 Tonnes of Rice, Space Tech: The Deal for North Korea Joining Russia's War." *The Straits Times*, 4 Nov. 2024, https://www.straitstimes.com/asia/east-asia/us200m-a-year-700000-tonnes-of-rice-space-tech-the-deal-for-north-korea-joining-russias-war
75. Luxmoore, Matthew, and Dasl Yoon. "North Korean Leader Kim Jong Un's Latest Gift to Russia Is Migrant Workers." *The Wall Street Journal*, 5 May 2025, www.wsj.com/world/asia/kim-jong-uns-latest-gift-to-russia-is-migrant-workers-916693a4
76. "Девелопер: количество строителей из Северной Кореи в России вырастет втрое [Developer: The Number of North Korean Construction Workers in Russia Will Triple]."

This influx has created a support ecosystem, with Russian companies now routinely seeking Korean-language interpreters and cultural liaisons. Moscow-based developer Strana Development, for instance, has posted vacancies for interpreters to facilitate communication on its construction sites.[77] The emergence of these roles signals more than just the normalization of this illicit labor trade; it may also point to a tactical shift in its operation.

The fact that Russian firms must source their own interpreters suggests they are increasingly engaging smaller, ad hoc units of North Korean workers, who can be integrated into existing workforces without procurement contracts that may draw scrutiny under international sanctions. This arrangement reveals a key tactic used by sanctioned North Korean companies, like GENCO, to continue generating profit.[78] This new model has reportedly increased the hardship faced by individual workers. They are now required to secure their own employment, forcing them to navigate a foreign labor market alone while still meeting demanding financial quotas for their company. Although the North Korean company no longer arranges contracts with firms, it continues to serve the state as a mechanism to supervise and exert control over an otherwise decentralized workforce (Expert 10).

---

77. "Девелопер: количество строителей из Северной Кореи в России вырастет втрое [Developer: The Number of North Korean Construction Workers in Russia Will Triple]." Недвижимость РИА Новости [RIA Novosti Realty], 26 June 2025, https://realty.ria.ru/20250626/chislo-2025542009.html

78. See *Section 3.6 Front Lines: Aliases and Operations in Russia* for examples of other North Korean companies that have been individually targeted by sanctions.

Excerpts from Interviews with Workers

> When UN sanctions blocked our work visas, we entered Russia by posing as students. On paper, we were doing practical training from a university, but in reality, we were working at construction sites. This wasn't a perfect solution, however. The Russian police, knowing the whole situation, would still crack down on us, and each time we had to bribe them to be released. I was once taken to the police station during a crackdown and was only able to get out after paying a bribe of 2,000 to 3,000 rubles. (Interview 2)

> We entered on student visas but worked at construction sites. The Russian university, as long as it received tuition fees, would forge documents regardless of our attendance. They created paperwork as if we were attending lectures every month to prepare for police crackdowns. The police, knowing this, would still find fault, saying, 'Why is a business major student wearing work clothes?' and use it as a pretext to extort money from us. In the end, the money we earned was spent on bribes everywhere. (Interview 6)

> We carried fake visas. Other North Korean companies that had already entered and signed contracts with Russian companies had their permits approved and had certificates. We couldn't get them, so we were illegal aliens, and if we got caught, we would be deported. To prevent that, we copied the documents of people who already had permits and carried someone else's papers as if they were our own…The Russian police knew everything but pretended not to. They can't really tell our faces apart, and they know the situation. Still, sometimes they would drag us to the police station to

'verify,' and then we'd be caught for sure. That's why we always carried 2,000 to 3,000 rubles in our pockets. If we got caught, we'd slip them 1,000 to 2,000 rubles, and they'd tell us to 'get lost.' (Interview 2)

CHAPTER 5
ONSITE MANAGEMENT AND WORKING CONDITIONS

The dispatch of North Korean workers to Russia involves the transplantation of the state's rigid, hierarchical control systems onto foreign soil. Once on-site, workers are absorbed into a multi-tiered command structure designed to maximize labor output and enforce total compliance. This structure, a microcosm of the North Korean state itself, dictates every facet of the workers' lives, from their daily tasks and financial autonomy to their access to healthcare and basic freedoms. The result is a system of exploitation where the line between state-mandated labor and forced labor becomes indistinguishable. Once dispatched outside, performing labor becomes non-negotiable, as all workers, even those who volunteered, must earn the minimum "loyalty fee" in exchange for the so-called privilege of going overseas.

The primary objective underpinning this entire apparatus is the prevention of defection, for which company managers are held personally responsible. This imperative drives a system of total control designed to isolate workers and strip them of their agency. For instance, workers are denied access to their own earnings and given only a minuscule allowance, a tactic to limit their financial capacity to flee. Similarly, the vast majority of workers are generally forbidden from securing their own work, which would create opportunities for unsanctioned contact with the outside world. The Ministry of State Security officer plays a crucial role in this system, enforcing not only loyalty but also ideological conformity to prevent defections abroad and the spread of dissent upon return. Workers are shielded from foreign influences and media to ensure they do not bring back ideas that could threaten the state's internal stability.

5.1 ONSITE MANAGEMENT: A NORTH KOREA OUTSIDE THE NORTH KOREAN STATE

At the apex of each overseas North Korean company is a leadership triad: a company president (사장/지배인), a Party secretary (당비서), and a Ministry of State Security officer (보위원), who often also holds the position of vice president (Interviews 2, 5, 6, 7, 12). Although the president manages business operations, his authority is subordinate to that of the Party secretary and the Ministry of State Security officer, whose primary mandate is to maintain state control over the workers (Interviews 6, 12). In practice, the president functions largely as an onsite manager, while a state official from the diplomatic mission serves as the company's legal representative in negotiations with major Russian firms (Expert 3). Within this hierarchy, the Party secretary directs ideological indoctrination, while the Ministry of State Security officer monitors the entire contingent, including the president, for any sign of dissent (Interviews 2, 6). This structure underpins all overseas companies, regardless of size.

Beneath this top tier, the hierarchy extends through several administrative and operational roles. Larger companies may have a planning officer (계획지도원) or finance officer (재정지도원/경리), a general coordinator (종합지도원), translators (통역사), drivers (운전사), and a medic (군의) (Interviews 2, 3, 5, 6, 7, 9, 11, 12, 15). The finance officer holds significant power due to their control over the company's money (Interviews 11, 12).

The workforce itself is organized into a subordinate structure. Workers are grouped into large units called worksites (직장/작업소), which are then subdivided into smaller work teams (작업반) (Interviews 2, 5, 7). A worksite may consist of over 100 individuals, while a work team can range from a handful to over 30 workers, with the configuration shifting based on the demands of a given project (Interviews 2, 3, 5, 8, 14). Each worksite is managed by a worksite manager (직장장/작업소장), who may be either a commissioned officer (장교) (for military-affiliated companies) or a civilian worker appointed pre-departure or promoted onsite based on capability (Interviews 3, 8, 11, 12). These managers provide updates on the status of the worksite directly to the company president, vice president, or general coordinator.

Work teams are led by a team leader (작업반장), who is appointed onsite by the worksite manager based on perceived loyalty and ability to drive productivity (Interview 2). In some cases, a cell secretary (세포비서) is appointed onsite within each work team to oversee grassroots ideological control and to report on the team's completion of routine ideological exercises (Interviews 2, 5). Meanwhile, certain worksites establish semi-autonomous "freelance" units (청부) consisting of an extreme minority of workers, which source their own work instead of relying on the company for work arrangements (대방) (Interviews 7, 8, 11, 12). These units are formed outside of the state's official orders and subject to higher quotas in exchange for greater mobility (Interviews 7, 11). The practice of forming semi-autonomous "freelance" units became more common in the post-sanctions period, especially during the COVID-19 pandemic, when it became difficult for work to be secured through company-to-company channels.

Figure 3. Sample Organizational Chart of Onsite Management

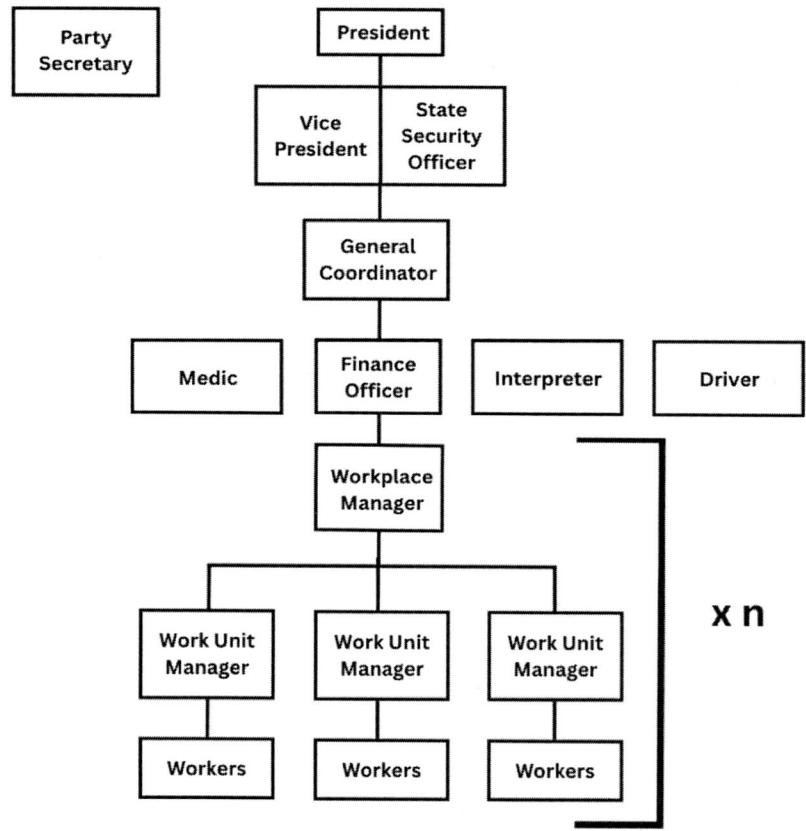

The company's administrative functions are typically run from a central "office," often a rented house or villa where senior managers reside (Interviews 6, 11). Workers are physically segregated from this office, living in separate and often makeshift accommodations at construction sites. They are summoned only for periodic ideological sessions or disciplinary action (Interviews 7, 8, 9). The reporting hierarchy is rigidly enforced: workers report issues to their team leader, who then reports to the worksite manager, creating a chain of command that restricts direct communication with senior leadership (Interview 12).

Despite this physical separation, the top-tiered management maintains constant and pervasive surveillance over the workers. The Ministry of State Security officer extends his reach by recruiting informants from the general workforce. These "spies" are tasked with monitoring their peers for any prohibited activities, such as watching foreign media, criticizing the government, or having unauthorized contact with outsiders (Interviews 1, 6, 8, 9, 14). This system of coerced peer surveillance effectively replicates the domestic *inminban* (people's group) system, fostering an atmosphere of deep-seated paranoia and preventing the formation of trust or solidarity among workers. Even worksite managers are subject to this surveillance and often pay bribes to the Ministry of State Security officer to secure a degree of operational freedom (Interviews 2, 6, 11, 12).

5.2 EXPLOITATIVE WORKING CONDITIONS

The labor system imposed on North Korean workers in Russia is deliberately structured to maximize remittances at the expense of basic rights to rest, fair pay, and safety. Rather than resulting from oversight or negligence, the working conditions reflect a state-engineered framework that prioritizes foreign currency generation over workers' physical and financial well-being (Interviews 3, 5, 7, 8, 9, 12, 14).

5.2.1 Working Hours and Rest

The concept of a standard workday does not exist: workers routinely toil 12 to 17 hours daily, seven days a week, driven not by clock time but by daily production quotas (Interviews 1, 2, 4, 6, 8, 9, 10, 14). While workers start their shifts at 8:00 AM, they work without a formal end time, continuing well past midnight to fulfill the demanding workloads (Interviews 2, 6, 8, 10, 14). Mid-day breaks are limited to a brief lunch period of 30 minutes to one hour. To avoid the time-consuming trip down and back up, workers often eat packed lunches directly on the upper levels of the buildings they are constructing (Interviews 3, 8).

Moreover, workers rarely take days off, as they are not guaranteed paid vacation or sick leave and constantly face pressure to meet remittance quotas (Interviews 4, 8, 10). At most, they are granted a few unpaid days of rest per year for major North Korean holidays, such as New Year's Day or the birthdays of Kim Il Sung and Kim Jong Il (Interviews 1, 3, 9, 11). In some cases, they may also rest on major Russian holidays because all operations are closed, giving them no other option. Workers who fall ill or are injured are expected to continue working unless their condition is life-threatening (Interviews 2, 3, 6, 12, 14). If they are forced to rest, they are not paid for that time and may even be punished for lost productivity (Interviews 1, 2, 8, 11).

Despite Russia's COVID-19 lockdowns, North Korean managers forced their workers to continue laboring in secret to meet government remittance quotas (Interviews 3, 6, 10). While Russian authorities halted work on many construction sites, workers were ordered to hide from monitoring drones and then sent back to work once the coast was clear (Interview 10). This practice blatantly violated local health regulations and showed that managers prioritized productivity at the expense of the workers' health and safety.

5.2.2 Compensation and Financial Autonomy

The financial exploitation of North Korean workers in Russia is systematic and multi-layered. Workers are never given an employment contract and have limited knowledge of the procurement values of their labor, as they are excluded from negotiations with Russian firms (Interviews 2, 3, 4, 8, 11, 12). Their nominal wages are subjected to a cascading series of deductions that leave them with only a small fraction of their earnings (Interviews 11, 14). Compensation is also highly inconsistent: monthly pay depends on a supervisor's subjective assessment of output and is further reduced by arbitrary levies (Interviews 2, 3).

Each worker's gross earnings—estimated at USD 600 to 1,000 per month—are first docked for the mandatory "loyalty payment" (국가계획분) to the North Korean government, an amount managers claim is between USD 500 and 800 (Interviews 3, 4, 6, 8, 9). In reality, however, interviewees found that the amount remitted to the central government is far lower, typically between USD 200 and 500 (Interviews 6, 7, 14). The remainder, or the difference between the claimed quota and the actual state remittance, is diverted to cover company operating costs, management salaries, contributions to the company's parent ministry in Pyongyang, and the company president's personal profit (Interview 14). This is in addition to illicit skimming, whereby supervisors under-report procurement values to their subordinates (Interviews 2, 11). As a result, workers may receive as little as ten percent of the value their labor commands on the Russian market (Interview 5). At times, they are also compelled to contribute to ad hoc state projects back home (e.g., building a monument in Pyongyang), further diminishing these meager earnings (Interviews 3, 8).

To keep even this pittance under strict managerial control, the companies also curtail every avenue of personal finance available to the workers. Workers are strictly forbidden from opening personal bank accounts (Interviews 2, 4, 7, 8, 9, 12, 14). This ban is enforced by the confiscation of their passports by the Party Secretary or the Ministry of State Security officer upon arrival, which prevents them from having the identification documents required to open a bank account (Interviews 1, 3, 4, 6, 11, 12). Furthermore, most workers cannot even retain their full earnings in cash, as Russian firms pay their wages in a lump sum directly to supervisors who exercise full discretion over distribution and access.

Workers are typically informed of their supposed earnings through a simple ledger, where they are forced to sign next to a number without ever seeing the actual money (Interviews 2, 6, 7, 12, 14). From these "paper earnings," they are given a meager monthly allowance of RUB 1,000 to 3,000 for all personal necessities (Interviews 6, 8, 14). This allowance is grossly insufficient, and requests for additional funds are almost always denied under the pretext that workers with money are more likely to become lazy or cause trouble (Interview 2). Given the delayed access to their earnings, a worker who was promised a total of USD 3,000 might only ultimately receive USD 2,000 at the end of a 3-

year assignment, while another received only USD 170 for an entire year of work (Interviews 1, 8).

Sanctions responses, namely the student visa scheme, have significantly exacerbated the financial precarity of North Korean workers in Russia, exposing them to exploitation not only by their own managers but also by Russian authorities. One interviewee, who was dispatched after the imposition of sanctions, recounted that he and his cohort were forced to use photocopies of work permits originally issued to pre-sanctions workers. During local police crackdowns, they had to pay bribes to avoid arrest for carrying fraudulent documents (Interview 1).

Following the repatriation deadline, companies increasingly relied on student visas to maintain a legal façade for incoming workers. Testimonies indicate that employers paid Russian universities not only for tuition but also for bribes to fabricate enrollment records for visa approval and "practical training" records to disguise commercial work as student internships (Interviews 3, 5, 6, 7). These expenses were deducted from the company's earnings—indirectly reducing the income of workers who already lacked any fixed or guaranteed wages (Interviews 6, 8). In cases where companies failed to arrange sponsorships, workers resorted to using duplicate or borrowed student visas belonging to other North Koreans who had recently arrived in Russia (Interviews 2, 7).

This system perpetuated a constant risk of detection. Workers carrying forged or reused documents were especially vulnerable to police inspections and often had to pay bribes of RUB 2,000 to 3,000 to avoid detention (Interviews 2, 6, 14). According to multiple accounts, these enforcement measures largely ceased after Russia's full-scale invasion of Ukraine in 2022, when sanctions enforcement against North Korean workers was deprioritized or informally suspended (Interviews 6, 14).

5.2.3 Workplace Safety and Access to Healthcare

A systemic disregard for the safety of workers has produced consistently hazardous workplace conditions. Interviewees uniformly report the absence of formal safety training or standardized protocols at construction sites. While Russian client companies may supply basic protective gear such as helmets and harnesses to comply with local regulations, North Korean management rarely provides such equipment independently (Interviews 3, 8, 11, 12). Moreover, when protective gear is available, workers may be discouraged from using it if they perceive it to impede productivity (Interview 1). The result is an alarmingly high incidence of serious injuries and fatalities, especially those caused by falls from heights (Interviews 1, 8, 9, 10).

Despite the frequency of injuries, access to adequate medical care remains systematically obstructed. This denial of treatment predates the 2017 UN sanctions, as North Korean companies have long failed to subsidize medical care for workplace-related injuries. Large companies may employ a designated medic (군의), but their capacity is limited to basic first aid (Interviews 1, 7). For anything beyond these minimal services, workers are left to self-treat or endure their conditions, primarily due to the prohibitive cost of professional care (Interviews 1, 10). Financial assistance, when provided, is not granted as a matter of policy but at the discretion of a company president or direct supervisor (Interviews 1, 8, 11). Additionally, the discovery of infectious diseases such as tuberculosis during medical examinations could lead to the expulsion of the entire workforce, incentivizing management to prevent workers from seeking formal healthcare altogether (Interview 6).

These factors have institutionalized a dangerous, emergency-only approach to health management. Hospital visits are thus reserved for life-threatening situations and are delayed as long as possible. This is partly influenced by Russia's policy of providing North Korean workers two days of free emergency care (Interviews 2, 3). The policy creates a perverse incentive to wait until medical conditions become critical in order to avoid the financial burden of treatment, which would otherwise be deducted from the worker's wages (Interview 2). This emergency-only approach is consistent with Article 8 of the 2007 bilateral labor agreement, which stipulates that Russia would only provide free emergency care and leave other healthcare matters to the North Korean state.

As workers continue to be dispatched to Russia despite sanctions, many are forced to rely on irregular visa arrangements—including student visas or forged documents—leaving them unable to assert even their right to emergency medical care guaranteed under the 2007 bilateral agreement on temporary labor activities. Interviewees report that even in cases of severe injury, such as broken bones, they refrain from seeking hospital treatment for fear that their improper documentation status will be discovered and lead to deportation (Interviews 2, 5, 8, 10).

The COVID-19 pandemic further highlighted the structural inadequacies in healthcare access. While some companies enforced basic health protocols, such as mask-wearing, workers were often required to cover the cost of masks through wage deductions (Interview 4). Vaccine access was similarly inconsistent: some companies arranged on-site vaccinations in response to a reported directive from Kim Jong Un (Interviews 2, 6, 10), while others provided no access at all (Interview 3).

5.3 USE OF VIOLENCE AT WORKPLACE

Physical violence is a routine and normalized feature of life for North Korean workers in Russia, employed by managers as a tool of discipline and control. Workers are frequently beaten by their superiors —including team leaders, worksite managers, and the Ministry of State Security officer—for a range of perceived infractions, such as working too slowly, making mistakes, or showing any sign of insubordination (Interview 1, 9, 10). One worker recalled being physically assaulted by the Ministry of State Security officer simply for an alleged failure to report a personal matter, illustrating how violence is used to enforce total obedience (Interview 9).

The high-stress, demanding environment also fosters violence among the workers themselves. Fights between workers are reported as a regular occurrence, often provoked by interpersonal tensions or the extreme psychological pressure under which they live and work (Interviews 2, 10). Such altercations are generally ignored by management unless they escalate to the point of disrupting productivity or attracting external attention. The pervasive threat of violence—from both superiors and peers—contributes to a constant atmosphere of fear, instability, and psychological distress.

Excerpts from Interviews with Workers

> We called ourselves the '365 Work Brigade.' That should tell you everything. We had no days off. The only break was one day for New Year's. That's it. We worked 365 days a year."(Interview 14)

> We worked seven days a week. We rested maybe one day a month. There were no holidays. On national holidays like New Year's or Kim Il Sung's birthday, we might get a day off, maybe three or four days a year in total. But that was only because the Russian sites were closed and we couldn't work anyway. It wasn't a paid day off. (Interview 3)

> Wages existed only on paper. Every month, they would tell us, 'You earned this much this month,' and make us sign the ledger, but we never actually saw the money. If you were sick and missed even a day of work, you got no pay for that month, and only a negative balance would accumulate in the ledger. Even after working diligently for three years, the negative balance continued, so it felt like we were working to pay off debt rather than earning money. What's more absurd is that if the ledger got wet from the rain and became unusable, the manager would just recreate it from memory, however he pleased. (Interview 6)

> For a year, I worked relentlessly, giving up alcohol and cigarettes and never even going to a store. The money I saved amounted to a mere 170 dollars. It was devastating to receive such a pittance after working until three or four in the morning. I heard other workers were earning 100 dollars a day, and I felt so wronged. They deducted 40,000 rubles a month from our pay for the 'plan,' but I later found out that the actual amount sent to the state was only 20,000 rubles. The rest was being pocketed by the manager and the site foreman. (Interview 8)

> As a site manager, I was also caught in a system of exploitation. The company demanded that we meet a quota, and I had to pressure the workers. I knew the real contract amounts with the Russian partners, so I would present much lower figures to the workers and pocket the difference. If I didn't, I wouldn't have been able to survive either. To meet the monthly quota of 7,500 dollars, the workers had to toil until the early hours of the morning, and I enriched myself with their blood and sweat. (Interview 12)

> The mid-level managers, like site foremen and work leaders, are also trapped in a structure where they have to exploit the workers to survive. They too must bribe their superiors and show loyalty to get another chance at being dispatched. For instance, if I buy a 100-won pair of socks for a worker and record it as 500 won in the ledger, the difference goes into my pocket and then up to my superiors. This chain of exploitation continues endlessly. (Interview 3)

> There was no safety training. If you got hurt, it was your own problem. The company provided nothing. I fell from a height of about 3 meters... my knee was shot, and

I couldn't walk. I was laid up like that for three months. After my injury, they told me to go to the hospital. But even at a regular hospital, you have to show your ID, your passport. All I had was that photocopy of someone else's documents. I refused to go. I thought it wasn't worth the risk. If I went to the hospital with those papers, my illegal status would be exposed immediately. There was no choice. Since I couldn't work for three months, I didn't earn any money. But they still demanded that I pay the annual loyalty fee of 7,500 dollars. They said it was non-negotiable. What could I do? The money I had earned before the accident was taken to cover that fee. (Interview 2)

A colleague of mine got hurt. He was using a grinder, and it slipped... it sliced his foot open. You could see the bone. He was bleeding a lot. But we couldn't go to the hospital. We had no passports, no way to prove who we were. We just wrapped his foot with a piece of his own clothing. A few days later, we got some bandages and wrapped it again. He just had to endure it and wait for it to heal on its own. That's how it was. (Interview 10)

CHAPTER 6
LIFE OUTSIDE OF WORKPLACE

North Korea's control over its overseas workers extends far beyond the workplace, encompassing every aspect of their personal lives. Workers are not permitted to choose where or how they live. Housing is not provided as a workplace benefit but deliberately used as a tool of transnational repression. This intent is evident in the inadequate, squalid conditions of the accommodations and in the severe restrictions on communication, movement, and access to information. As a result, workers remain in a state of near-total dependency on their supervisors and are shielded from meaningful exposure to foreign influences while abroad.

6.1 HOUSING AND PRIVACY

The vast majority of North Korean workers abroad are housed in accommodations assigned by the company, typically located directly at or near the worksite. The most common accommodations are converted shipping containers, often less than two meters (approximately six feet) in width, where up to 30 workers are crammed into a single unit outfitted with stacked bunk beds (Interviews 1, 2). Others are forced to reside in the basements or unfinished floors of the very buildings they are constructing (Interviews 3, 8). These living spaces are squalid and severely inadequate, frequently lacking insulation or basic heating—a dire hardship during Russia's brutal winters, when temperatures routinely fall far below freezing (Interviews 3, 7). Personal hygiene is a constant challenge: workers report being able to bathe only once a week, often with cold water, leading to cracked skin and significant physical discomfort in subzero temperatures (Interview 3). Overcrowding and lack of sanitation also result in infestations of lice and bedbugs, contributing to both physical and psychological discomfort (Interview 6).

In addition to being forced into group living arrangements, North Korean workers are denied privacy and subjected to constant surveillance of their personal activities. Every North Korean company is assigned a Ministry of State Security officer whose primary role is to monitor the workforce. This surveillance is bolstered by a network of workers chosen by the security officer to spy on their colleagues. These informants are strategically embedded within each work unit, sometimes at a ratio as high as one for every five workers, and are tasked with reporting any signs of ideological deviation, unauthorized interactions with locals, or attempted escape (Interviews 1, 6, 8, 9). The result is an atmosphere of constant suspicion and fear, replicating the mechanisms of control found inside North Korea itself.

Ultimately, this system of repression is upheld through violence. Workers risk beatings from the Ministry of State Security officer for even minor infractions (such as failing to disclose personal matters upon questioning) or from team leaders for perceived laziness or disobedience. Such acts of brutality serve as deliberate demonstrations of power, reinforcing a rigid hierarchy built on coercion and fear (Interviews 1, 9, 10).

6.2 ACCESS TO FOOD AND BASIC NECESSITIES

North Korean workers are generally prohibited from purchasing food on their own. Instead, companies provide a limited selection of raw ingredients, and workers must prepare meals in communal makeshift kitchens, often set up in repurposed shipping containers (Interviews 1, 2, 3, 6). The food is of poor quality and nutritionally insufficient, with a monotonous diet consisting primarily of rice, cabbage, potatoes, and pork skin (Interviews 3, 8). In one extreme case, workers survived on nothing but bread for an entire year, resulting in malnourishment and psychological fatigue (Interview 12). The quantity is frequently inadequate, given the physically demanding nature of the labor. As a result, some field supervisors secretly arrange unauthorized side jobs to help workers earn additional income to supplement their meager rations (Interview 1).

Other basic necessities, such as soap, toothpaste, and clothing, are also subject to strict control. Workers are not granted the financial freedom to purchase these items on their own. Instead, they must submit requests to their managers, who purchase the goods on their behalf (Interviews 2, 3, 7). In some cases, workers receive a modest monthly stipend of RUB 1,000 to 2,000 (approximately USD 10 to 20) to buy items from a designated store (Interviews 1, 7). This arrangement not only limits personal autonomy but also creates opportunities for exploitation, as managers can inflate prices and deduct inflated costs directly from workers' earnings (Interview 3).

6.3 MOVEMENT, INFORMATION, AND COMMUNICATION

To maintain ideological control and prevent defections, North Korean authorities systematically restrict workers' movement, communication, and access to information. Upon arrival in Russia, the Ministry of State Security officer or the Party secretary confiscates the passports and other personal documents of workers, a measure intended to immobilize them and force dependency (Interviews 1, 2, 4, 6, 12). Workers are left with, at most, paper photocopies of their personal documents, which effectively hold no legal standing (Interviews 2, 3, 7). This legal precarity has worsened in the post-sanctions era, with many relying on photocopies of other people's work permits or fraudulent student visas (Interview 2).

The mobility of workers is restricted not only by the lack of official personal documents but also by the requirement to obtain prior approval from worksite managers for any travel beyond the designated worksite and living quarters (Interview 1, 3, 6, 8). To leave the worksite or living quarters, workers need to receive managerial approval by disclosing the purpose of their travel in advance. Even with permission, they must typically stay within a 100- to 200-meter radius and move in pairs or groups to enable mutual surveillance (Interviews 1, 3, 6, 8, 9, 12). In some cases, workers became temporarily exempt from these distance limitations during the COVID-19 pandemic when company-led procurement became less reliable. Under this exception, workers were allowed to travel to larger wholesale markets to buy groceries or to secure work from individual clients (e.g., those seeking help with home renovations) (Interview 2). Unauthorized travel may be treated as an act of defection and punished severely, most notably through forced repatriation.

North Korean workers are prohibited from possessing personal mobile phones or electronic devices (Interviews 1, 3, 4, 9, 10). While managers are allowed to use basic phones (limited to calls and texts) for work communications, everyone is prohibited from using smartphones or other internet-enabled devices. Despite the prohibition, many workers secretly obtain used smartphones through various means: receiving them as gifts from other migrant workers (e.g., those from CIS countries), picking up unattended devices, or purchasing them with money earned from selling North Korean cigarettes (Interviews 1, 2, 3, 9, 12). For many workers, these devices serve as a crucial means of entertainment and stress alleviation, providing a rare connection to the broader world.

This restriction on devices is enforced by informants who search for unauthorized possession and inspect browsing histories, sometimes even while their colleagues are asleep (Interview 1). Punishments for using internet-enabled devices vary depending on the perceived severity of the offense: mere possession may result in confiscation, while accessing prohibited content, such as South Korean media, is considered a political crime and may lead to immediate repatriation (Interviews 2, 6, 8, 9, 10). However, enforcement is not always consistent, as workers have been able to bribe the Ministry of State Security officer to avoid punishment. During the COVID-19 pandemic, when repatriation was temporarily suspended, surveillance reportedly became more lenient overall (Interviews 1, 2).

North Korea controls not only the access of overseas workers to outside information, but also their communication to family and acquaintances remaining back home. The primary method of contact is through letters, which are inspected and censored by North Korean customs (Interviews 1, 2, 6, 11). These letters are often hand-delivered by entrusted intermediaries returning to North Korea. These intermediaries may include managers, diplomats, or airline staff. As the process of delivery often exceeds three months, many workers feel discouraged from pursuing routine communication with family and acquaintances back home (Interviews 1, 2, 7, 11).

To remit money home, workers must hand cash to informal couriers, who charge commissions starting at 10 percent (Interview 7). Confirmation of receipt relies on a written letter or a verbal message relayed through intermediaries, leaving workers in prolonged uncertainty (Interview 7). For some military workers, sending letters or money was not an option at all (Interview 1). The lack of reliable and unhindered communication channels leave workers in a constant state of worry over the well-being of the families whom they were working to support.

6.4 IDEOLOGICAL INDOCTRINATION

To counteract exposure to foreign ideas and reinforce loyalty to the state, North Korean overseas workers are required to participate in regular ideological indoctrination sessions. The most frequent of these is the *saenghwal chonghwa*, or "life review" session, which is intended to take place weekly (Interviews 2, 6, 7, 9). During these meetings, workers are expected to engage in mutual criticism and self-criticism, which are intended to enforce discipline and discourage the formation of private solidarity. In addition to these weekly sessions, workers are periodically subjected to political lectures, typically held monthly, in which they are briefed by the Party secretary on current state policies and Party directives using materials sent directly from North Korea (Interviews 2, 3, 6, 9). Some groups also conduct daily 30-minute morning meetings to read state-approved news reports on Kim Jong Un's activities (Interview 6).

However, the implementation of these sessions varies. Although the ideological programming is formally mandatory, work obligations often take priority. As a result, many sites do not conduct sessions on a consistent weekly basis. Instead, worksite managers frequently consolidate the material into a single, extended session held once per month (Interviews 3, 4). In some instances, the sessions are reduced to a bureaucratic formality: the cell secretaries, who are appointed onsite by worksite managers, may simply collect signatures or brief statements from workers to document compliance, without holding an actual meeting (Interview 2). These documents are delivered to and maintained by the Party secretary. Notably, some managers deliberately soften the tone of criticism, concerned that excessive psychological pressure could drive workers to defect (Interview 1). This pragmatic approach reflects the underlying tension between the state's ideological demands and the economic imperative to maximize labor output.

Excerpts from Interviews with Workers

> The living quarters were not fit for humans. When we were building a 20-story apartment, we lived on the unfinished first floor. A colleague of mine even fell from the second floor. Fortunately, he wasn't seriously injured, but we had to spend every night in that dangerous environment. (Interview 12)

> We lived in a shipping container at the construction site. That's the cheapest option. Usually, about five or six of us lived together. It was a standard-sized container. We had two sets of military-style bunk beds facing each other, with just enough space for one or two people to walk between them. Once you put four of those in, the container was completely full. In the winter, it was cold, but we had two or three electric radiators. Russia has plenty of electricity, so we didn't suffer from the cold as long as the power didn't go out. (Interview 2)

> The winters in Irkutsk drop to -40 degrees Celsius, but we lived in a place that wasn't even a proper house, more like a warehouse. There were no proper plumbing facilities, so we had to melt snow in the bitter cold to get water. We bathed maybe once a month, if that, and even then, it was just a quick wash in the hallway with water heated by an electric heater. I couldn't stand the miserable life, so I protested, 'I'd rather go back to North Korea,' and the site manager had to come and persuade me for three hours to stay. (Interview 9)

> We ate pigskin for three meals a day. It wasn't the delicacy you might find in South Korea, but the thick, tough skin from the slaughterhouse, usually used for animal feed. We had to boil it for a long time to render the fat and make it somewhat edible. In the mornings, no

one had an appetite, so we would trade the leftover rice with foreign workers for alcohol. The only silver lining was that, as the cook, I could at least provide some alcohol to the others using the leftover food. (Interview 10)

Surveillance was systematic and constant. The state security agent monitored us directly, and also gathered information through spies planted among the workers. There was one spy for every five workers. After a while, you could get a sense of who the spies were. In a system where everyone watches everyone else, you always had to be careful about what you said. (Interview 6)

We couldn't leave the premises. Going out was not allowed. Even if you reported it and got approval, it was impossible. There was no reason to get approval in the first place. If we needed necessities, we had to tell the site manager, and he would buy them for us. Individual actions were absolutely forbidden. Only those at the site manager level or above had some freedom of movement. (Interview 3)

I was able to send money to my family. The company's financial officer handled it. I would ask him, and he would arrange it. To confirm that the money was received, the overseas dispatch department in North Korea would contact my family and then send a fax to our company in Russia. I couldn't contact them directly, of course. Everything went through the company. The manager used his personal connections in North Korea to make it happen. If I wanted to send 300 dollars, I had to give the manager an extra 90 dollars as a commission. The commission rate was about 30%. (Interview 5)

Only managers, like the work team leaders and above, were allowed phones, and even then, they were just basic phones for calls and texts. Later, smartphones were permitted for 'work purposes'—like sending photos and documents—but with the strict condition that we were not to use the internet. Of course, there was no way for them to really check that. But if someone saw you and reported it to the state security agent, you were in trouble. The punishment for watching outside media was severe. First, they'd confiscate the phone. In serious cases, they'd repatriate you. After the COVID-19 pandemic started, they couldn't send people back, so confiscation was the only punishment. (Interview 6)

CHAPTER 7
PROCESS OF REPATRIATION AND REINTEGRATION INTO NORTH KOREA

Returning to North Korea, whether at the end of the labor term or for a short-term visit, is far from a simple homecoming. It is a tightly controlled process involving extensive interrogation, ideological re-acclimation, and reassertion of state authority. All returning workers—regardless of their performance abroad or demonstrated loyalty—are treated with inherent suspicion due to their exposure to foreign influences. They are subjected to mandatory investigations and ideological evaluations. This chapter examines the protocols and experiences involved in the repatriation and reintegration of North Korean workers returning from Russia.

7.1 STANDARD REENTRY AND REINTEGRATION PROCESS

Workers return to North Korea for a range of reasons. While some are fully repatriated after the end of their labor terms, many return temporarily for administrative purposes or personal leave (Interviews 9, 12). Following the imposition of the 2017 UN sanctions, numerous workers were recalled to North Korea only to be redeployed under new visa categories, such as student visas (Interviews 3, 4, 6, 10). Short-term returns for personal reasons, such as family visits, are generally limited to managerial staff (Interviews 11, 12). For general workers, such visits are rare due to the high travel costs—reportedly up to USD 1,500 for a round trip—and the loss of company revenue from unmet remittance quotas during their absence (Interviews 9, 14). As a result, most refrain from or are discouraged from taking personal leave (Interview 9).

Upon reentry into North Korea, all workers are subjected to a rigorous debriefing process. For a period lasting from several days to up to a month, they must submit detailed reports documenting their activities while abroad. These reports are reviewed by the provincial office of the Ministry of State Security or the local Party committee affiliated with their dispatching enterprise (Interviews 3, 6, 8). The reports function as ideological confessions, outlining any exposure to foreign influence or instances of misconduct, and are used to assess the returning worker's political reliability (Interview 7). Corruption is pervasive throughout this process. Bribes are commonly used to shorten or mitigate the severity of the debriefing period. One worker reported that a payment of USD 100 could exempt them from the month-long requirement to write reports (Interview 3).

`To reinforce state control, strict regulations govern what workers may bring back from abroad. They are prohibited from importing electronic devices, digital storage media such as USBs and SD cards, foreign publications, and personal photographs (Interviews 4, 6, 8, 10). All items originating from South Korea or the United States are explicitly banned, and clothing or merchandise with a discernible Western aesthetic—such as blue jeans—is also subject to confiscation (Interviews 1, 6). In response to severe domestic shortages, workers often attempt to bring back Russian pharmaceuticals (Interview 11), but these are frequently seized at customs unless bribes are paid (Interview 6).

For military-affiliated workers, the reintegration process is particularly harsh. Instead of returning home, they are confined to the barracks of their dispatching unit (Interviews 3, 10). There, they face abuse and extortion by officers seeking money or goods acquired during their time abroad (Interviews 3, 10). One worker recounted being treated "worse than a dog" and forced to shovel coal in his underwear during the winter as punishment for not bringing back sufficient funds (Interview 10).

7.2 FORCED REPATRIATION

The forced repatriation of North Korean workers—especially those who attempt to defect—is conducted under a bilateral agreement serving Pyongyang's interest in preventing escape. Signed in 2016, the "Agreement on the Transfer and Receipt of Illegal Entrants and Residents" created a formal mechanism for Russia to return to North Korean custody any nationals who violate local laws on entry, exit, or residence, effectively eliminating Russia as a potential safe haven for defectors.[79] This policy is further reinforced by a systemic practice in which North Korean authorities confiscate workers' passports and other legal documents upon arrival in Russia. Deprived of valid identification, these workers are treated as immigration offenders under Russian law. In the absence of legal protections for individuals fleeing human rights abuses, the Russian police are far more likely to arrest and hand them over to North Korean officials than to assess the circumstances of their status or the risks they may face upon return (Interviews 3, 4, 6, 8, 9, 10, 12; Experts 8, 9).

Moreover, North Korean companies actively participate in the pursuit of defectors, as any escape is viewed as a failure of management and control (Interview 12). One example is a case in which a company president personally led multiple search efforts to locate an escaped worker (Interview 10). For those in hiding, the constant threat of discovery by these pursuit teams is a major source of fear (Interviews 9, 10). Interviewees reported witnessing or hearing about captured workers being repatriated under heavy physical restraint (Interviews 11, 12). To prevent further escape attempts during transit, the Ministry of State Security officials may immobilize the detainee by placing their

---

79. See Appendix 3a/3b for the full text in Russian/English.

arms and legs in full-body plaster casts, disguising them as medical patients who had to be carried onto the plane (Interview 12).

Russian human rights lawyers have documented multiple cases in which defectors were abducted and beaten by North Korean agents on Russian soil or handed over to North Korean authorities by Russian officials. These incidents occurred even when the workers had formally applied for asylum and explicitly expressed fears of torture or execution upon return. In several cases, forced repatriation was prevented only through emergency intervention by human rights lawyers and the UN Refugee Agency. The most recent case reported by the Civic Assistance Center—a Russian human rights organization consulted for this project—occurred in 2017. Between 2011 and 2019, only one North Korean citizen was granted refugee status by the Russian government.

Forced repatriation is not limited to defectors; it is also the standard punishment for serious rule violations, such as watching South Korean media (Interviews 6, 7, 8). Once returned to North Korea, individuals are treated as political criminals. They undergo a coercive interrogation by the Ministry of State Security, during which they are questioned on their activities abroad—especially any contact with South Koreans, Christians, or foreign organizations.[80] Following this interrogation, they are imprisoned in detention facilities rampant with forced labor, torture, and violence (Interview 12).[81] In some cases, they may be executed by a firing squad (Interview 9).

7.3 REPATRIATION OF THE INJURED AND DECEASED

North Korea's treatment of its injured and deceased overseas workers starkly illustrates a system in which human life is valued primarily for

---

80. This process of interrogation has been consistently documented by NKDB across more than 8,000 cases of forced repatriation stored in the Unified Human Rights Database.
81. According to NKDB's Unified Human Rights Database, over 60% of recorded cases of arbitrary detention in North Korea are linked to charges related to unauthorized travel, including attempted defection.

its economic utility. Workers who suffer debilitating injuries that prevent them from laboring for an extended period—typically over a month—are deemed financial liabilities and are promptly repatriated (Interview 14). While companies may cover the initial hospital costs, the unwritten policy is clear: a worker who cannot contribute to the mandatory "loyalty payments" must be returned (Interview 14).

This process is also exploited for political purposes. In some of the most chilling accounts, captured defectors have had their limbs intentionally broken by security officers and placed in casts, then repatriated under the guise of medical returnees. This tactic both conceals grave human rights violations and prevents escape attempts during transit (Interview 12).

The treatment of deceased workers is equally callous, motivated by efforts to avoid the costs of cremation and repatriation of remains. In one harrowing case from 2019, a company president coerced four workers into staging a fake cremation by burning leftover pig bones, which were then presented in an urn to the deceased worker's family as his remains (Interview 14). When this deception was exposed, the president received only a temporary demotion. His record of meeting state revenue quotas was deemed more valuable than accountability for gross violations of human dignity, reflecting a broader culture of impunity (Interview 14).

7.4 IMPACT OF THE COVID-19 PANDEMIC ON ABILITY TO RETURN

The COVID-19 pandemic and the subsequent closure of North Korea's borders fundamentally disrupted the system of overseas labor control. With the state refusing reentry to its own citizens, North Korean authorities lost their most powerful tool of coercion: the threat of forced repatriation (Interviews 2, 3, 5, 12). This shift had an immediate impact in Russia. As several interviewees noted, worksite managers and even Ministry of State Security officers could no longer punish workers for infractions such as watching foreign media, since the threat of repatriation was no longer enforceable (Interviews 2, 5, 7). As a result, control within overseas enterprises weakened, and workers became less fearful of reprisal (Interview 3).

Although this shift inadvertently granted workers a degree of autonomy, the closure of the border also imposed a profound psychological toll. With travel between Russia and North Korea suspended, the few informal channels through which workers had previously communicated with their families—such as sending letters or money with returning colleagues—were abruptly severed (Interviews 2, 3, 6). Stranded indefinitely in a foreign country during a global health crisis, workers were left with no reliable way to learn about the well-being of their loved ones, heightening their sense of isolation and anxiety (Interview 4). The pandemic, therefore, not only altered the balance of power within the labor system but also deepened the emotional and psychological hardship of the workers trapped abroad. In one case, a worker who died during the pandemic could not be returned home and had to be cremated in Russia (Interview 4).

Excerpts from Interviews with Workers

After completing 11 years of military service, I was dispatched to Russia, but life there was no different from that of an animal. Especially when I returned to North Korea for a month's leave, the officers beat me and dragged me by my hair for not bringing back money. They subjected me to all kinds of humiliation, like forcing me to load and unload coal in my underwear in the freezing cold. The memory of that horrific experience and the inhumane labor exploitation by the manager [redacted] ultimately led me to defect. (Interview 10)

When you return, you have to write a confession. If you have money, you can get away with it. The state security agents demand money, so if you give them a bribe, you can get out of writing it. If you don't have money, you have to write it. For those who can't pay, they are forced to write self-criticisms for a month, detailing their life abroad. (Interview 8)

> When a worker dies on the job, in Russia, they either cremate the body and send it to the family or send the body frozen. But cremation costs money, right? ...Because Russia was on lockdown ahead of Victory Day in May, they couldn't handle the body for several days. As the body started to spread, they gave up and decided not to take the body, but they still had to give something to the family in North Korea. So what did he do? He gathered four workers from his company who were unskilled and not earning any money, got them drunk on barbecue and alcohol. Then he took the bones from the pork they had for the barbecue, burned them, and put the ashes in a sealed container, passing them off as the cremated remains of the deceased worker. He gave the other workers 200 dollars each as hush money. Is that what a human being does? (Interview 12)

> During COVID, you couldn't go back. Even if you died, you couldn't go back. They would just cremate the body there in Russia and send the ashes later. (Interview 6)

CHAPTER 8
APPLICATION OF INTERNATIONAL HUMAN RIGHTS AND LABOR LAWS

The legal analysis of the working and human rights conditions of North Korean workers in Russia rests upon a fundamental principle: the supremacy of the peremptory norms of international law over Russia's domestic legislation and bilateral agreements. Russia cannot invoke its domestic laws or arrangements with North Korea to justify derogation from its obligations under international human rights treaties. This chapter establishes the legal hierarchy that governs Russia's responsibilities to protect North Korean workers on its soil, demonstrating the precedence of peremptory norms over conflicting domestic laws or bilateral agreements.

8.1 HIERARCHY OF DOMESTIC AND INTERNATIONAL OBLIGATIONS

8.1.1 Position of International Treaties in the Russian Legal Order

Adopted in 1993, the Russian Constitution established the precedence of international agreements within the national legal framework. Article 15(4), as originally adopted in 1993, stated:

"The universally recognized norms of international law and international treaties and agreements of the Russian Federation shall be a component part of its legal system. If an international treaty or agreement of the Russian Federation establishes other rules than those envisaged by law, the rules of the international agreement shall be applied."[82]

This provision accorded international treaties ratified by Russia a higher normative status than conflicting domestic legislation, including the Labor Code. In principle, this hierarchy required Russian authorities and courts to give effect to treaty-based obligations. As a result, the rights enshrined in ratified international instruments, such as the International Covenant on Civil and Political Rights (ICCPR) and International Labour Organization (ILO) conventions, were to be respected within the nation's jurisdiction and could not lawfully be curtailed by inconsistent statutes or administrative practice.

Over time, however, Russia's commitment to universal human rights was progressively eroded by a shift toward an isolationist approach to international law. In 2015, a federal constitutional law empowered the Constitutional Court to declare judgments by the European Court of Human Rights (ECHR) and other international bodies "non-enforceable" if they were deemed incompatible with the Constitution.[83] Although Article 15(4) continues to recognize the authority of treaties, the 2020 amendments to Articles 79 and 125 explicitly empowered the Constitutional Court to determine the enforceability of interstate decisions, further weakening the domestic effect of treaty-based human rights protections.[84] These developments

---

82. Russian Federation. *Constitution of the Russian Federation*. 12 Dec. 1993, http://www.constitution.ru/en/10003000-01.htm

83. Russian Federation. *Federal Law No.7-FKZ of 14 December 2015 On Amendments to the Federal Constitutional Law "on the Constitutional Court of the Russian Federation." Official Publication of Legal Acts*, http://publication.pravo.gov.ru/Document/View/0001201512150010

84. Jefferies, Isabelle. "Russia's Constitutional Amendment from an International Law Perspective." *Public International Law & Policy Group*, 1 Mar. 2021, https://www.

entrenched a framework of rejecting external accountability, marking a decisive departure from the constitutional vision of 1993.

In parallel, Russia has increasingly prioritized its bilateral relations with North Korea over its obligations under multilateral human rights treaties. The 2007 bilateral agreement on temporary labor activities exemplifies this trend, as it delegated Russia's human rights obligations to North Korean authorities, in breach of its positive duty to protect individuals within its jurisdiction.[85] Although the agreement nominally affirms that North Korean workers should receive treatment equivalent to Russian nationals, Article 6 assigns oversight of wages and working conditions to North Korean officials—a provision incompatible with Russia's obligations under the ICCPR and ILO core conventions.

A similar approach underlies the 2016 bilateral agreement on the transfer of illegal entrants and residents.[86] This agreement has been invoked to justify the forcible return of North Korean defectors to the custody of North Korean authorities, undermining the principle of *non-refoulement*, a *jus cogens* norm of international law insofar as it prohibits return where there is a risk of torture or other cruel, inhuman, or degrading treatment. By failing to assess asylum claims or the risk of torture, Russian authorities have facilitated *refoulement* in violation of their obligations under the 1951 Refugee Convention and the Convention against Torture.[87]

These practices of privileging domestic laws and bilateral arrangements are incompatible with the core principles of the

---

publicinternationallawandpolicygroup.org/lawyering-, justice-1 Marblog/. 2021/2021, 3/1/https://russias-constitutional-amendment-from-an-international-law-perspective
85. See Appendix 2a/2b for the full text in Russian/English.
86. See Appendix 3a/3b for the full text in Russian/English.
87. United Nations. *Convention relating to the Status of Refugees*. 28 July 1951. United Nations Treaty Series, vol. 189, p. 137. Entered into force 22 June 1954. Ratified by the USSR on 2 Feb. 1993 (binding on the Russian Federation as successor state);
United Nations. *Convention against Torture and Other Cruel, Inhuman or Degrading Treatment or Punishment*. 10 Dec. 1984. United Nations Treaty Series, vol. 1465, p. 85. Entered into force 26 June 1987. Ratified by the USSR on 3 Mar. 1987 (binding on the Russian Federation as successor state).

international legal order. Article 103 of the UN Charter establishes that Charter obligations take precedence over conflicting obligations from other international agreements,[88] while the Vienna Convention on the Law of Treaties prohibits states from invoking internal law as justification for failing to perform treaty obligations (Article 27), and nullifies treaties that conflict with peremptory (*jus cogens*) norms of international law (Article 53).[89]

8.1.2 Primacy of *Jus Cogens* and *Erga Omnes* Obligations

While Russia adopts an arbitrary approach to *jus cogens* norms, international law affirms their absolute and non-derogable character. Article 53 of the Vienna Convention on the Law of Treaties defines a *jus cogens* norm as one that is "accepted and recognized by the international community of States as a whole as a norm from which no derogation is permitted."[90] Under Articles 53 and 64 of the Convention, a treaty is void if it conflicts with a *jus cogens* norm at the time of its inception, while an existing treaty also becomes void if a new, conflicting *jus cogens* norm emerges.

The prohibitions of slavery and torture are recognized as having *jus cogens* status, a view affirmed by the International Law Commission.[91] If the conditions of North Korean workers in Russia amount to slavery, as argued in Section 8.2, any provision within the 2007 bilateral agreement on temporary labor that facilitates or tolerates these practices is void *ab initio*. Consequently, Russia cannot invoke this agreement to justify its failure to prevent the enslavement of North Korean nationals, as the agreement would be invalid due to its conflict with a higher, non-derogable norm.

---

88. United Nations. Charter of the United Nations. 26 June 1945. Entered into force 24 Oct. 1945. Ratified by the USSR on 24 Oct. 1945 (binding on the Russian Federation as successor state).
89. United Nations. Vienna Convention on the Law of Treaties. 23 May 1969. United Nations Treaty Series, vol. 1155, p. 331. Entered into force 27 Jan. 1980. Ratified by the USSR on 29 Apr. 1986 (binding on the Russian Federation as successor state).
90. Ibid.
91. United Nations, General Assembly. Report of the International Law Commission. 12 Aug. 2022, A/77/10.

Similarly, the prohibition of torture underpins Russia's obligation to uphold the principle of *non-refoulement*. Any practice of returning defectors to North Korean authorities on the basis of the 2016 bilateral agreement contravenes this obligation by exposing individuals to a substantial risk of torture. As *jus cogens* norms, the prohibitions of slavery and torture impose not only a negative obligation to refrain from violations but also a positive obligation to cooperate in ending them.[92] Russia's complicity in these breaches is examined further in Section 8.3 through the international framework of state responsibility.

Moreover, the prohibitions of slavery and torture generate obligations that extend beyond the interests of the directly affected states. The prohibition of slavery constitutes an *erga omnes* obligation, owed by every state to the international community as a whole, as affirmed by the International Court of Justice in *Barcelona Traction, Light and Power Company, Limited* (*Belgium v. Spain*, 1970).[93] The obligation to prosecute or extradite acts of torture under the Convention against Torture has been recognized by the Court as an obligation *erga omnes partes*, owed to all treaty parties collectively, in *Questions relating to the Obligation to Prosecute or Extradite* (*Belgium v. Senegal*, 2012).[94] Together, these rulings establish that other states may possess a basis to

---

92. Ibid.
93. In *Barcelona Traction, Light and Power Company, Limited* (*Belgium v. Spain*, 1970), Belgium brought a claim on behalf of Belgian shareholders alleging that Spain had harmed a Canadian company, Barcelona Traction. The ICJ dismissed the claim for lack of standing, holding that only the State of incorporation (Canada) could exercise diplomatic protection. However, in its reasoning, the Court made a landmark distinction between obligations owed to particular States and those owed to the international community as a whole. It identified prohibitions against aggression, genocide, slavery, and racial discrimination as obligations *erga omnes*, enforceable by all States because of the fundamental rights at stake.

See *Barcelona Traction, Light and Power Company, Limited (Belgium v. Spain)*. International Court of Justice, 5 Feb. 1970. *ICJ Reports 1970*, p. 3.
94. In *Questions relating to the Obligation to Prosecute or Extradite* (*Belgium v. Senegal*, 2012), the ICJ addressed Senegal's failure to prosecute or extradite former Chadian president Hissène Habré, accused of widespread torture. Belgium, as a State party to the Convention against Torture, argued that Senegal had violated its treaty obligations by sheltering Habré. The Court agreed, affirming that the prohibition of torture is a *jus cogens* norm and that under the Convention the obligation to prosecute or extradite is owed *erga omnes partes*—to all States parties collectively. In other words, every State has a legal interest in ensuring compliance, even absent direct injury.

demand accountability from North Korea and Russia for perpetrating or facilitating such abuses against workers.[95]

8.2 ESCALATION FROM FORCED LABOR TO SERVITUDE AND ENSLAVEMENT

A precise legal classification of the human rights abuses suffered by North Korean workers in Russia is essential for identifying avenues through which both Russia and North Korea may be held accountable. Applying the International Labour Organization's (ILO) indicators reveals that the workers' conditions satisfy the criteria for forced labor. However, a more in-depth analysis, which draws on the jurisprudence of international courts such as the European Court of Human Rights, shows that these conditions go beyond the threshold of forced labor and amount to more severe violations, including servitude and, ultimately, the "crime against humanity" of enslavement. This section unpacks the layers of exploitation by applying established international definitions and precedents to the documented facts, demonstrating how the situation meets the legal standards for forced labor, servitude, and slavery, respectively.

8.2.1 Threshold of Forced Labor Based on ILO Indicators

The internationally recognized definition of forced labor is articulated in ILO Convention No. 29, which defines it as "all work or service which is exacted from any person under the menace of any penalty and for which the said person has not offered himself voluntarily."[96] While the ILO generally evaluates forced labor based on the overall context and the cumulative presence of multiple indicators, it also acknowledges that, in certain cases, a single, particularly severe

---

See *Questions relating to the Obligation to Prosecute or Extradite (Belgium v. Senegal)*. International Court of Justice, 20 July 2012. *ICJ Reports 2012*, p. 422.

95. While any state may be entitled to demand accountability, compelling North Korea or Russia to answer for these breaches before a body like the ICJ remains contingent on securing their consent to its jurisdiction

96. International Labour Organization. Forced Labour Convention, 1930 (No. 29). 28 June 1930; entered into force 1 May 1932. Ratified by the USSR on 23 June 1956 (binding on the Russian Federation as successor state).

indicator—such as physical violence—may be sufficient to establish a situation of forced labor (Experts 6, 7). Furthermore, even where a worker initially appears to "consent" to employment, such consent is rendered invalid if obtained through deception or if the working and living conditions are coercive or abusive.

This framework accurately characterizes the experience of North Korean workers abroad. They are denied access to employment contracts and remain uninformed about their actual wages and working hours, thereby falling victim to deception. Upon arrival in Russia, they are subjected to coercive and abusive practices, including threats of punishment. The ILO has identified 11 operational indicators of forced labor, and the conditions experienced by North Korean workers correspond to nearly all of them, demonstrating a systematic, rather than incidental, imposition of forced labor.[97]

Table 7. Application of ILO Forced Labor Indicators

ILO Indicator	Evidence from Conditions of North Korean Workers in Russia
Abuse of Vulnerability	The state-controlled nature of the workers' lives, combined with their lack of financial autonomy and fear of reprisals against their families, creates a profound vulnerability systematically exploited by authority figures. In the post-sanctions context, their undocumented status in Russia further exacerbates this vulnerability.
Deception	Workers are denied formal employment contracts and kept uninformed about their eventual placement, wages, and working hours. Although they are informally promised substantial earnings, they ultimately receive only a fraction of their due pay.

---

97. International Labour Office. *ILO Indicators of Forced Labour*. International Labor Organization, 1 Oct. 2012, https://www.ilo.org/sites/default/files/wcmsp5/groups/public/%40ed_norm/%40declaration/documents/publication/wcms_203832.pdf

Restriction of Movement	Workers are prohibited from leaving the worksite without authorization and are kept under constant surveillance by managers and state security agents. Any movement is restricted to short distances expressly approved in advance.
Isolation	Personal phones are confiscated, correspondence is censored, contact with local residents is prohibited, and a coerced system of peer surveillance undermines trust and solidarity among workers.
Physical & Sexual Violence	Company managers, including state security officers, routinely beat workers for slow performance, perceived insubordination, or even minor infractions of rules.
Intimidation & Threats	The ever-present threat of forced repatriation for any infraction serves as a primary tool of control, while families remaining in North Korea are effectively held as collateral to ensure compliance.
Retention of Identity Documents	Passports are systematically confiscated upon arrival, leaving workers undocumented and discouraging them from escaping or seeking legal protection from local authorities.
Withholding of Wages	Up to 90% of workers' wages are withheld as so-called "loyalty payments" and "operating fees," leaving them with only a meager allowance (sometimes as little as $10–$20 per month). They are compelled to sign wage ledgers acknowledging earnings, the majority of which they never receive.
Debt Bondage	Although not a classic case of debt bondage, the requirement to pay substantial bribes for overseas dispatch creates an initial debt that workers are forced to repay through their labor. The mandatory "loyalty fees" operate as a perpetual debt to the state, ensuring continued control and exploitation.

Abusive Living & Working	Workers are housed in cramped, unsanitary shipping containers without proper heating, provided no safety equipment for hazardous construction work, and denied adequate medical care.
Excessive Overtime	Workers are forced to labor 12–17 hours a day, seven days a week, far exceeding the international standard of an eight-hour day and 48-hour work week. They are denied any regular rest days, in breach of the requirement for at least one rest day in every seven-day period.

8.2.2 Framework of Servitude: Comparison with *F.M. and Others v. Russia*

The conditions faced by North Korean workers in Russia transcend the baseline of forced labor and amount to servitude. Under international human rights law, servitude is understood as an "aggravated form of forced labor" involving a greater deprivation of liberty (Expert 8). In *Siliadin v. France* (2005), the European Court of Human Rights (ECtHR) established the defining characteristics of servitude: an obligation to provide services imposed by coercion, a deprivation of freedom of movement, and the victim's perception that they cannot alter their circumstances. This creates a sense of permanence, from which escape appears impossible.[98]

F.M. and Others v. Russia (2024) is a particularly relevant ECtHR case for understanding Russia's accountability for the servitude of migrant workers on its soil.[99] Although Russia withdrew from the ECtHR in September 2022, the Court retains jurisdiction over violations that occurred before its withdrawal.[100] Accordingly, the ruling in *F.M. and*

---

98. *Siliadin v. France*. No. 73316/01, European Court of Human Rights, 26 Oct. 2005, https://hudoc.echr.coe.int/?i=001-69891
99. *F.M. and Others v. Russia*. Nos. 71671/16 and 40190/18, European Court of Human Rights, 10 Dec. 2024, https://hudoc.echr.coe.int/eng?i=002-14414
100. Article 58(2) of the European Convention on Human Rights states: "Such a denunciation shall not have the effect of releasing the High Contracting Party concerned from its obligations under this Convention in respect of any act which,

Others v. Russia remains significant in positioning the ECtHR as a mechanism of accountability vis-à-vis Russia. In *F.M. and Others v. Russia*, the Court found Russia in violation of Article 4 of the European Convention on Human Rights for failing to protect female migrant workers from Kazakhstan and Uzbekistan who were trafficked and held in servitude.[101] The Court identified several key elements that collectively met the threshold for servitude, which is prohibited by Article 4 of the Convention:

- Forced, unpaid, and excessive labor under conditions of violence and coercion;

- Seizure of identity documents, leaving victims legally powerless and dependent;

- Confinement to the workplace, where victims lived and worked under constant surveillance;

- Inability to change their condition, creating a feeling of permanence and hopelessness.

While the acts of servitude were committed by private actors, the Court found that the state violated Article 4 (prohibition of servitude) by failing to fulfill its positive obligations. This failure resulted from the deficient criminalization of trafficking, the absence of effective victim protections, and the authorities' failure to investigate credible suspicions or *prima facie* evidence. Moreover, the ECtHR held that Russia's inaction reflected a gender- and status-based bias, thereby violating Article 14's prohibition of discrimination in conjunction with

---

being capable of constituting a violation of such obligations, may have been performed by it before the date at which the denunciation became effective."

See Council of Europe. *European Convention on Human Rights*. 4 Nov. 1950. Entered into force 3 Sept. 1953. Ratified by the Russian Federation on 5 May 1998 and withdrawn on 16 Sept. 2022, https://www.echr.coe.int/documents/d/echr/convention_ENG

101. "Russia Ceases to Be Party to the European Convention on Human Rights." Council of Europe, 16 Sept. 2022, www.coe.int/en/web/portal/-/russia-ceases-to-be-party-to-the-european-convention-on-human-rights

Article 4's protections. In *F.M. and Others v. Russia*, the failure of domestic authorities to treat irregular female foreign workers as potential victims of trafficking demonstrated a discriminatory attitude that facilitated their exploitation. According to a lawyer who worked on the case, Russian authorities are more likely to prosecute such individuals for their documentation status than to offer them victim protections (Expert 8).

When presented with the facts documented in this report, the aforementioned lawyer noted that the situation of North Korean workers in Russia parallels that of the migrant workers in *F.M. and Others v. Russia*, both groups being victims of trafficking for the purpose of servitude (Expert 8). Like the victims in *F.M. and Others v. Russia*, North Korean workers meet all three elements of the international definition of trafficking: the "act," as they are recruited and transported into Russia from North Korea; the "means," as they are subjected to coercion through confiscation of personal documents, restrictions on movement, and threats of punishment; and the "purpose," as they are exploited for labor.

The lawyer emphasized, however, that the situation of North Korean workers is more severe than in *F.M. and Others v. Russia* because it is embedded in a state-sponsored system, rather than perpetrated by private actors: the North Korean state recruits the workers, dispatches minders to confine and monitor them, and systematically expropriates their wages. Within this system, Russia functions not merely as a bystander but as an active collaborator. It manipulates its student visa policy to circumvent sanctions and routinely returns escapees to North Korean authorities, the very perpetrators of the abuses. In this context, Russia's responsibility shifts from passive tolerance to active complicity in a state-run system of trafficking for servitude, as further argued in Section 8.3.

8.2.3 "Crime Against Humanity" of Enslavement

The exploitation of North Korean workers in Russia constitutes more than forced labor and servitude; it rises to the level of slavery, reflecting the North Korean state's systematic exercise of powers akin to ownership over its citizens abroad. This characterization was affirmed by the Office of the United Nations High Commissioner for Human Rights (UN OHCHR), which defined slavery in accordance with the 1926 Slavery Convention as "the status or condition of a person over whom any or all of the powers attaching to the right of ownership are exercised."[102] The UN OHCHR clarifies that the element of ownership involves "not only 'legal ownership'—a status abolished worldwide—but a lived condition in which one individual exercises over another powers that are similar to or attach themselves to the right of ownership."

The powers attaching to the right of ownership are demonstrably exercised over North Korean workers:

- **The Power to Buy, Sell, or Transfer:** North Korean authorities function as a broker, negotiating contracts and "selling" the labor of its citizens to Russian firms. Workers are excluded from these negotiations and kept uninformed about the terms of the labor procurement. Moreover, they are denied employment contracts, which leads to information asymmetry undermining their capacity to consent.

- **The Power to Control and Manage a Person as an Asset:** North Korean authorities strip workers of their legal identity and personal agency by confiscating their passports upon

---

102. United Nations Office of the High Commissioner for Human Rights. *Forced labour by the Democratic People's Republic of Korea*. July 2024, https://www.ohchr.org/sites/default/files/documents/countries/korea-republic/forced-labour-democratic-peoples-republic-korea-en.pdf.
    United Nations. *Slavery Convention*. 7 Dec. 1953. *United Nations Treaty Series*, vol. 212, p. 17. Entered into force 7 July 1955. Ratified by the USSR on 8 Aug. 1956 (binding on the Russian Federation as successor state).

arrival in Russia and severely restricting their movement to prevent escape. These practices resemble the actions of an owner managing property rather than an employer managing employees.

- **The Power to Appropriate Labor and Profit:** North Korean authorities seize up to 90% of the workers' earnings, not as tax but as a direct appropriation of the economic value they produce. Moreover, the workers are not allowed to retain and manage their own finances.

- **The Power to Mistreat, Neglect, or Dispose:** North Korean authorities enforce labor productivity through physical and psychological violence, while systematically denying workers adequate safety protections and medical care. Moreover, workers who fail to meet quotas or become unproductive due to serious injuries or illness are often repatriated arbitrarily.

Together, these practices establish a coercive and dehumanizing system in which workers are treated not as individuals with rights, but as state-controlled property. This exceeds the threshold of forced labor or servitude and satisfies the definition of slavery under international human rights law. Slavery is expressly prohibited under Article 4 of the Universal Declaration of Human Rights, Article 8 of the International Covenant on Civil and Political Rights (ICCPR), and Article 4 of the European Convention on Human Rights (ECHR).[103] Both North Korea and Russia are bound by the ICCPR and UDHR, and although Russia has withdrawn from the ECtHR, acts occurring prior to its withdrawal remain within the Court's jurisdiction.

---

103. United Nations General Assembly. *Universal Declaration of Human Rights.* 10 Dec. 1948, G.A. Res. 217 A (III), U.N. Doc. A/RES/217(III);

United Nations. *International Covenant on Civil and Political Rights.* 16 Dec. 1966. *United Nations Treaty Series*, vol. 999, p. 171. Entered into force 23 Mar. 1976. Ratified by the USSR on 16 Oct. 1973 (binding on the Russian Federation as successor state);

Council of Europe. *European Convention on Human Rights.* 4 Nov. 1950. Entered into force 3 Sept. 1953. Ratified by the Russian Federation on 5 May 1998 and withdrawn on 16 Sept. 2022.

Moreover, the Rome Statute of the International Criminal Court (ICC) classifies enslavement as a crime against humanity under Article 7(1)(c).[104] Although jurisdictional limitations—such as the fact that neither North Korea nor Russia is a party to the Rome Statute—currently preclude prosecution before the ICC, the elements of enslavement as a crime against humanity are clearly satisfied:

Element 1: The perpetrator exercised any or all of the powers attaching to the right of ownership over one or more persons... or imposed a similar deprivation of liberty.

→ As described above, North Korea imposes such powers by arbitrarily selling the workers' labor, confiscating their documents, restricting their movement, and denying them any financial autonomy.

Element 2: The conduct was part of a widespread or systematic attack directed against a civilian population.

→ North Korea's labor export program involves an estimated 15,000 workers in Russia alone and is operated through the coordination of numerous state actors that manage the entire procedure, from recruitment to on-site control. Russia's complicity is also systematic, demonstrated by its 2007 bilateral agreement with North Korea on temporary labor activities, its institutionalized fraudulent "student visa" scheme for sanctions evasion, and its 2016 bilateral agreement to transfer defectors back to North Korean authorities.

Element 3: The perpetrator knew that the conduct was part of, or intended it to be part of, such an attack.

→ North Korean authorities intentionally exploit the workers' vulnerability as a matter of state policy, using the money extorted from their earnings to fund state initiatives. Russian authorities and private actors facilitate the program through a fraudulent "student visa" scheme, active complicity in the face of abuses, and cooperation in the

---

104. United Nations. *Rome Statute of the International Criminal Court.* 17 July 1998. *United Nations Treaty Series*, vol. 2187, p. 3. Entered into force 1 July 2002. Russia signed on 13 Sept. 2000 but withdrew its signature on 16 Nov. 2016; it is therefore not a state party.

forced repatriation of defectors. Both states are aware—or cannot credibly deny awareness—of the systematic nature and consequences of these actions. The exploitative nature of the program is widely documented by UN bodies and human rights organizations, making claims of ignorance by state authorities implausible.

In sum, the treatment of North Korean workers abroad constitutes the "crime against humanity" of enslavement under international criminal law. Although current jurisdictional constraints limit the feasibility of immediate criminal accountability through the ICC, these findings support the classification of the situation as a crime against humanity and underscore the urgent need for international action, including sustained monitoring of the workers' conditions, strengthened global cooperation to protect their rights, and the pursuit of accountability through universal jurisdiction.

8.3 WEB OF ACCOUNTABILITY: STATE AND CORPORATE RESPONSIBILITY

The systematic exploitation of North Korean workers in Russia generates a complex web of legal accountability that extends beyond North Korea, the principal perpetrator, to include Russia as the host state and the corporate actors that profit from this forced labor. While the North Korean government orchestrates the system, the Russian government's active complicity, coupled with corporate participation, creates multiple avenues for pursuing accountability under international law.

8.3.1 State Responsibility of Russia

Russia bears direct and multifaceted responsibility for the human rights violations occurring within its territory. This responsibility arises both from its failure to fulfill positive obligations to protect individuals under its jurisdiction and, more seriously, from its active complicity in North Korea's internationally wrongful acts. Under its obligations pursuant to ratified treaties, including the ICCPR, ICESCR, CAT, Palermo Protocol, and numerous ILO Conventions, Russia must exercise due diligence to prevent, investigate, punish, and remedy human rights violations, whether committed by state or private actors.

Russia has demonstrably failed to meet these obligations. As confirmed in *F.M. and Others v. Russia* and emphasized by Russian human rights lawyers, the domestic legal system is "completely inadequate to deal with forced labor and human trafficking" (Experts 8, 9). It lacks meaningful prevention mechanisms, does not properly criminalize trafficking, and offers no effective victim protection framework. Rather than receiving protection, North Korean workers who flee are prosecuted as irregular migrants, and laws that criminalize assistance to irregular migrants further isolate them from potential aid and justice (Experts 8, 9).

Moreover, Russia's role extends beyond mere failure to protect. Its conduct constitutes active complicity in North Korea's commission of internationally wrongful acts, thereby engaging its responsibility under the customary international law reflected in Article 16 of the International Law Commission's Articles on the Responsibility of States for Internationally Wrongful Acts (ARSIWA).[105] This provision establishes that a State incurs responsibility when it knowingly aids or assists another State in the commission of such an act. Russia's actions meet each element of this standard:

1. The state must actually provide aid or assistance that facilitates the commission of the wrongful act by the other state. Russia facilitates North Korea's system of modern-day slavery through formally ceding oversight of working conditions, orchestrating the fraudulent student visa scheme, and transferring captured defectors to North Korean authorities despite credible allegations of abuse. Furthermore, Russian local police have accepted or extorted bribes from North

---

105. United Nations International Law Commission. *Draft Articles on Responsibility of States for Internationally Wrongful Acts, with Commentaries*. 2001. *Official Records of the General Assembly*, Fifty-sixth Session, Supplement No. 10 (A/56/10). Annexed to UNGA Resolution 56/83 of 12 Dec. 2001.

Korean managers and workers in exchange for overlooking labor violations and documentation fraud.

2. The assisting state must be aware of the circumstances that make the act wrongful. The exploitative nature of North Korea's labor export program is well-documented by the UN Commission of Inquiry on Human Rights in the DPRK, the UN Panel of Experts assisting the 1718 Sanctions Committee, and numerous human rights organizations. Asylum claims and legal complaints filed by North Korean defectors and Russian lawyers have further underscored these abuses, making it implausible for Russian authorities to claim ignorance (Expert 9).

3. The act must be one that would also be considered internationally wrongful if the assisting state had committed it directly. The act of enslavement constitutes a violation of *jus cogens* norms and is prohibited under treaties binding on Russia. If Russia were to commit the same act independently, it would constitute an internationally wrongful act.

Multiple international mechanisms exist to hold Russia accountable for these breaches:

- **ILO Supervisory Bodies:** While individuals cannot file complaints directly, workers' or employers' organizations may submit representations to the ILO under Article 24 of its Constitution. Additionally, other ILO member states or the ILO Governing Body may file complaints under Article 26, which can trigger the establishment of a Commission of Inquiry—the ILO's highest-level investigative mechanism—to examine a member state's failure to comply with its obligations under ratified conventions, such as Convention No. 29 on Forced Labour (C029). The Committee of Experts on the Application of Conventions and Recommendations (CEACR) monitors Russia's compliance with its reporting obligations under ratified ILO instruments and, in its 2021 and 2024 observations, raised concerns over the vulnerability of migrant workers in Russia to forced labor and exploitation, particularly due to gaps in law enforcement.[106]

- **UN Human Rights Treaty Bodies:** Individuals or their representatives can file complaints ("individual communications") against Russia with the Human Rights Committee (under the ICCPR), the Committee on the Elimination of Racial Discrimination (under ICERD), and the Committee Against Torture (under CAT), as Russia has accepted these procedures.[107] While domestic remedies must typically be exhausted, this requirement may be waived if such remedies are unavailable or ineffective, which is demonstrably the case for these workers in Russia. Even if individual complaints are challenging, civil society can submit information for Russia's periodic reviews before these treaty bodies and during its Universal Periodic Review (UPR) to generate official scrutiny and recommendations.

- **The International Court of Justice (ICJ):** The ICJ offers a potential avenue for inter-state claims. Russia has accepted the ICJ's jurisdiction for disputes under the Convention Against

---

106. International Labour Organization, Committee of Experts on the Application of Conventions and Recommendations. *Observation on the Russian Federation under the Forced Labour Convention, 1930 (No. 29)*. Adopted 2020, published 109th ILC session (2021). NORMALEX, https://normlex.ilo.org/dyn/nrmlx_en/f?p=1000:13100:0::NO:13100:P13100_COMMENT_ID,P11110_COUNTRY_ID,P11110_COUNTRY_NAME,P11110_COMMENT_YEAR:4046649,102884,Russian%20Federation,2020.

International Labour Organization, Committee of Experts on the Application of Conventions and Recommendations. *Observation on the Russian Federation under the Forced Labour Convention, 1930 (No. 29)*. Adopted 2024, published 113th ILC session (2025). NORMALEX, https://normlex.ilo.org/dyn/nrmlx_en/f?p=1000:13100:0::NO:13100:P13100_COMMENT_ID,P13100_COUNTRY_ID:4417505,102884.

107. United Nations Office of the High Commissioner for Human Rights. *Treaty Body Database: Acceptance of Individual Complaints Procedures for Russian Federation*. OHCHR, https://tbinternet.ohchr.org/_layouts/15/TreatyBodyExternal/Treaty.aspx?CountryID=144&Lang=en

Torture and ICERD.[108] Based on the emerging doctrine of *erga omnes partes* obligations, affirmed in ICJ cases like *Questions relating to the Obligation to Prosecute or Extradite (Belgium v. Senegal, 2012)*, any state party to these conventions could potentially bring a claim against Russia for its role in facilitating acts that violate these treaties, even without being directly injured.[109]

- **The European Court of Human Rights (ECtHR):** The ECtHR retains jurisdiction over all violations committed by Russia prior to its withdrawal on September 16, 2022. The landmark ruling in *F.M. and Others v. Russia* establishes a powerful precedent that can be leveraged in future cases filed on behalf of North Korean workers for abuses that occurred on Russian territory before this date.

---

108. Article 21 of the Convention against Torture and Article 22 of the International Convention on the Elimination of All Forms of Racial Discrimination grant the International Court of Justice jurisdiction over disputes.

See United Nations. *Convention against Torture and Other Cruel, Inhuman or Degrading Treatment or Punishment*. 10 Dec. 1984. *United Nations Treaty Series*, vol. 1465, p. 85. Entered into force 26 June 1987. Ratified by the USSR on 3 Mar. 1987 (binding on the Russian Federation as successor state);

United Nations. *International Convention on the Elimination of All Forms of Racial Discrimination*. 7 Mar. 1966. *United Nations Treaty Series*, vol. 660, p. 195. Entered into force 4 Jan. 1969. Ratified by the USSR on 4 Feb. 1969 (binding on the Russian Federation as successor state).

109. *Questions relating to the Obligation to Prosecute or Extradite (Belgium v. Senegal)*, supra note 94, pp. 117.

Table 8. Russia's Key International Obligations

Ratified International Legal Instrument	Key Articles and Obligations
Slavery Convention	**Art. 2 & 5:** Obligation to prevent and suppress slavery in all its forms, including forced labor.
Palermo Protocol (Trafficking)	**Art. 6:** Obligation to aid victims of trafficking. **Art. 9 & 10:** Obligation to prevent and combat trafficking by launching policies and programs and by promoting information exchange among law enforcement.
ICCPR	**Art. 2:** Guarantee of the Convention rights to all individuals within the State's territory and effective remedy for rights violations. **Art. 7:** Prohibition of torture and cruel, inhuman, or degrading treatment. **Art. 8:** Prohibition of forced labor or compulsory labor, servitude, and slavery. **Art. 26:** Obligation to guarantee equal protection before the law without discrimination.
ICESCR	**Art. 6:** Obligation to protect the right to freely chosen work. **Art. 7:** Obligation to guarantee just and favorable conditions of work, including fair wages, a safe environment, and reasonable working hours. **Art. 8:** Obligation to protect the right to form and join trade unions.

ICERD	**Art. 5(e)(i):** Obligation to protect the rights to work, to free choice of employment, to just and favorable conditions of work, to equal pay for equal work, without discrimination based on national origin.
CAT	**Art. 2 & 16:** Obligation to take effective measures to prevent torture and other acts of cruel, inhuman, or degrading treatment or punishment.
ECHR (pre-Sept. 2022)	**Art. 4 & 14:** Prohibition of slavery, servitude, and forced labor, and prohibition of discrimination in the enjoyment of Convention rights.
Key ILO Conventions	**C029 (Art. 1, 25 & 26):** Obligation to suppress the use of forced or compulsory labor in all its forms within the shortest possible period, make forced labor criminally punishable, and apply the Convention to all territories under its sovereignty or jurisdiction. **C105 (Art. 1 & 2):** Prohibition of the use of forced labor for economic development. **P029 (Art. 1-5):** Obligation to take effective measures to prevent and eliminate forced labor; prevent abuses and fraudulent practices in recruitment; support due diligence in both public and private sectors; address root causes that heighten risks of forced or compulsory labor; identify, release, protect, and rehabilitate victims; guarantee remedies to victims regardless of legal status, and protect them from prosecution for crimes committed under coercion; and cooperate internationally to prevent and eliminate all forms of forced and compulsory labor. **C081 (Art. 1 & 2):** Obligation to maintain a system of labor inspection in industrial and commercial workplaces to monitor workplace conditions.

C087 (Art. 1 & 2): Obligation to protect the right to form and join trade unions.

C098 (Art. 1 & 2): Obligation to protect the right to engage in collective bargaining and enjoy adequate protection against acts of anti-union discrimination.

C100 (Art. 1 & 2): Obligation to ensure equal remuneration for work of equal value.

C095 (Art. 5, 6, 8, 9 & 14): Obligation to ensure that workers are paid directly, retain full freedom to dispose of their wages, and are informed of all wage conditions prior to employment. Prohibition of arbitrary deductions from wages and of deductions made for obtaining or retaining employment.

C111 (Art. 1): Prohibition of discrimination in employment and occupation, including on the basis of national origin.

C144 (Art. 1 & 2): Obligation to maintain tripartite consultation mechanisms to ensure cooperation among government, employers, and workers in shaping labor standards.

C155 (Art. 1-3): Obligation to promote a safe and healthy working environment and to ensure the well-being of all workers.

C187 (Art. 1 & 2): Obligation to promote occupational safety and health and prevent work-related injuries, illnesses, and deaths, and take active steps to progressively achieve a safe and healthy working environment.

8.3.2 Corporate Responsibility of Russian and Other Companies

The legal landscape is rapidly evolving to address the role of corporate actors in human rights abuses. While most international treaties do not impose binding obligations directly on companies, a robust and authoritative framework for responsible business conduct has emerged. This framework exposes companies to significant legal, financial, and reputational risks if they fail to uphold human rights standards.

The UN Guiding Principles on Business and Human Rights (UNGPs) set the global benchmark for corporate responsibility to "respect" human rights.[110] This responsibility operates independently of a state's own human rights duties and urges companies to conduct human rights due diligence (HRDD) to identify, prevent, mitigate, and account for adverse human rights impacts in which they are involved. HRDD comprises four core components: (1) identifying and assessing actual or potential adverse human rights impacts; (2) integrating and acting on the findings; (3) tracking the effectiveness of responses and obtaining feedback from affected stakeholders; and (4) communicating transparently about how impacts are being addressed.

Russian developers employing North Korean workers, such as Strana Development and Eskadra, are complicit in forced labor, servitude, and other serious human rights abuses by directly benefiting from these violations. Their advantages, such as accelerated construction timelines and reduced management costs, are made possible by excessive working hours imposed on North Korean workers and by ceding day-to-day oversight to North Korean managers. The conditions of these workers are extensively documented by the UN Panel of Experts assisting the 1718 DPRK Sanctions Committee, human rights organizations, and global media. In light of the well-established nature of these abuses, claims of plausible deniability are legally and ethically indefensible.

---

110. United Nations. *Guiding Principles on Business and Human Rights: Implementing the United Nations "Protect, Respect and Remedy" Framework.* HR/PUB/11/04, 2011. Endorsed by the UN Human Rights Council in Resolution 17/4, 16 June 2011.

Moreover, the framework of corporate responsibility is shifting from "soft law" to "hard law." The new EU Corporate Sustainability Due Diligence Directive (EU CS3D), which entered into force in July 2024, transforms the voluntary standards of the UNGPs into legally binding obligations for certain companies.[111] The directive applies to large EU companies as well as non-EU companies generating significant turnover in the EU market. If any Russian firms involved—or their parent companies—meet the EU CS3D's jurisdictional thresholds, they could face administrative sanctions and civil liability in the EU for failing to identify, prevent, mitigate, and account for forced labor in their value chains. Enforcement is twofold: national supervisory authorities may impose administrative penalties, and affected parties may bring civil actions against companies that intentionally or negligently breach their due diligence obligations. The directive thus marks a significant legal development, embedding corporate human rights responsibilities in a binding regulatory framework and signaling a broader global shift toward mandatory human rights due diligence (mHRDD).

---

111. European Union. *Directive (EU) 2024/1760 of the European Parliament and of the Council of 13 June 2024 on Corporate Sustainability Due Diligence. Official Journal of the European Union,* 5 July 2024.

CHAPTER 9
CONCLUSION

9.1 SYNTHESIS OF FINDINGS ON THE POST-SANCTIONS CONTEXT

In sum, the report has found that UN sanctions prohibiting work authorizations for North Korean nationals have proven ineffective in Russia. Russia continues to employ North Korean workers and permits their wages to be systematically expropriated by Pyongyang to finance illicit WMD programs. In doing so, Russia has engineered sanctions evasion mechanisms that undermine the security objectives of the UN measures. Instead of issuing work permits, Russian authorities now admit North Koreans on "student visas" to circumvent restrictions. Consequently, tens of thousands of workers remain in Russia under conditions nearly identical to the pre-sanctions era, preserving a key financial pipeline for the North Korean state.

North Korean workers in Russia endure conditions amounting to forced labor, servitude, and the crime against humanity of enslavement as defined under international law. The North Korean state siphons off their earnings while imposing total control through onsite minders, seized identity documents, assigned housing, and severe restrictions on movement, communication, and access to information. The irregular status of workers under sanctions evasion mechanisms exacerbates their vulnerability to abuse and exploitation. In particular, the "student visa" scheme forces workers to bear the costs of a corrupt ecosystem involving Russian schools, brokers, and local law enforcement.

This system of transnational repression is sustained by the complicity of Russian state and corporate actors, who delegate oversight of working conditions to North Korean authorities and willfully disregard credible reports of abuse. Since the imposition of sanctions, this complicity has deepened, with Russian officials openly collaborating with North Korean counterparts to fabricate student documents and broker labor arrangements. Thus, in practice, the blanket ban has become counterproductive: it incentivizes Russian stakeholders to exploit loopholes rather than genuinely comply with international law when also faced with persistent needs for cheap workforce.

Seven years after the adoption of sanctions, the security environment has grown increasingly complex. North Korean soldiers are now fighting in Russia, adding to the presence of laborers whose expropriated wages are diverted to prohibited weapons programs. The 2024 Treaty on Comprehensive Strategic Partnership formalizes this deepening Russia–North Korea alliance with a mutual defense pact, openly defying international norms and further enabling human rights abuses.

This critical juncture demands the exploration of a more holistic strategy than our current sanctions regime. Rather than relying solely on a blanket ban, the international community should adopt measures that ensure employment functions as the exercise of workers' fundamental rights and cannot be exploited by the state as a geopolitical instrument. By equipping North Korean workers with more agency, such as control over their wages, the international community would prevent North Korea from weaponizing its labor export program and more effectively address the intertwined threats that it poses to security and human rights.

9.2 POLICY RECOMMENDATIONS

The following recommendations are directed to the multiple actors whose direct action, complicity, or negligence have enabled the system of exploitation described in this report. They are structured by stakeholder to create a system of mutual accountability, wherein each party can encourage others to improve the labor and human rights conditions of North Korean workers. Collectively, these recommendations seek to shift the policy paradigm from a blanket prohibition on work authorization for North Korean nationals toward principled, rights-based engagement grounded in international legal frameworks.

9.2.1 Recommendations to the Government of Russia

1. Dismantle sanctions evasion mechanisms and cooperate with the international community in establishing a principled framework for employing North Korean nationals.

Russia should cease the practice of designating North Korean workers as "students" to evade sanctions and instead issue appropriate work visas that accurately reflect the purpose of their entry and employment. Furthermore, Russia should cooperate with the international community to establish a monitored framework under which host countries may employ North Korean nationals only upon the adoption of binding wage protection mechanisms. These mechanisms must guarantee that workers directly receive their remuneration and that wages are safeguarded against diversion into the financing of illicit WMD programs. By working with the UN Security Council to pursue this approach to the employment of North Korean nationals, Russia would better fulfill its obligations under the UN Charter toward international peace and security, while simultaneously advancing the protection of migrant workers' rights in line with ILO Convention No. 95 on the Protection of Wages.[112]

---

112. International Labour Organization. *Protection of Wages Convention, 1949 (No. 95)*. 1 July 1949; entered into force 24 Sept. 1952. Ratified by the USSR on 4 May 1951 (binding on the Russian Federation as successor state).

2. Enact legislation mandating human rights due diligence to address the responsibility of corporations for the abuse and exploitation of workers whose services they employ or benefit from.

Russia should adopt comprehensive legislation requiring corporations operating within its jurisdiction to conduct mandatory human rights due diligence. Grounded in the UN Guiding Principles on Business and Human Rights, such legislation should obligate corporations to systematically identify, prevent, and mitigate risks of severe human rights abuses across their operations and supply chains. This requirement would apply to both corporations directly hiring North Korean employees and those subcontracting the labor services of North Korean corporations. Under this framework, corporations would be held responsible for the failure to exhaust possible safeguards against violations of basic labor rights, such as the right to fair remuneration and decent working conditions.

The legislation must include robust mechanisms for enforcement, including administrative penalties for non-compliance, civil liability provisions guaranteeing victims meaningful access to remedies, and independent bodies tasked with handling reports of non-compliance. In parallel, Russia should amend its bilateral agreement with North Korea on temporary labor activities to align with the new law, removing provisions that delegate oversight of working conditions to North Korean authorities. By mandating human rights due diligence for corporations, Russia would take a concrete step toward fulfilling its obligations under ILO Convention No. 29 on Forced Labor and its Protocol of 2014.[113]

---

113. International Labour Organization. *Forced Labour Convention, 1930 (No. 29)*. 28 June 1930; entered into force 1 May 1932. Ratified by the USSR on 23 June 1956 (binding on the Russian Federation as successor state);

International Labour Organization. Protocol of 2014 to the Forced Labour Convention, 1930 (P029). Adopted 11 June 2014, entered into force 9 Nov. 2016. Ratified by the Russian Federation on 17 Jan. 2019.

3. Enforce accountability for corrupt practices by universities and local police who facilitate sanctions evasion or ignore credible allegations of abuse in exchange for bribes.

Russia should enforce existing anti-corruption and abuse-of-power legislation against universities and local police implicated in sanctions evasion and the exploitation of North Korean workers. University administrators who falsify student records in exchange for bribes should be investigated and prosecuted under Criminal Code Article 204 on commercial bribery, Article 292 on official forgery, and, where applicable, Article 290 on bribe-taking by public officials.[114] Likewise, law enforcement officers who ignore credible allegations of abuse in exchange for bribes from North Korean managers, or who extort bribes from North Korean workers through threats, should be investigated and prosecuted under Criminal Code Article 285 on abuse of official powers, Article 286 on exceeding official powers, and Article 290 on bribe-taking by public officials. These measures should be implemented within the framework of Federal Law No. 273-FZ of 25 December 2008 "On Counteracting Corruption."[115] By holding these actors accountable, Russia would also be fulfilling its binding obligations under the UN Convention against Corruption, which requires the criminalization and prosecution of corruption and abuse of official functions.[116]

4. Strengthen legal protection for victims of trafficking and remove barriers to assistance.

Russia must expand and strengthen protections for all victims of human trafficking, guaranteeing access to remedies, shelter, and legal assistance regardless of immigration status. These protections are

---

114. Russian Federation. *Federal Law No. 63-FZ, Criminal Code of the Russian Federation*. 13 June 1996, amended on 31 July 2025. *ConsultantPlus*, http://www.consultant.ru/document/cons_doc_LAW_10699/
115. Russian Federation. *Federal Law No. 273-FZ, On Counteracting Corruption*. 25 Dec. 2008. *ConsultantPlus*, http://www.consultant.ru/document/cons_doc_LAW_82959
116. United Nations. United Nations Convention against Corruption. Adopted 31 Oct. 2003, entered into force 14 Dec. 2005. United Nations Treaty Series, vol. 2349, pp. 41. Ratified by the Russian Federation on 9 May 2006.

particularly critical for North Korean workers, whose passports are routinely confiscated by managers upon arrival. Without access to their personal documents, those who leave the workplace cannot prove their legal status and are often treated as immigration offenders rather than victims of trafficking. To address this treatment, Russia should formally extend coverage under Federal Law No. 119-FZ "On State Protection of Victims, Witnesses, and Other Participants in Criminal Proceedings" to all trafficked persons, ensuring their safety and ability to pursue legal remedies.[117]

In parallel, Russia should amend Article 322.1 of the Criminal Code to decriminalize the provision of humanitarian assistance to migrants whose legal status is irregular as a result of trafficking or the forcible deprivation of personal documents.[118] These reforms would close systemic gaps identified in international jurisprudence, including *F.M. and Others v. Russia*, and bring Russia's practice into compliance with its binding obligations under the UN Palermo Protocol, which requires states to guarantee effective protection and support for victims of trafficking.[119]

5. Fully uphold the principle of *non-refoulement* by ending all practices that enable the repatriation of North Korean defectors at risk.

Russia must fully comply with the principle of *non-refoulement*, recognizing it not only as a prohibition on forced repatriation but as a positive obligation to identify and protect individuals at risk. This requires ensuring that the situation of North Korean defectors is formally assessed before any transfer to the custody of North Korean companies or authorities. To achieve that objective, Russia should

---

117. Russian Federation. *Federal Law No. 119-FZ, On State Protection of Victims, Witnesses, and Other Participants in Criminal Proceedings*. 20 Aug. 2004. Garant Legal Information System, https://base.garant.ru/12136633
118. Russian Federation, *supra* note 114, pp. 141.
119. United Nations. *Protocol to Prevent, Suppress and Punish Trafficking in Persons, Especially Women and Children, Supplementing the United Nations Convention against Transnational Organized Crime*. Adopted 15 Nov. 2000, entered into force 25 Dec. 2003. United Nations Treaty Series, vol. 2237, p. 319. Ratified by the Russian Federation on 26 May 2004.

rescind—or at minimum revise—its 2016 bilateral agreement with North Korea on the transfer of "illegal" entrants and residents to require refugee status determination (RSD) procedures as a legal prerequisite for any handover.

Russia should also cooperate closely with the UN Refugee Agency (UNHCR) to guarantee the full and uncompromised implementation of RSD procedures, including a rigorous assessment of the risk of torture or persecution. Furthermore, Russia should commit to transparency by publicly reporting to international bodies on the measures taken to uphold the principle of *non-refoulement* and on the outcomes of asylum proceedings for North Korean nationals. Implementing these safeguards is essential for Russia to comply with its binding obligations under the 1951 Refugee Convention, its 1967 Protocol, and Article 3 of the Convention against Torture, which prohibit returning any person to a state where they face a risk of torture.[120]

6. Reinforce commitment to international labor and human rights standards through ratification of other treaties.

To signal a stronger commitment to protecting migrant worker rights, Russia should ratify the International Convention on the Protection of the Rights of All Migrant Workers and Members of Their Families, as well as the 1954 Convention Relating to the Status of Stateless Persons and the 1961 Convention on the Reduction of Statelessness. Furthermore, Russia should demonstrate its commitment to combating the crime against humanity of enslavement by ratifying the Rome Statute of the International Criminal Court.

---

120. United Nations. *Convention Relating to the Status of Refugees*. Adopted 28 July 1951, entered into force 22 Apr. 1954. *United Nations Treaty Series*, vol. 139, p. 137. Acceded to by the USSR on 2 Feb. 1993 (binding on the Russian Federation as successor state).

United Nations. *Protocol Relating to the Status of Refugees*. Adopted 31 Jan. 1967, entered into force 4 Oct. 1967. *United Nations Treaty Series*, vol. 606, p. 267. Acceded to by the USSR on 2 Feb. 1993 (binding on the Russian Federation as successor state).

United Nations. *Convention against Torture and Other Cruel, Inhuman or Degrading Treatment or Punishment*. 10 Dec. 1984. *United Nations Treaty Series*, vol. 1465, p. 85. Entered into force 26 June 1987. Ratified by the USSR on 3 Mar. 1987 (binding on the Russian Federation as successor state).

9.2.2 Recommendations to the Government of North Korea

1. Increase the agency and representation of workers in determining pay and other working conditions.

To transition from coercion to lawful labor relations, North Korea must guarantee that all employment is grounded in transparent, enforceable contracts and the genuine consent of workers. Dispatching companies must be required to provide each worker with a written employment contract prior to departure that specifies a clear payment and disbursement schedule, including fixed monthly salaries or transparent methods for calculating project-based pay. These contracts must also define working hours, guarantee vacation and sick leave, provide comprehensive insurance for workplace injuries, and outline consequences for breaches by either party, with deference to ILO standards. Guaranteeing these contractual rights is a critical step toward dismantling state-sponsored forced labor and fostering just working conditions, in line with the state's obligations under Article 8 of the ICCPR and Article 7 of the ICESCR.[121]

2. Protect the financial autonomy of workers by banning practices that force dependency and by ensuring full control over wages.

North Korea must penalize debt bondage practices by company managers, including situations where workers are compelled to repay flight or other preliminary expenses as loans. It should also eliminate wage theft by prohibiting managers from serving as intermediaries in the disbursement of wages. Moreover, North Korea must abolish exploitative deductions by replacing the fixed "loyalty remittance" system with a transparent and equitable graduated income tax framework, where remittances are proportional and collected only after wages are received. To prevent arbitrariness, workers must be clearly informed in advance of any lawful deductions. At the same time, North Korea must not restrict how workers manage their

---

121. United Nations. *International Covenant on Economic, Social and Cultural Rights*. Adopted 16 Dec. 1966, entered into force 3 Jan. 1976. *United Nations Treaty Series*, vol. 993, p. 3. Acceded to by the Democratic People's Republic of Korea on 14 Sept. 1981.

earnings, but guarantee their freedom to dispose of wages at their discretion.

3. Immediately cease the diversion of labor export revenues to WMD programs.

The diversion of workers' earnings to North Korea's illicit weapons programs undermines both international security and the fundamental rights of workers. As a condition for renewed engagement with the international community, North Korea must provide verifiable proof that revenues from overseas labor (i.e., equitable tax revenues as proposed in the previous recommendation) are not used for weapons development. It should cooperate with international partners to establish wage protection mechanisms managed by a trusted third party, such as the United Nations, to ensure revenues are directed toward healthcare and education, and social welfare. It should undergo independent audits of labor revenue flows in order to demonstrate compliance with obligations under the UN Charter toward international peace and security.

4. Respect workers' right to privacy by ending surveillance and control beyond the workplace.

North Korea must end practices that undermine the boundary between work and personal life and subject workers to total control. Workers should retain possession of their personal documents, including passports, visas, and identification, in order to be protected from coercion and forced dependency on managers. They must be allowed to freely choose their residence, rather than being confined to employer-controlled dormitories or living arrangements. Outside working hours, workers should have the right to move freely, communicate with others, and engage in personal activities without requiring prior approval. These safeguards are consistent with ICCPR Articles 12 and 17, which guarantee freedom of movement and freedom from arbitrary interference in private life.[122]

---

122. United Nations. *International Covenant on Civil and Political Rights*. 16 Dec. 1966. *United Nations Treaty Series*, vol. 993, p. 3. Acceded to by the Democratic People's Republic of Korea on 14 Sept. 1981.

5. Ensure the access of workers to effective mechanisms of reporting and recourse for abuses committed by company managers and state security officers overseas.

North Korea must provide overseas workers with a safe, independent, and impartial mechanism for reporting abuses and seeking recourse against company managers and state security officers. A taskforce, independent of dispatching companies and their parent ministries, should be periodically deployed to receive complaints and investigate violations such as wage theft and violence. Based on its findings, the taskforce should ensure that victims receive appropriate remedies, such as the restitution of wages, and that perpetrators are penalized through fines or criminal sentences. Throughout the process, victims must be guaranteed anonymity and protection from retaliation. Such measures would align both with North Korea's domestic Law on Complaints and Petitions and with its obligations under ICCPR Article 2(3) on the right to an effective remedy.[123]

6. Eliminate discriminatory and corrupt practices in the selection of overseas workers.

North Korea must abolish selection criteria that discriminate on the basis of *songbun* (hereditary social class), *todae* (family lineage), marital status, disability, or other personal characteristics unrelated to work performance. The state must also dismantle the system of institutionalized corruption that makes bribery an informal prerequisite for dispatch. The selection process should be transparent, merit-based, and grounded in professional skills and qualifications, ensuring that all citizens have equal and fair access to overseas work opportunities. Such reforms are essential to uphold the principles of equality and non-discrimination under Article 2 of the ICCPR and Articles 2 and 7 of the ICESCR.[124]

---

123. Ibid.
124. United Nations. *International Covenant on Economic, Social and Cultural Rights.* Adopted 16 Dec. 1966, entered into force 3 Jan. 1976. *United Nations Treaty Series*, vol. 993, p. 3. Acceded to by the Democratic People's Republic of Korea on 14 Sept. 1981;
    United Nations. International Covenant on Civil and Political Rights. ea on 14 Sept. 1981;16 Dec. 1966. United Nations Treaty Series, vol. 999, p. 171. Entered into force 23 Mar. 1976. Acceded to by the Democratic People's Republic of Korea on 14 Sept. 1981.

7. Reinforce commitment to international labor and human rights standards through ratification of other treaties.

North Korea should seek membership in the International Labour Organization and ratify its core conventions, including the Forced Labour Convention (No. 29), Abolition of Forced Labour Convention (No. 105), Freedom of Association Convention (No. 87), and Discrimination (Employment and Occupation) Convention (No. 111). It should also accede to outstanding human rights treaties, such as the Convention against Torture, and ratify the Rome Statute of the International Criminal Court to signal a commitment to combatting crimes against humanity, including enslavement.

9.2.3 Recommendations to Other Governments and Multilateral Bodies

1. Transition from a blanket ban on the work authorization of North Korean nationals to a principled engagement framework for their employment.

Given the limitations of existing measures, the UN Security Council should consider a principled engagement framework that permits member states to employ North Korean nationals only if they are covered by mandatory, independently monitored wage protection mechanisms. In theory, such a framework would not only reduce the incentive for the Russian state and corporations to evade compliance, but also limit their ability to justify non-compliance on humanitarian grounds. The framework could be built on two complementary mechanisms involving escrow accounts and in-kind compensation.

Mechanism 1: Require host-country firms to deposit compensation for the labor services of North Korean workers into UN escrow accounts.

Firms hiring the services of North Korean companies would be required to deposit compensation into escrow accounts managed by the UN. Only North Korean workers themselves would be authorized to access funds from these accounts through debit cards or other traceable instruments. This arrangement would replace the current system in which Russian firms pay lump sums to North Korean managers, who often commit wage theft or make arbitrary deductions before redistributing wages to workers.

This mechanism would be designed to address the shortcomings of the 1995 Oil-for-Food Programme, which allowed Iraq to sell oil on the international market in exchange for food, medicine, and other humanitarian necessities.[125] Unlike this precedent, the proposed mechanism for the North Korean context would restrict the role of the North Korean government in selecting foreign firms. One of the central flaws of the Oil-for-Food Programme was that Saddam Hussein's regime retained control over the choice of oil buyers and suppliers, enabling collusion and kickbacks.[126] To avoid repeating this mistake, all foreign firms employing North Korean labor should be pre-approved through an independent vetting process, requiring full ownership disclosure and licensing under a uniform set of criteria.

Mechanism 2: Use international humanitarian agencies to provide in-kind compensation for the labor of North Korean workers hired abroad.

Wages owed to North Korean workers could be provided partially or fully as in-kind benefits, with the UN and other vetted humanitarian organizations delivering food, housing, and other daily necessities in host countries. This arrangement, modeled on a "Food-for-Work" program, would ensure that workers directly benefit from their labor and experience improved living conditions, while also preventing

---

125. United Nations Security Council. *Resolution 986 (1995)*. 14 Apr. 1995, S/RES/986.
126. Otterman, Sharon. "Iraq Oil-for-Food Scandal." *Council on Foreign Relations*, 28 Oct. 2005, https://www.cfr.org/backgrounder/iraq-oil-food-scandal

North Korean managers from financially exploiting them.[127] Looking ahead, international actors could also pilot a carefully designed program for non-monetary remittances to workers' dependents remaining in North Korea. Such a program would allow workers to send humanitarian resources to support their families, but would require unprecedented levels of transparency and monitoring. Any expansion would be strictly contingent on verified success and governed by a pre-established termination protocol to halt operations immediately if its integrity were compromised. Ultimately, in-kind compensation would not only reduce the risk of wage redirection by the North Korean government, but also address the poor living conditions faced by workers abroad and support their underlying goal of providing for their families back home.

2. Introduce or strengthen mandatory human rights due diligence for corporations, as well as market restrictions on business activities involving North Korean forced labor.

The European Commission should leverage the Forced Labour Regulation (FLR) to issue early guidance identifying risk indicators of "state-imposed" forced labor, with explicit reference to the situation of North Korean workers.[128] Although EU member states no longer directly employ North Korean labor due to UN sanctions, their supply chains remain vulnerable in sectors such as construction, textiles, and agriculture. To address this risk, the Commission's guidance should direct member states and national enforcement bodies to promote supply chain mapping, mandate third-party audits, and incorporate information provided by NGOs and international bodies. Because the FLR entered into force on 13 December 2024 but will only become fully

---

127. The International Labour Organization has published Terms of Reference for Guidelines regarding Food for Work Programmes.
See Van Esch, Wilma, Jan Fransen, Jane Tournée, and David Mason. *TOR for Guidelines on Food for Work Programmes*. International Labour Organization, May 1997, https://www.ilo.org/sites/default/files/wcmsp5/groups/public/%40ed_emp/%40emp_policy/%40invest/documents/instructionalmaterial/wcms_asist_6036.pdf

128. European Union. *Regulation (EU) 2023/1115 of the European Parliament and of the Council of 31 May 2023 on Prohibiting Products Made with Forced Labour on the Union Market. Official Journal of the European Union.*

operative on 14 December 2027, early guidance during this transitional period is essential to shape enforcement expectations and ensure harmonized compliance once the regulation is fully applied.

In parallel, EU member states should move swiftly to transpose and enforce the Corporate Sustainability Due Diligence Directive (CS3D), explicitly classifying the use of North Korean labor in supply chains as a severe and likely human rights risk that triggers enhanced due diligence obligations.[129] The Directive entered into force on 25 July 2024, with national transposition required by 26 July 2026 and phased application beginning on 26 July 2027 for the largest companies, extending through 26 July 2029. To ensure meaningful implementation, member states should require responsible disengagement where remediation is not feasible, and condition lawful economic engagement on verifiable supplier compliance with international labor standards. In cases involving North Korean or other migrant-sourced labor, this compliance should include participation in wage protection mechanisms.

The United States Congress should enact a North Korean Forced Labor Prevention Act, modeled on the Uyghur Forced Labor Prevention Act (UFLPA), to establish a rebuttable presumption of forced labor for all goods produced wholly or in part with North Korean labor, including labor performed outside North Korea.[130] Pending such legislation, U.S. Customs and Border Protection (CBP) should prioritize enforcement under Section 307 of the Tariff Act and apply UFLPA-level traceability and documentation standards to shipments with North Korea-linked inputs.[131]

Finally, other jurisdictions should adopt comparable measures that combine mandatory human rights due diligence with import prohibitions on products and services made with forced labor. Such

---

129. European Union. *Directive (EU) 2024/1760 of the European Parliament and of the Council of 13 June 2024 on Corporate Sustainability Due Diligence and Amending Directive (EU) 2019/1937 and Regulation (EU) 2023/2859. Official Journal of the European Union.*
130. United States. *Uyghur Forced Labor Prevention Act*. Public Law No. 117-78, 135 Stat. 1525, 23 Dec. 2021.
131. United States. *Tariff Act of 1930*, Public Law No. 71-361, 46 Stat. 689, 17 June 1930.

coordinated action is necessary to close global enforcement gaps and prevent displacement of North Korean forced labor into less regulated markets.

3. Establish a "Safe Harbor Protocol" for North Korean workers fleeing from work posts in Russia.

EU member states sharing a land border with Russia—Estonia, Latvia, Lithuania, and Finland—together with neighboring transit states such as Mongolia and Kazakhstan, should work with countries like South Korea, the United Kingdom, Canada, and the United States, in establishing a Safe Harbor Protocol for North Korean workers fleeing from work posts in Russia. Under this protocol, bordering states would guarantee safe passage and temporary protection through diplomatic agreements grounded in international refugee law; create dedicated consular programs to expedite applications for asylum and refugee status; and establish temporary protection hubs with the support of the UN Refugee Agency and International Organization for Migration, drawing on Emergency Transit Facility models.[132] South Korea should take the lead in diplomatic arrangements, leveraging its statutory mandate to provide overseas protection and resettlement for North Korean defectors. This Protocol is critically urgent given Russia's bilateral agreement with North Korea on the transfer of North Korean defectors and consistent denial of refugee status to those at risk. By anchoring responsibility with both bordering states and South Korea, the Safe Harbor Protocol would operationalize the principle of *non-refoulement* and create a viable humanitarian corridor for those defecting from work posts in Russia.

4. Increase support to civil society organizations and aid groups working on the rights of North Korean and other migrant workers.

States and international organizations should increase funding to the civil society organizations and legal aid groups in Russia and

---

132. United Nations High Commissioner for Refugees. *Emergency transit facilities. UNHCR Resettlement Handbook*, https://www.unhcr.org/resettlement-handbook/4-managing-resettlement-activities/4-9-emergency-transit-facilities-etf/

neighboring countries that work to protect all migrant workers. Strengthening these on-the-ground networks is critical for providing direct assistance, legal support, and safe pathways for victims of trafficking and forced labor, fulfilling the international community's collective obligation to protect vulnerable populations under frameworks like the UN Palermo Protocol.[133]

9.2.4 Recommendations to Corporations

1. Conduct enhanced human rights due diligence to identify, prevent, mitigate, and account for the risk of forced labor and other abuses when contracting with global suppliers.

Corporations must act as responsible actors in the global community by conducting enhanced human rights due diligence, as urged by the UN Guiding Principles on Business and Human Rights. This effort should include attending to credible third-party information on suppliers and industries at risk, as well as ensuring transparency in the sourcing of products and services throughout their supply chains, recognizing that many inputs may be linked to the forced labor of North Koreans and other vulnerable groups worldwide. Under emerging mandatory due diligence frameworks, such as the EU Corporate Sustainability Due Diligence Directive (CS3D), the failure to implement such measures exposes companies active in the EU market to substantial legal, financial, and reputational consequences, including civil liability.

2. Implement wage protection mechanisms when employing the services of North Korean workers.

Corporations must end the practice of making lump-sum payments to North Korean managers when compensating groups of workers. Instead, they should contractually require the use of wage protection mechanisms—such as UN-managed escrow accounts proposed in this

---

133. United Nations. *Protocol to Prevent, Suppress and Punish Trafficking in Persons, Especially Women and Children, Supplementing the United Nations Convention against Transnational Organized Crime.* Adopted 15 Nov. 2000, entered into force 25 Dec. 2003. *United Nations Treaty Series*, vol. 2237, p. 319.

report or other independently monitored, traceable systems—that guarantee wages reach individual workers directly. Given the well-documented nature of wage theft and exploitative practices imposed by North Korean authorities, the failure to ensure wage protection exposes corporations to significant legal, financial, and reputational consequences, including potential import bans under the U.S. Tariff Act (Section 307) and the EU Forced Labour Regulation.[134]

3. Monitor worksites and seek remediation for poor or exploitative working conditions when employing the services of North Korean workers.

Corporations contracting with North Korean suppliers should conduct regular, independent monitoring of worksites, particularly in high-risk sectors such as construction, shipbuilding, and agriculture, to verify compliance with labor and safety standards and to detect coercive practices. Where abuses are identified, corporations must seek remediation from North Korean management. If remediation is denied or obstructed, companies should responsibly disengage from such procurement relationships in accordance with the UN Guiding Principles on Business and Human Rights and other standards on responsible business conduct.

4. Guarantee insurance for worksite injuries when employing North Korean workers directly or hiring them through labor contracts.

Corporations should provide insurance coverage for worksite injuries, or at minimum require such coverage to be provided by North Korean management as a contractual condition, when employing the labor services of North Korean workers. This safeguard is particularly critical in high-risk sectors such as construction, where workplace accidents are frequent and where North Korean workers are denied access to adequate medical care.

---

134. United States. *Tariff Act of 1930*, Public Law No. 71-361, 46 Stat. 689, 17 June 1930;
European Union. *Regulation (EU) 2023/1115 of the European Parliament and of the Council of 31 May 2023 on Prohibiting Products Made with Forced Labour on the Union Market.* Official Journal of the European Union.

Together, these recommendations form a framework for principled engagement amid escalating challenges to global governance on peace, security, and human rights. The deepening military partnership between North Korea and Russia, coupled with their sanctions evasion tactics, risks entrenching exploitative systems and transnational repression of North Korean workers. The proposed framework outlines a path to hold these states accountable while also creating incentives for them to demonstrate, through concrete actions, a genuine commitment to international norms. At its core, it affirms that protecting workers' dignity and ensuring global security are mutually reinforcing goals. By empowering workers, the international community can weaken the authoritarian networks that profit from their labor, and direct Russia and North Korea toward greater respect for human rights as the foundation for responsible participation in the global order.

BIBLIOGRAPHY

Treaties, Laws, and Documents from Multilateral Bodies

Council of Europe

Council of Europe. *European Convention on Human Rights*. Adopted 4 November 1950 in Rome; entered into force 3 September 1953.

European Union

European Union. *Directive (EU) 2024/1760 of the European Parliament and of the Council of 13 June 2024 on Corporate Sustainability Due Diligence*. Official Journal of the European Union, 5 July 2024.

International Labour Organization

International Labour Organization. *ILO Indicators of Forced Labour*. Geneva: International Labour Office, 1 October 2012.
—. *Forced Labour Convention, 1930 (No. 29)*. Adopted 28 June 1930.
—. *Weekly Rest (Industry) Convention, 1921 (No. 14)*. Adopted 17 November 1921.
—. *Forty-Hour Week Convention, 1935 (No. 47)*. Adopted 22 June 1935.
—. *Labour Inspection Convention, 1947 (No. 81)*. Adopted 11 July 1947.
—. *Freedom of Association and Protection of the Right to Organise Convention, 1948 (No. 87)*. Adopted 9 July 1948.
—. *Protection of Wages Convention, 1949 (No. 95)*. Adopted 1 July 1949.
—. *Right to Organise and Collective Bargaining Convention, 1949 (No. 98)*. Adopted 1 July 1949.
—. *Equal Remuneration Convention, 1951 (No. 100)*. Adopted 29 June 1951.
—. *Abolition of Forced Labour Convention, 1957 (No. 105)*. Adopted 25 June 1957.
—. *Weekly Rest (Commerce and Offices) Convention, 1957 (No. 106)*. Adopted 26 June 1957.
—. *Discrimination (Employment and Occupation) Convention, 1958 (No. 111)*. Adopted 25 June 1958.
—. *Tripartite Consultation (International Labour Standards) Convention, 1976 (No. 144)*. Adopted 21 June 1976.
—. *Occupational Safety and Health Convention, 1981 (No. 155)*. Adopted 22 June 1981.
—. *Promotional Framework for Occupational Safety and Health Convention, 2006 (No. 187)*. Adopted 15 June 2006.
—. *Protocol of 2014 to the Forced Labour Convention, 1930 (P029)*. Adopted 11 June 2014.

United Nations

United Nations. *Charter of the United Nations*. Adopted 26 June 1945 in San Francisco; entered into force 24 October 1945.

—. *Universal Declaration of Human Rights*. Adopted 10 December 1948 (General Assembly Resolution 217 A (III)).

—. *Convention relating to the Status of Refugees*. Adopted 28 July 1951; entered into force 22 April 1954.

—. *Protocol Relating to the Status of Refugees*. Adopted 31 January 1967; entered into force 4 October 1967.

—. *Convention relating to the Status of Stateless Persons*. Adopted 28 September 1954; entered into force 6 June 1960.

—. *Convention on the Reduction of Statelessness*. Adopted 30 August 1961; entered into force 13 December 1975.

—. *Slavery Convention*. Adopted 25 September 1926 by the League of Nations; entered into force 9 March 1927.

—. *International Convention on the Elimination of All Forms of Racial Discrimination (ICERD)*. Adopted 21 December 1965 by the General Assembly; entered into force 4 January 1969.

—. *International Covenant on Civil and Political Rights (ICCPR)*. Adopted 16 December 1966 by the General Assembly (Resolution 2200A (XXI)); entered into force 23 March 1976.

—. *International Covenant on Economic, Social and Cultural Rights (ICESCR)*. Adopted 16 December 1966 by the General Assembly (Resolution 2200A (XXI)); entered into force 3 January 1976.

—. *Convention against Torture and Other Cruel, Inhuman or Degrading Treatment or Punishment (UNCAT)*. Adopted 10 December 1984 by the General Assembly; entered into force 26 June 1987.

—. *Protocol to Prevent, Suppress and Punish Trafficking in Persons, Especially Women and Children, Supplementing the United Nations Convention against Transnational Organized Crime*. Adopted 15 November 2000; entered into force 25 December 2003.

—. *Rome Statute of the International Criminal Court*. Adopted 17 July 1998; entered into force 1 July 2002.

—. *United Nations Convention against Corruption (UNCAC)*. Adopted 31 October 2003 by the General Assembly; entered into force 14 December 2005.

—. *Vienna Convention on the Law of Treaties*. Adopted 23 May 1969; entered into force 27 January 1980.

United Nations Reports and Resolutions

—. *Report of the International Law Commission on the Work of Its Seventy-Third Session (A/77/10)*. 12 August 2022; published in *Yearbook of the International Law Commission, 2022, Vol. II, Part Two*.

—. *Report of the Detailed Findings of the Commission of Inquiry on Human Rights in the Democratic People's Republic of Korea*. 7 February 2014, A/HRC/25/CRP.1.

—. *Draft Articles on Responsibility of States for Internationally Wrongful Acts, with*

Commentaries. Adopted 2001; published in *Yearbook of the International Law Commission, 2001, Vol. II, Part Two*.

—. *Forced Labour by the Democratic People's Republic of Korea*. United Nations Office of the High Commissioner for Human Rights, July 2024.

—. *Resolution 2371 (2017)*. Adopted 5 August 2017, S/RES/2371(2017).

—. *Resolution 2375 (2017)*. Adopted 11 September 2017, S/RES/2375(2017).

—. *Resolution 2397 (2017)*. Adopted 22 December 2017, S/RES/2397(2017).

—. *Final Report of the Panel of Experts Established Pursuant to Resolution 1874, Submitted Pursuant to Resolution 2680 (2023)*. 7 March 2024, UN doc. S/2024/215.

International Court Cases

Barcelona Traction, Light and Power Company, Limited (Belgium v. Spain). International Court of Justice, Judgment of 5 February 1970, *ICJ Reports 1970*.

Questions relating to the Obligation to Prosecute or Extradite (Belgium v. Senegal). International Court of Justice, Judgment of 20 July 2012, *ICJ Reports 2012*.

Siliadin v. France. European Court of Human Rights, Judgment of 26 October 2005, Application no. 73316/01.

F.M. and Others v. Russia. European Court of Human Rights, Judgment of 10 December 2024, Applications nos. 71671/16 and 40190/18.

Other Legal Documents

Bilateral Agreements between the Russian Federation and the Democratic People's Republic of Korea

Agreement on the Temporary Labor Activities of Citizens of One State in the Territory of the Other State. Signed by the Russian Federation and the Democratic People's Republic of Korea, 31 August 2007.

Agreement on the Transfer and Receipt of Illegal Entrants and Residents. Signed by the Russian Federation and the Democratic People's Republic of Korea, 2 February 2016.

Treaty on Comprehensive Strategic Partnership. Signed by the Russian Federation and the Democratic People's Republic of Korea, 19 June 2024.

Domestic Laws of the Russian Federation

Russian Federation. *Constitution of the Russian Federation*. Adopted 12 December 1993; entered into force 25 December 1993.

—. Federal Law No. 16-FZ. *On Amendments to the Federal Law "On the Legal Status of Foreign Citizens in the Russian Federation."* 6 February 2020.

—. Federal Law No. 63-FZ. *Criminal Code of the Russian Federation*. 13 June 1996.

—. Federal Law No. 109-FZ. *On Migration Registration of Foreign Citizens and Stateless Persons in the Russian Federation*. 18 July 2006.

—. Federal Law No. 110-FZ. *On Amendments to the Federal Law "On the Legal Status of Foreign Citizens in the Russian Federation."* 18 July 2006.

—. Federal Law No. 115-FZ. *On the Legal Status of Foreign Citizens in the Russian Federation*. 25 July 2002.

—. Federal Law No. 119-FZ. *On State Protection of Victims, Witnesses, and Other Participants in Criminal Proceedings*. 20 August 2004.

—. Federal Law No. 273-FZ. *On Counteracting Corruption*. 25 December 2008.

—. Federal Law No. 7-FKZ. *On Amendments to the Federal Constitutional Law "On the Constitutional Court of the Russian Federation."* 14 December 2015.

—. Presidential Decree No. 156. "About Enhancement of Public Administration in the Sphere of Control of Drug Trafficking, Psychotropic Substances and Their Precursors and in the Sphere of Migration." 5 April 2016.

Domestic Laws of the Democratic People's Republic of Korea

Democratic People's Republic of Korea. *Regulations on External Economic Projects*. Cabinet Decision No. 49, 1 July 2020.

Academic Articles and Reports

An, Kyeong-mo. "'새로운 전략적 노선' 이후 북한의 국가전략: 균형전략으로의 재전환과 그 함의" [North Korea's National Strategy After the 'New Strategic Line': Reconversion to a Balancing Strategy and Its Implications]. 한국정치연구 [*Korean Political Research*], vol. 32, no. 1, 2023.

Armenzoni, Alessio, et al. *Brothers in Arms: Estimating North Korean Munitions Deliveries to Russia*. Open Source Centre, 15 April 2025.

Bezik, Igor V. "Участие граждан КНДР в хозяйственном освоении советского Дальнего Востока (1950-е начало 1960-х гг.)" [The Participation of the Citizens of the DPRK in the Economic Development of the Soviet Far East (early 1950s–early 1960s)]. *Известия Восточного Института* [*Oriental Journal Institute*], vol. 17, no. 1, 2011.

Byeon, Woisuk, and Jeongpil Heo. "김정은 시기 북한군의 주요 활동 변화 연구: 비군사활동을 중심으로" [A Study on the Major Changes in North Korean Military Activities during the Kim Jong Un Era: Focusing on Non-Military Activities]. 보훈학술논총 [*Journal of Patriots and Veterans Affairs in the Republic of Korea*], vol. 24, no. 1, 2025.

Cha, Du Hyeogn. *Implications of the DPRK-Russia 'Treaty on Comprehensive Strategic Partnership'*. The Asan Institute for Policy Studies, 8 October 2024.

Chudinovskikh, Olga, and Oxana Kharaeva. "Migration Policy towards Skilled Labor in the Russian Federation." *BRICS Journal of Economics*, vol. 1, no. 2, 2020.

Chung, Young Chul. "북한 경제의 변화 시장, '돈주', 그리고 국가의 재등장" [Changes in North Korea's Economy: Markets, 'Donju,' and the Reemergence of the State]. 역사비평 [*Critical Review of History*], no. 126, 2019.

Database Center for North Korean Human Rights. *Human Rights and North Korea's Overseas Laborers: Dilemmas and Policy Challenges*. 2015.

—. *The North Korea Outside the North Korean State*. 2016.

Jefferies, Isabelle. *Russia's Constitutional Amendment from an International Law Perspective*. Public International Law & Policy Group, 1 March 2021.

Kim, Kwang Jin. "The Defector's Tale: Inside North Korea's Secret Economy." *World Affairs*, vol. 174, no. 3, 2011.

Kim, Unique. *Introducing a Human Rights Paradigm: The Human Cost of North Korea's Support of the Russo-Ukrainian War*. Database Center for North Korean Human Rights, 23 December 2024.

Lankov, Andrei. "North Korean Labor Export to the USSR/Russia: Why the Project Has Survived Against All Odds." *Russia in Global Affairs*, vol. 18, no. 3, 2020.

—. "Северокорейские рабочие в России: критерии отбора и мотивация работников" [North Korean Workers in Russia: Selection Criteria and Motivation]. *Вестник Санкт-Петербургского университета. Международные отношения* [*Vestnik of Saint Petersburg University. International Relations*], vol. 13, no. 2, 2020.

Lee, Seungwon. "김정은 시대 북한의 군민관계 변화에 관한 연구: 조선인민군 사회적 역할의 변화양상과 특성을 중심으로" [A Study on the Changes in the Military-Civil Relations of North Korea in the Era of Kim Jong Un: A Focus on the Changing Patterns in the Social Role and Characteristics of the KPA]. PhD dissertation, University of North Korean Studies, 2022.

Lim, Soo-ho. 북한 경제전략 변화의 정치동학 [*Political Dynamics of Changes in North Korea's Economic Strategy*]. Institute for National Security Strategy, 2021.

Park, Chan Hong. *Conditions of Labor and Human Rights: North Korean Overseas Laborers in Russia*. Database Center for North Korean Human Rights, 2016.

Ri, Chang-ha. "사회주의기업책임관리제는 우리 식의 독특한 기업관리방법" [Our Unique Method of Enterprise Management: The Socialist Enterprise Responsibility Management System]. *Journal of Philosophy and Economics*, no. 2, 2018.

Troyakova, Tamara G. "Рабочая сила из КНДР на российском Дальнем Востоке: история и современное состояние" [Workers from DPRK in the Russian Far East: History and Current Situation]. *Ойкумена* [*Ojkumena: Regional Researches*], no. 2, 2017.

News Articles

"$263m a Year, 700,000 Tonnes of Rice, Space Tech: The Deal for North Korea Joining Russia's War." *The Straits Times*, 4 November 2024.

"Александр Новиков: северокорейские мигранты идеальные работники" [Alexander Novikov: North Korean Migrants—Ideal Workers]. *Аргументы Недели* [*Arguments of the Week*], 4 June 2025.

Balmforth, Thom. "Exclusive: Ukraine Sees Marked Improvement in Accuracy of Russia's North Korean Missiles." *Reuters*, 6 February 2025.

Beech, Samantha. "China and Russia Veto New UN Sanctions on North Korea for First Time Since 2006." *CNN*, 27 May 2022.

"Девелопер: количество строителей из Северной Кореи в России вырастет втрое" [Developer: The Number of North Korean Construction Workers in Russia Will Triple]. *Недвижимость РИА Новости* [*RIA Novosti Realty*], 26 June 2025.

Fifield, Anna. "He Ran North Korea's Secret Moneymaking Operation. Now He Lives in Virginia." *The Washington Post*, 13 July 2017.

Garamone, Jim. "Pentagon Says 10K North Korean Troops in Kursk Oblast." *U.S. Department of Defense*, 4 November 2024.

"General Assembly Overwhelmingly Adopts Resolution Demanding Russian Federation Immediately End Illegal Use of Force in Ukraine, Withdraw All Troops." *United Nations, Meetings Coverage and Press Releases*, 2 March 2022.

Gordon, Michael R. "Russia Blocks Extension of North Korea Sanctions Monitoring." *Wall Street Journal*, 28 March 2024.

Guinto, Joel, and Jean Mackenzie. "N Korea Confirms It Sent Troops to Fight for Russia in Ukraine War." *BBC News*, 28 April 2025.

Higgins, Andrew. "North Koreans in Russia Work 'Basically in the Situation of Slaves'." *The New York Times*, 11 July 2017.

Jung, Chul-hwan. "Exclusive: Captured North Korean Soldiers Speak Out on Deployment to Russia." *The Chosun Daily*, 20 February 2025.

"Как нанять в России рабочих из Северной Кореи в 2025 году: пошаговая инструкция" [How to Hire Workers from North Korea in Russia in 2025: A Step-by-Step Guide]. *Business.ru*, n.d.

Kang, Taejun. "Russia Pays North Korean Soldiers about $2,000 a Month: South's Spy Agency." *Radio Free Asia*, 23 October 2024.

Khoroshavin, Kosmos, and Dylan Carter. "Workers of the World: Modern-Day Slave Labor Is Being Imported from North Korea into Russia Despite a UN Ban." *The Insider*, 20 June 2025.

Kim, Dae-hoon. "북한 노동당 39호실 '김정은 통치자금' 총괄하는 곳" [Room 39 of North Korea's Workers' Party: The Organization Managing Kim Jong-un's Slush Fund]. *Hankyung*, 14 February 2016.

Kim, Jieun. "North Korean Authorities Begin to Distribute Russian Flour Rations." *Radio Free Asia*, 20 November 2024.

Kim, Tong-Hyung. "A Timeline of the Complicated Relations between Russia and North Korea." *AP News*, 13 September 2024.

"경애하는 김정은동지께서 조선로동당 중앙위원회 2013년 3월전원회의에서 하신 보고" [Report by Respected Comrade Kim Jong Un at the March 2013 Plenary Meeting of the Workers' Party of Korea Central Committee]. *Rodong Sinmun*, 2 April 2013.

"김정은 동지의 지도밑에 조선로동당 중앙위원회 제7기 제3차전원회의 진행" [7th Plenary Meeting of the 3rd Central Committee of the Workers' Party of Korea Held under the Guidance of Comrade Kim Jong Un]. 조선중앙통신[*Korean Central News Agency*], 21 April 2018.

Lim, Jeong-won. "Video Shows North Korean Workers Working in Russia in Violation of UN Sanctions." *Korea JoongAng Daily*, 15 April 2025.

Luxmoore, Matthew, Dasl Yoon, and Kate Vtorygina. "North Korean Leader Kim Jong Un's Latest Gift to Russia Is Migrant Workers." *Wall Street Journal*, 5 May 2025.

Moon, Dong-hui. "북, '김정은 비자금' 39호실 돈줄인 대흥총국 평양종합무역회사 인사 교체" [North Korea Replaces Personnel at Daehung General Bureau's Pyongyang General Trading Company, a Key Cash Source for Kim Jong-un's Slush Fund, Office 39]. *Daily NK*, 2 May 2025.

Ng, Kelly. "What We Know about North Korean Troops Fighting Russia's War." *BBC News*, 24 December 2024.

"North Korea: UN Imposes Fresh Sanctions over Missile Tests." *BBC News*, 23 December 2017.

"N.Korea to Send Workers to Russian Drone Factory to Gain Expertise." *NHK WORLD-JAPAN News*, 19 June 2025.

"Ольга Кириллова: более 300 тысяч украинцев получили гражданство РФ с 2014 года" [Olga Kirillova: Over 300,000 Ukrainians Obtained Russian Citizenship Since 2014]. *Interfax*, 3 October 2017.

Osborn, Andrew. "Russia Says It Missed U.N. Deadline to Repatriate North Korean Workers." *Reuters*, 24 January 2020.

Pourahmadi, Adam, and Audry Jeong. "Zelensky Offers to Release Captured North Korean Soldiers in Exchange for Ukrainian Soldiers Held in Russia." *CNN*, 13 January 2025.

Пыханов, Иван [Pykhanov, Ivan]. "В России ищут переводчиков с северокорейского для работы в МГИМО и на стройках" [In Russia, They Are Seeking Translators from North Korean for Work at MGIMO and on Construction Sites]. *Daily Storm*, 3 July 2025.

"Russia Ceases to Be Party to the European Convention on Human Rights." *Council of Europe*, 16 September 2022.

Troianovski, Anton. "North Korea Will Send 5,000 Workers to Russia, Kremlin Says." *The New York Times*, 17 June 2025.

United States, Department of the Treasury. "Treasury Sanctions Perpetrators of Serious Human Rights Abuse on International Human Rights Day." 1 December 2021.

Viner, Katharine. "Ukraine War Briefing: North Korea Ratifies Landmark Mutual Defence Pact with Russia." *The Guardian*, 12 November 2024.

APPENDICES

APPENDIX 1A. TREATY ON COMPREHENSIVE STRATEGIC PARTNERSHIP (RUSSIAN ORIGINAL)

Контрагент: КНДР

Дата подписания: 19.06.2024

Дата вступления в силу: 04.12.2024

Действие: Действует

ДОГОВОР О ВСЕОБЪЕМЛЮЩЕМ СТРАТЕГИЧЕСКОМ ПАРТНЕРСТВЕ МЕЖДУ РОССИЙСКОЙ ФЕДЕРАЦИЕЙ И КОРЕЙСКОЙ НАРОДНО-ДЕМОКРАТИЧЕСКОЙ РЕСПУБЛИКОЙ

Российская Федерация и Корейская Народно-Демократическая Республика, далее именуемые Сторонами,

исходя из общего стремления и желания сохранять исторически сформировавшиеся традиции российско-корейской дружбы и сотрудничества, выстраивать устремленные в будущее межгосударственные отношения новой эпохи, тем самым способствуя процветанию и благополучию народов двух стран, выражая уверенность, что развитие отношений всеобъемлющего стратегического партнерства Сторон отвечает коренным интересам их народов и вносит вклад в обеспечение мира, региональной и глобальной безопасности и стабильности,

подтверждая свою приверженность целям и принципам Устава ООН, а также другим общепризнанным принципам и нормам международного права,

подтверждая стремление защищать международную справедливость от гегемонистских устремлений и попыток навязывания однополярного миропорядка, установить многополярную международную систему, основанную на добросовестном сотрудничестве государств, взаимном уважении интересов, коллективном решении международных проблем, культурно-цивилизационном многообразии, верховенстве международного права в международных отношениях, совместными усилиями противодействовать любым вызовам, ставящим под угрозу существование человечества,

стремясь путем упрочения товарищеских дружественных двусторонних связей, а также расширения и укрепления сотрудничества во всех сферах вывести российско-корейские отношения на устойчивый уровень, способствующий региональному и международному миру и процветанию,

договорились о нижеследующем:

Статья 1

Стороны на постоянной основе поддерживают и развивают с учетом законодательства своих государств и их международных обязательств отношения всеобъемлющего стратегического партнерства, базирующиеся на принципах взаимного уважения государственного суверенитета и территориальной неприкосновенности, невмешательства во внутренние дела, равенства и других принципах международного права, касающихся дружественных отношений и сотрудничества между государствами.

Статья 2

Стороны путем диалога и переговоров, в том числе на высшем уровне, обмениваются мнениями по вопросам двусторонних отношений и международной повестки дня, представляющим взаимный интерес, а также укрепляют совместную координацию и взаимодействие на международных площадках.

Стремясь к установлению глобальной стратегической стабильности и нового справедливого и равноправного международного порядка, Стороны поддерживают тесную коммуникацию друг с другом и укрепляют тактическое и стратегическое взаимодействие.

Статья 3

Стороны сотрудничают друг с другом в целях обеспечения прочного регионального и международного мира и безопасности.

В случае возникновения непосредственной угрозы совершения против одной из Сторон акта вооруженной агрессии Стороны по требованию одной из Сторон незамедлительно задействуют двусторонние каналы для проведения консультаций с целью координации своих позиций и согласования возможных практических мер по оказанию помощи друг другу для содействия устранению возникшей угрозы.

Статья 4

В случае если одна из Сторон подвергнется вооруженному нападению со стороны какого-либо государства или нескольких государств и окажется таким образом в состоянии войны, то другая Сторона незамедлительно окажет военную и иную помощь всеми имеющимися в её распоряжении средствами в соответствии со статьёй 51 Устава ООН и согласно законодательству Российской Федерации и Корейской Народно-Демократической Республики.

Статья 5

Каждая из Сторон обязуется не заключать с третьими государствами соглашения, направленные против суверенитета, безопасности, территориальной неприкосновенности, права на свободный выбор и развитие политической, социальной, экономической и культурной систем и других ключевых интересов другой Стороны, а также не принимать участие в таких действиях.

Стороны не допускают использования своей территории третьими государствами в целях нарушения суверенитета, безопасности, территориальной неприкосновенности другой Стороны.

Статья 6

Стороны поддерживают миролюбивую политику и меры друг друга, направленные на защиту их государственного суверенитета, обеспечение их безопасности и стабильности, отстаивание их права на развитие, а также активно сотрудничают друг с другом в проведении такой политики, нацеленной на установление справедливого многополярного нового миропорядка.

Статья 7

Руководствуясь целями поддержания международного мира и безопасности, Стороны проводят консультации и сотрудничают друг с другом в рамках международных организаций, в том числе ООН и её специализированных учреждений, по вопросам глобального и регионального развития, которые прямо или косвенно могут представлять вызов общим интересам и безопасности Сторон.

Стороны сотрудничают и поддерживают на взаимной основе членство каждой Стороны в соответствующих международных и региональных организациях.

Статья 8

Стороны создают механизмы по проведению совместных мероприятий в целях укрепления обороноспособности в интересах предотвращения войны и обеспечения регионального и международного мира и безопасности.

Статья 9

Стороны взаимодействуют в целях совместного противостояния множащимся вызовам и угрозам в сферах стратегического значения, в том числе продовольственной и энергетической безопасности, безопасности в сфере информационно-коммуникационных технологий (далее — ИКТ), изменения климата, здравоохранения и цепочек поставок.

Статья 10

Стороны способствуют расширению и развитию сотрудничества в торгово-экономической, инвестиционной и научно-технической областях.

Стороны прилагают усилия для увеличения объемов взаимной торговли, создают благоприятные условия для экономического сотрудничества в таможенной, валютно-финансовой и других сферах, а также поощряют и защищают взаимные инвестиции в соответствии с Соглашением между Правительством Российской Федерации и Правительстзом Корейской Народно-Демократической Республики о поощрении и взаимной защите капиталовложений от 28 ноября 1996 года.

Стороны оказывают содействие особым/свободным экономическим зонам Российской Федерации и Корейской

Народно-Демократической Республики и организациям с их участием.

Стороны развивают обмены и сотрудничество, а также активно поощряют совместные исследования в области науки и технологий, включая такие сферы, как космос, биология, мирная атомная энергия, искусственный интеллект, информационные технологии и иные.

Статья 11

Стороны поддерживают развитие межрегионального и приграничного сотрудничества в сферах, представляющих обоюдный интерес, исходя из его особой важности для расширения всего комплекса двусторонних отношений.

Стороны создают благоприятные условия для установления прямых связей между регионами Российской Федерации и Корейской Народно-Демократической Республики, содействуют взаимному ознакомлению с их экономическим и инвестиционным потенциалами, в том числе путем проведения бизнес-миссий, конференций, выставок, ярмарок и других совместных межрегиональных мероприятий.

Статья 12

Стороны укрепляют обмены и сотрудничество в области сельского хозяйства, образования, здравоохранения, спорта, культуры, туризма и иных областях, осуществляют взаимодействие в сфере охраны окружающей среды, предотвращения и ликвидации последствий стихийных бедствий.

Статья 13

Стороны развивают сотрудничество в вопросах взаимного признания стандартов, протоколов испытаний и сертификатов соответствия, прямого применения стандартов, обмена опытом и новейшими достижениями в сфере обеспечения единства измерений, обучения экспертов и содействия признанию результатов испытаний между Российской Федерацией и Корейской Народно-Демократической Республикой.

Статья 14

Каждая из Сторон защищает законные права и интересы находящихся на её территории юридических лиц и граждан другой Стороны.

Стороны сотрудничают по вопросам оказания правовой помощи по гражданским и уголовным делам, выдачи и передачи лиц, осуждённых к лишению свободы, а также реализации договорённостей в сфере возвращения активов, полученных преступным путём.

Статья 15

Стороны углубляют контакты между законодательными, исполнительными и правоохранительными органами двух стран, проводят обмен опытом и мнениями в сфере принятия и применения законов и по другим вопросам, представляющим взаимный интерес.

Статья 16

Стороны противодействуют применению односторонних принудительных мер, в том числе экстерриториального характера, и считают их введение незаконным и противоречащим Уставу ООН и нормам международного права. Стороны координируют усилия и взаимодействуют в целях поддержки многосторонних инициатив, направленных на исключение практики применения таких мер в международных отношениях.

Стороны гарантируют неприменение односторонних принудительных мер, направленных прямо или косвенно на одну из Сторон, физических и юридических лиц такой Стороны или их собственность, находящуюся под юрисдикцией такой Стороны, товары, работы, услуги, информацию, результаты интеллектуальной деятельности, в том числе исключительные права на них, происходящие из одной Стороны, предназначенные для другой Стороны.

Стороны воздерживаются от присоединения к односторонним принудительным мерам или поддержки таких мер любой третьей стороны, если такие меры затрагивают или направлены прямо или косвенно на одну из Сторон, физических и юридических лиц такой Стороны или их собственность, находящуюся под юрисдикцией такой третьей стороны, товары, происходящие из одной Стороны, предназначенные для другой Стороны, и (или) работы, услуги, информацию, результаты интеллектуальной деятельности, в том числе исключительные права на них, предоставляемые поставщиками другой Стороны.

В случае если в отношении одной из Сторон вводятся односторонние принудительные меры любой третьей стороной, Стороны предпринимают практические усилия для снижения рисков, устранения или минимизации прямого и косвенного воздействия таких мер на взаимные экономические связи, физических или юридических лиц Сторон или их собственность, находящуюся в юрисдикции Сторон, товары, происходящие из одной Стороны, предназначенные для другой Стороны, и (или) работы, услуги, информацию, результаты интеллектуальной деятельности, в том числе исключительные права на них, предоставляемые поставщиками Сторон. Стороны также предпринимают шаги по ограничению распространения информации, которая может быть использована такой третьей стороной для введения и эскалации таких мер.

Статья 17

Стороны взаимодействуют в борьбе с международным терроризмом и другими вызовами и угрозами, в том числе экстремизмом, транснациональной организованной преступностью, торговлей людьми и захватом заложников, незаконной миграцией, незаконными финансовыми потоками, легализацией (отмыванием) доходов, полученных преступным путем, финансированием терроризма и финансированием распространения оружия массового уничтожения, противоправными акциями, создающими угрозу безопасности гражданской авиации и морского судоходства, нелегальным оборотом товаров, денежных средств и денежных инструментов, а также незаконным оборотом наркотических средств, психотропных веществ и их прекурсоров, оружия, культурных и исторических ценностей.

Статья 18

Стороны взаимодействуют в сфере международной информационной безопасности, стремятся к укреплению двустороннего сотрудничества, в том числе посредством развития соответствующей нормативно-правовой основы и углубления межведомственного диалога.

Стороны способствуют формированию системы обеспечения международной информационной безопасности, в том числе путем выработки универсальных юридически обязывающих документов.

Стороны выступают за равные права для государств в управлении информационно-телекоммуникационной сетью «Интернет», а также против злонамеренного использования ИКТ с целью опорочить достоинство и репутацию суверенных государств и посягнуть на их суверенные права, считают неприемлемыми любые попытки ограничить суверенное право на регулирование и обеспечение безопасности национальных сегментов глобальной сети.

Стороны расширяют сотрудничество в сфере противодействия использованию ИКТ в преступных целях, включая обмен информацией для предупреждения, выявления, пресечения и расследования преступлений и иных правонарушений, связанных с использованием ИКТ.

Стороны координируют действия и совместно продвигают инициативы в рамках международных организаций и иных переговорных площадок, сотрудничают в области цифрового развития, обмениваются информацией и создают условия для взаимодействия компетентных органов Сторон.

Статья 19

Стороны сотрудничают в области печати и издательской деятельности.

Стороны поощряют продвижение русской и корейской литературы в своих государствах, способствуют изучению русского языка в Корейской Народно-Демократической Республике и корейского языка в Российской Федерации, а также содействуют взаимному ознакомлению и общению между народами Российской Федерации и Корейской Народно-Демократической Республики.

Статья 20

Стороны содействуют широкому сотрудничеству в медиасфере в целях повышения уровня знаний о жизни народов двух стран, продвижения в глобальном медиапространстве объективной информации о Российской Федерации и Корейской Народно-Демократической Республике и двустороннем сотрудничестве, дальнейшего формирования благоприятных условий для взаимодействия между национальными средствами массовой информации, укрепления координации в деле противодействия дезинформации и агрессивным информационным кампаниям.

Статья 21

Стороны активно сотрудничают в целях заключения и последующей реализации отраслевых соглашений, направленных на выполнение настоящего Договора, а также соглашений в иных областях, не предусмотренных настоящим Договором.

Статья 22

Настоящий Договор подлежит ратификации и вступает в силу с даты обмена ратификационными грамотами.

С даты вступления в силу настоящего Договора прекращается действие Договора о дружбе, добрососедстве и сотрудничестве между Российской Федерацией и Корейской Народно-Демократической Республикой от 9 февраля 2000 года.

Статья 23

Настоящий Договор действует бессрочно.

Если одна из Сторон намерена прекратить действие настоящего Договора, то она должна уведомить об этом другую Сторону в письменной форме. Действие Договора прекращается через год с даты получения другой Стороной письменного уведомления.

Совершено в г. Пхеньяне 13 июня 2024 года в двух экземплярах, каждый на русском и корейском языках, причем оба текста имеют одинаковую силу.

Source: Ministry of Foreign Affairs of the Russian Federation, *Official Internet Portal of Legal Information,* https://www.mid.ru/ru/

foreign_policy/international_contracts/international_contracts/
2_contract/62546/

APPENDIX 1B. TREATY ON COMPREHENSIVE STRATEGIC PARTNERSHIP (ENGLISH TRANSLATION)

Counterparty: DPRK

Date of signature: 19.06.2024

Date of entry into force: 04.12.2024

Status: In Force

The Democratic People's Republic of Korea and the Russian Federation, hereinafter referred to as the Parties, based on common desire and commitment to preserve the historically formed traditions of Korean–Russian friendship and cooperation to build future-oriented interstate relations of a new era, thereby promoting the prosperity and well-being of the peoples of the two countries;

expressing confidence that the development of relations of a comprehensive strategic partnership of the Parties meets the fundamental interests of their peoples and contributes to ensuring peace, regional and global security and stability;

reaffirming their commitment to the purposes and principles of the UN Charter, as well as other generally recognized principles and norms of international law;

reaffirming the desire to protect international justice from hegemonic aspirations and attempts to impose a unipolar world order, to establish a multipolar international system based on good faith cooperation of states, mutual respect for interests, collective resolution of international problems, cultural and civilizational diversity, the supremacy of international law in international relations, and by joint efforts to counteract any challenges that threaten the existence of humanity;

seeking, through strengthening comradely and friendly bilateral ties, as well as expanding and strengthening cooperation in all areas, to bring North Korean–Russian relations to a sustainable level conducive to regional and international peace and prosperity, have agreed on the following:

Article 1

The Parties constantly support and develop, taking into account the legislation of their states and their international obligations, relations of comprehensive strategic partnership based on the principles of mutual respect for state sovereignty and territorial integrity, non-interference in internal affairs, equality and other principles of international law relating to friendly relations and cooperation between states.

Article 2

The Parties, through dialogue and negotiations, including at the highest level, will exchange views on issues of bilateral relations and the international agenda of mutual interest, and also strengthen joint coordination and interaction in international platforms.

In an effort to establish global strategic stability and a new fair and equitable international order, the Parties will maintain close communication with each other and strengthen tactical and strategic cooperation.

Article 3

The Parties shall cooperate with each other to ensure lasting regional and international peace and security.

In the event of an immediate threat of an act of armed aggression against one of the Parties, the Parties, at the request of one of the Parties, shall immediately use bilateral channels for consultations in order to coordinate their positions and agree on possible practical measures to assist each other to help eliminate the emerging threat.

Article 4

If one of the Parties is subjected to an armed attack by any state or several states and thus finds itself in a state of war, the other Party will immediately provide military and other assistance with all means at its disposal in accordance with Article 51 of the UN Charter and in accordance with legislation of the Democratic People's Republic of Korea and the Russian Federation.

Article 5

Each Party vows not to enter into agreements with third states directed against the sovereignty, security, territorial integrity, right to free choice and development of political, social, economic and cultural systems and other key interests of the other Party, and not to take part in such actions.

The Parties do not allow third states to use their territory for the purpose of violating the sovereignty, security, or territorial integrity of the other Party.

Article 6

The Parties support each other's peaceful policies and measures aimed at protecting their state sovereignty, ensuring their security and stability, defending their right to development, and also actively cooperating with each other in pursuing such policies aimed at establishing a fair multipolar new world order.

Article 7

Guided by the goals of maintaining international peace and security, the Parties will consult and cooperate with each other within the framework of international organizations, including the UN and its specialized agencies, on issues of global and regional development that directly or indirectly may pose a challenge to the common interests and security of the Parties.

The Parties shall cooperate and mutually support the membership of each Party in relevant international and regional organizations.

Article 8

The Parties create mechanisms for joint activities to strengthen defense capabilities in the interests of preventing war and ensuring regional and international peace and security.

Article 9

The Parties will interact to jointly confront growing challenges and threats in areas of strategic importance, including food and energy security, information and communications technology (ICT) security, climate change, healthcare and supply chains.

Article 10

The Parties will promote the expansion and development of cooperation in trade, economic, investment, scientific and technical fields.

The Parties will make efforts to increase the volume of mutual trade, create favorable conditions for economic cooperation in customs, monetary and financial and other areas, and also encourage and protect mutual investments in accordance with the Agreement between the Government of the Democratic People's Republic of Korea and the Government of the Russian Federation on the promotion and mutual protection of investments of November 28, 1996.

The Parties will provide assistance to special/free economic zones of the Democratic People's Republic of Korea and the Russian Federation and organizations with their participation.

The Parties will develop exchanges and cooperation, and also actively encourage joint research in the field of science and technology, including such areas as space, biology, peaceful nuclear energy, artificial intelligence, information technology and others.

Article 11

The Parties will support the development of interregional and cross-border cooperation in areas of mutual interest, based on its special importance for expanding the entire range of bilateral relations.

The Parties will create favorable conditions for establishing direct connections between the regions of the Democratic People's Republic of Korea and the Russian Federation, promote mutual awareness of their economic and investment potential, including through business missions, conferences, exhibitions, fairs and other joint interregional events.

Article 12

The Parties will strengthen exchanges and cooperation in the field of agriculture, education, healthcare, sports, culture, tourism and other areas, cooperate in the field of environmental protection, prevention and relief from natural disasters.

Article 13

The Parties will develop cooperation in matters of mutual recognition of standards, test reports and certificates of conformity, direct application of standards, exchange of experience and the latest achievements in the field of ensuring uniformity of measurements, training of experts and promoting the recognition of test results between the Democratic People's Republic of Korea and the Russian Federation.

Article 14

Each Party will protect the legal rights and interests of legal entities and citizens of the other Party located on its territory.

The Parties will cooperate on the provision of legal assistance in civil and criminal cases, the extradition and transfer of persons sentenced to imprisonment, as well as the implementation of agreements in the field of return of assets obtained by criminal means.

Article 15

The Parties will deepen contacts between the legislative, executive and law enforcement bodies of the two countries, exchanging experiences and opinions in the field of adoption and application of laws and on other issues of mutual interest.

Article 16

The Parties will oppose the use of unilateral coercive measures, including those of an extraterritorial nature, and consider their introduction illegal and contrary to the UN Charter and international law. The Parties will coordinate efforts and interact in order to support multilateral initiatives aimed at eliminating the practice of using such measures in international relations.

The Parties will guarantee the non-application of unilateral coercive measures aimed directly or indirectly at one of the Parties, individuals and legal entities of such Party or their property under the jurisdiction of such Party, goods, work, services, information, results of intellectual activity, including exclusive rights to them, originating from one Party, intended for the other Party.

The Parties shall refrain from joining unilateral enforcement measures or supporting such measures of any third party if such measures affect or are directed directly or indirectly at one of the Parties, individuals and legal entities of such Party or their property under the jurisdiction of such third party, goods originating from one Party, intended for the other Party, and/or works, services, information, results of intellectual activity, including exclusive rights to them, provided by suppliers of the other Party.

If unilateral coercive measures are introduced against one of the Parties by any third party, the Parties shall make practical efforts to reduce the risks, eliminate or minimize the direct and indirect impact of such measures on mutual economic relations, individuals or legal entities of the Parties or their property located in the jurisdiction Parties, goods originating from one Party, intended for the other Party, and/or works, services, information, results of intellectual activity, including exclusive rights to them provided by suppliers of the Parties.

The Parties shall also take steps to limit the dissemination of information that could be used by such third parties to impose and escalate such measures.

Article 17

The Parties will cooperate in the fight against international terrorism and other challenges and threats, including extremism, transnational organized crime, human trafficking and hostage-taking, illegal migration, illicit financial flows, legalization (laundering) of proceeds from crime, terrorist financing and financing of proliferation of weapons of mass destruction, illegal actions that pose a threat to the safety of civil aviation and maritime navigation, illegal trafficking of goods, funds and monetary instruments, as well as illegal trafficking of narcotic drugs, psychotropic substances and their precursors, weapons, cultural and historical values.

Article 18

The Parties will interact in the field of international information security and strive to strengthen bilateral cooperation, including through the development of an appropriate regulatory framework and deepening interdepartmental dialogue.

The Parties will contribute to the formation of a system for ensuring international information security, including through the development of universal legally binding documents.

The Parties will advocate equal rights for states in managing the Internet information and telecommunications network, as well as against the malicious use of information and communication technologies (ICT) in order to discredit the dignity and reputation of sovereign states and encroach on their sovereign rights, and will consider unacceptable any attempts to limit the sovereign right to regulate and ensure security of the national segments of the global network.

The Parties will expand cooperation in the field of combating the use of ICTs for criminal purposes, including the exchange of information to prevent, detect, suppress and investigate crimes and other offenses related to the use of ICTs.

The Parties will coordinate actions and jointly promote initiatives within international organizations and other negotiation platforms, cooperate in the field of digital development, exchange information and create conditions for interaction between the competent authorities of the Parties.

Article 19

The Parties will cooperate in the field of printing and publishing activities.

They will encourage the promotion of Korean and Russian literature in their respective states, promote the study of the Korean language in the Russian Federation and the Russian language in the Democratic

People's Republic of Korea, and promote mutual acquaintance and communication between the peoples of the Democratic People's Republic of Korea and the Russian Federation.

Article 20

The Parties will promote broad cooperation in the media sphere to increase knowledge about the lives of the peoples of the two countries, promote objective information about the Democratic People's Republic of Korea and the Russian Federation and bilateral cooperation in the global media space, further create favorable conditions for interaction between national media, and strengthen coordination in countering disinformation and aggressive information campaigns.

Article 21

The Parties will actively cooperate in order to conclude and subsequently implement sectoral agreements aimed at implementing this Agreement, as well as agreements in other areas not provided for by this Agreement.

Article 22

This Agreement is subject to ratification and enters into force on the date of exchange of instruments of ratification.

From the date of entry into force of this Agreement, the Treaty on Friendship, Good-Neighbourliness and Cooperation between the Democratic People's Republic of Korea and the Russian Federation of February 9, 2000, shall cease.

Article 23

This Agreement is valid for an indefinite period.

If one of the Parties intends to terminate this Agreement, it must notify the other Party in writing. The Agreement is terminated one year from the date of receipt of written notice by the other Party.

Signed in Pyongyang on June 13, 2024, in two copies, each in Korean and Russian, both texts being equally authentic.

Signed on behalf of the Democratic People's Republic of Korea – Kim Jong Un

Signed on behalf of the Russian Federation – Vladimir Putin

Source: English translation provided by Sputnik, https://sputnikglobe.com/20240620/full-text-of-russia-north-korea-strategic-agreement--1119035258.html

APPENDIX 2A. AGREEMENT ON THE TEMPORARY LABOR ACTIVITIES OF CITIZENS OF ONE STATE IN THE TERRITORY OF THE OTHER STATE (RUSSIAN ORIGINAL)

Контрагент: КНДР

Дата подписания: 31.08.2007

Дата вступления в силу: 29.12.2009

Действие: ДЕЙСТВУЕТ

Соглашение
между Правительством Российской Федерации и Правительством Корейской Народно-Демократической Республики о временной трудовой деятельности граждан одного
государства на территории другого государства

Правительство Российской Федерации и Правительство Корейской Народно-Демократической Республики, далее именуемые Сторонами,

руководствуясь духом и принципами, закрепленными в Договоре о дружбе, добрососедстве и сотрудничестве между Российской

Федерацией и Корейской Народно-Демократической Республикой от 9 февраля 2000 года,

исходя из стремления к развитию двустороннего экономического сотрудничества, желая обеспечить благоприятные условия для временной трудовой деятельности граждан одного государства на территории другого государства,

согласились о нижеследующем:

Статья 1

Действие настоящего Соглашения распространяется на граждан Российской Федерации и граждан Корейской Народно-Демократической Республики (далее - работники), постоянно проживающих соответственно в Российской Федерации и в Корейской Народно-Демократической Республике (далее - государства постоянного проживания), которые на законном основании въехали на территорию государства другой Стороны (далее - принимающее государство) с целью осуществления временной трудовой деятельности в соответствии с договорами о выполнении работ или об оказании услуг (далее - договоры), заключенными между физическими или юридическими лицами принимающего государства (далее - заказчики) и юридическими лицами государства постоянного проживания, далее именуемыми исполнителями работ (подрядчиками), в порядке, установленном законодательством государства постоянного проживания.

Статья 2

1. Органами Сторон, ответственными за реализацию настоящего Соглашения (далее - компетентные органы), являются:

с Российской Стороны - Федеральная миграционная служба и Министерство здравоохранения и социального развития Российской Федерации;

с Корейской Стороны – Министерство внешней торговли Корейской Народно-Демократической Республики.

Стороны незамедлительно уведомляют друг друга по дипломатическим каналам об изменении своих компетентных органов.

2. Компетентные органы образуют совместную рабочую группу для решения вопросов, связанных с реализацией настоящего Соглашения.

По мере необходимости совместная рабочая группа проводит заседания поочередно в Российской Федерации и Корейской Народно-Демократической Республике.

Регламент работы совместной рабочей группы и положение о ней утверждаются компетентными органами.

3. Компетентные органы обмениваются информацией об изменениях в законодательстве, связанном с привлечением и использованием иностранной рабочей силы в Российской Федерации и Корейской Народно-Демократической Республике.

Статья 3

Работники должны быть не моложе 18 лет и иметь соответствующий медицинский сертификат об отсутствии у них заболеваний наркоманией и инфекционных заболеваний, представляющих опасность для окружающих, а также об отсутствии у них заболевания, вызываемого вирусом иммунодефицита человека (ВИЧ-инфекции).

Статья 4

1. Трудовая деятельность работника осуществляется в соответствии с законодательством принимающего государства.

2. Работники могут заниматься трудовой деятельностью в принимающем государстве при наличии разрешения на работу,

выдаваемого в соответствии с законодательством принимающего государства.

Статья 5

1. Въезд, выезд, пребывание и режим передвижения работников по территории принимающего государства регулируются законодательством этого государства и международными договорами, участниками которых являются Стороны.

2. Компетентные органы предпринимают возможные меры для ускорения выполнения процедур, связанных с оформлением документов, необходимых для осуществления трудовой деятельности работников в принимающем государстве.

3. В случае если одна из Сторон будет вынуждена ввести ограничение численности работников государства другой Стороны, компетентные органы этой Стороны заблаговременно информируют об этом компетентные органы другой Стороны.

Статья 6

Оплата и другие условия труда работников регулируются договорами, заключаемыми этими работниками и исполнителями работ (подрядчиками).

Условия труда работников не должны быть менее благоприятными, чем те, которые предусмотрены для граждан принимающего государства, выполняющих аналогичную работу у того же заказчика.

Статья 7

Работники имеют право на освобождение от работы в дни официальных праздников государства постоянного проживания. Положения, регулирующие вопросы освобождения от работы в эти дни, должны содержаться в договоре, заключаемом заказчиком и исполнителем работ (подрядчиком).

Статья 8

1. Социальное и медицинское страхование работников, а также возмещение вреда, причиненного работникам в результате несчастного случая на производстве, профессионального заболевания или иного ухудшения здоровья, возникшего при исполнении ими своих трудовых обязанностей во время работы в принимающем государстве, осуществляются исполнителями работ (подрядчиками) и соответствующими органами государства постоянного проживания и регулируются законодательством государства их постоянного проживания, если отдельным международным договором между Сторонами не предусмотрено иное.

2. Пенсионное обеспечение работников осуществляется в соответствии с законодательством государства их постоянного проживания.

Статья 9

1. Положения договоров, относящиеся к медицинскому обслуживанию работников, не должны ограничивать их права в области охраны здоровья, установленные законодательством принимающего государства.

2. Работники имеют право на получение скорой (неотложной) медицинской помощи при внезапных острых состояниях и заболеваниях, угрожающих жизни больного или здоровью окружающих, несчастных случаях, отравлениях, травмах, родах и неотложных состояниях в период беременности. Данный вид медицинской помощи предоставляется работнику беспрепятственно, бесплатно и в необходимом объеме в лечебно-профилактических учреждениях принимающего государства.

Другие виды медицинской помощи оказываются работникам в соответствии с законодательством принимающего государства и международными договорами между Сторонами, а также за счет работников и средств исполнителя работ (подрядчика), если это предусмотрено договором.

Статья 10

1. В случае смерти работника исполнитель работ (подрядчик) при содействии заказчика организует и оплачивает перевозку тела (останков) умершего в государство постоянного проживания и несет все расходы, связанные с провозом, пересылкой и переводом его имущества и выплатой компенсации в соответствии с законодательством государства постоянного проживания.

Заказчик незамедлительно (в течение трех дней) уведомляет о смерти работника дипломатическое представительство или консульское учреждение государства постоянного проживания в принимающем государстве и компетентные органы по месту регистрации работника и предоставляет документ, подтверждающий смерть.

2. В случае если смерть работника наступила по вине заказчика, заказчик несет ответственность в соответствии с законодательством принимающего государства, а также оплачивает все расходы, связанные с перевозкой тела умершего и его имущества из принимающего государства в государство постоянного проживания.

Статья 11

Работники могут приобретать иностранную валюту на внутреннем валютном рынке принимающего государства, а также переводить и перевозить с собой заработанные средства в иностранной валюте в государство постоянного проживания в соответствии с законодательством принимающего государства.

Статья 12

Налогообложение доходов работников в период пребывания в принимающем государстве регулируется Соглашением между Правительством Российской Федерации и Правительством Корейской Народно-Демократической Республики об избежании двойного налогообложения в отношении налогов на доходы и капитал от 26 сентября 1997 г.

Статья 13

Работникам в принимающем государстве гарантируются права, свободы, правовая защита и личная безопасность, установленные законодательством принимающего государства для иностранных граждан и соответствующими международными договорами между Сторонами.

Работники во время пребывания в принимающем государстве должны соблюдать его законодательство, в том числе касающееся правил пребывания иностранных граждан.

Статья 14

Ввоз на территорию принимающего государства и вывоз с его территории работниками товаров, включая личное имущество, осуществляются в соответствии с законодательством принимающего государства, если договорами между Российской Федерацией и Корейской Народно-Демократической Республикой не установлено иное.

Статья 15

1. Работник обязан покинуть принимающее государство по истечении срока действия визы, если на момент истечения срока действия визы им не получено разрешение на ее продление.

В случае возникновения объективных причин, препятствующих своевременному выезду работника из принимающего государства по истечении разрешенного периода пребывания (например, тяжелая болезнь работника, смерть близкого родственника в принимающем государстве), он обязан покинуть принимающее государство незамедлительно после принятия обусловленных сложившимися обстоятельствами мер.

2.В случае уклонения работника от выезда из принимающего государства по истечении разрешенного периода пребывания и при отсутствии объективных причин он подлежит ответственности в соответствии с законодательством принимающего государства.

Статья 16

Споры относительно толкования и применения положений настоящего Соглашения решаются путем консультаций между компетентными органами.

Статья 17

Вопросы, связанные с реализацией настоящего Соглашения, регулируются отдельным соглашением (протоколом), заключаемым между компетентными органами.

Статья 18

1.Настоящее Соглашение вступает в силу с даты получения последнего письменного уведомления о выполнении Сторонами внутригосударственных процедур, необходимых для его вступления в силу, и действует в течение 5 лет, по истечении которых автоматически продлевается на последующие годичные периоды до тех пор, пока одна из Сторон не менее чем за 6 месяцев до истечения очередного годичного периода не уведомит в письменной форме по дипломатическим каналам другую Сторону о своем намерении прекратить его действие.

2. Изменения, вносимые в настоящее Соглашение по взаимному согласию Сторон, оформляются протоколами к нему, которые вступают в силу в порядке, предусмотренном пунктом 1 настоящей статьи.

3. В случае прекращения действия настоящего Соглашения разрешения на работу, выданные в период его действия, остаются в силе до истечения указанного в них срока. Прекращение действия настоящего Соглашения не затрагивает реализацию договоров о выполнении работ или об оказании услуг, заключенных до прекращения его действия.

Совершено в г. Москве «31» августа 2007 года (Чучхе 96 года) в двух экземплярах, каждый на русском и корейском языках, причем оба текста имеют одинаковую силу.

За Правительство Российской Федерации

За Правительство Корейской Народно-Демократической Республики

Source: ConsultantPlus, https://www.consultant.ru/document/cons_doc_LAW_94253/

APPENDIX 2B. AGREEMENT ON THE TEMPORARY LABOR ACTIVITIES OF CITIZENS OF ONE STATE IN THE TERRITORY OF THE OTHER STATE (ENGLISH TRANSLATION)

Counterparty: DPRK

Date of signature: 31.08.2007

Date of entry into force: 29.12.2009

Status: In Force

Agreement
between the Government of the Russian Federation and the
Government of the Democratic People's Republic of Korea
on the Temporary Labor Activities of Citizens of One State in the
Territory of the Other State

The Government of the Russian Federation and the Government of the Democratic People's Republic of Korea, hereinafter referred to as the Parties,

guided by the spirit and principles enshrined in the Treaty of Friendship, Good Neighborliness and Cooperation between the Russian Federation and the Democratic People's Republic of Korea of 9 February 2000, proceeding from the desire to develop bilateral economic cooperation, wishing to ensure favorable conditions for the temporary labor activities of citizens of one state in the territory of the other state, have agreed as follows:

Article 1

The present Agreement applies to citizens of the Russian Federation and citizens of the Democratic People's Republic of Korea (hereinafter - workers), who are permanently residing respectively in the Russian Federation and in the Democratic People's Republic of Korea (hereinafter - states of permanent residence), and who have lawfully entered the territory of the other Party's state (hereinafter - host state) for the purpose of engaging in temporary labor activities in accordance with contracts for the performance of works or the provision of services (hereinafter - contracts), concluded between natural or legal persons of the host state (hereinafter - clients) and legal persons of the state of permanent residence, hereinafter referred to as contractors, in the manner established by the legislation of the state of permanent residence.

Article 2

1. The authorities of the Parties responsible for the implementation of this Agreement (hereinafter – competent authorities) are:

– on the Russian Side: the Federal Migration Service and the Ministry of Health and Social Development of the Russian Federation;

– on the Korean Side: the Ministry of Foreign Trade of the Democratic People's Republic of Korea.

The Parties shall promptly notify each other through diplomatic channels of any changes to their competent authorities.

2. The competent authorities shall establish a joint working group to address matters related to the implementation of this Agreement.

As necessary, the joint working group shall hold meetings alternately in the Russian Federation and in the Democratic People's Republic of Korea.

The rules of procedure of the joint working group and its statute shall be approved by the competent authorities.

3. The competent authorities shall exchange information on changes in legislation related to the recruitment and use of foreign labor in the Russian Federation and the Democratic People's Republic of Korea.

Article 3

Workers must be no younger than 18 years old and must possess an appropriate medical certificate confirming the absence of drug addiction and communicable diseases that pose a danger to others, as well as the absence of a disease caused by the human immunodeficiency virus (HIV infection).

Article 4

1. The labor activity of the worker shall be carried out in accordance with the legislation of the host state.

2. Workers may engage in labor activity in the host state only if they possess a work permit issued in accordance with the legislation of the host state.

Article 5

1. The entry, exit, stay, and movement regime of workers within the territory of the host state shall be regulated by the legislation of that state and by international treaties to which both Parties are signatories.

2. The competent authorities shall undertake appropriate measures to expedite procedures related to the issuance of documents necessary for the workers to carry out labor activities in the host state.

3. In the event that one of the Parties is compelled to introduce a restriction on the number of workers from the other Party's state, the competent authorities of that Party shall inform the competent authorities of the other Party in advance.

Article 6

The remuneration and other working conditions of the workers shall be governed by contracts concluded between those workers and the contractors.

The working conditions of the workers must not be less favorable than those established for nationals of the host state performing similar work for the same client.

Article 7

Workers shall have the right to be released from work on official holidays of their state of permanent residence. The provisions regulating the release from work on such days must be included in the contract concluded between the client and the contractor.

Article 8

1. Social and medical insurance for workers, as well as compensation for harm caused to workers as a result of occupational accidents, occupational diseases, or other health deterioration occurring during the performance of their duties while working in the host state, shall be provided by the contractors and the relevant authorities of the state of permanent residence and shall be regulated by the legislation of that state, unless otherwise provided by a specific international agreement between the Parties.

2. Pension provision for workers shall be carried out in accordance with the legislation of the state of their permanent residence.

Article 9

1. The provisions of the contracts related to the medical services for the workers shall not limit their health protection rights established by the legislation of the host state.

2. Workers shall have the right to receive emergency (urgent) medical care in cases of sudden acute conditions and diseases that threaten the life of the patient or the health of others, accidents, poisonings, injuries, childbirth, and urgent conditions during pregnancy.

This type of medical care shall be provided to the worker without hindrance, free of charge, and in the necessary amount in healthcare institutions of the host state.

Other types of medical care shall be provided to the workers in accordance with the legislation of the host state and international treaties between the Parties, as well as at the expense of the workers and the executor of work (contractor), if stipulated in the contract.

Article 10

1. In case of the death of a worker, the executor of work (contractor), with the assistance of the client, shall organize and pay for the transportation of the body (remains) of the deceased to the state of permanent residence, and shall bear all expenses related to the transportation, shipment and transfer of his/her property, and the payment of compensation in accordance with the legislation of the state of permanent residence.

The client shall immediately (within three days) notify the diplomatic mission or consular office of the state of permanent residence in the host state, as well as the competent authorities at the place of registration of the worker, and shall provide a document confirming the death.

2. In case the worker's death occurred due to the fault of the client, the client shall bear responsibility in accordance with the legislation of the host state and shall also pay all expenses related to the transportation

of the body and property of the deceased from the host state to the state of permanent residence.

Article 11

Workers may purchase foreign currency on the domestic foreign exchange market of the host state and may transfer or carry with them the earned funds in foreign currency to the state of permanent residence in accordance with the legislation of the host state.

Article 12

The taxation of workers' income during their stay in the host state shall be governed by the Agreement between the Government of the Russian Federation and the Government of the Democratic People's Republic of Korea on the Avoidance of Double Taxation with respect to Taxes on Income and Capital, dated September 26, 1997.

Article 13

Workers in the host state shall be guaranteed the rights, freedoms, legal protection, and personal security established by the legislation of the host state for foreign citizens and by the relevant international treaties between the Parties.

Workers must comply with the legislation of the host state during their stay, including the rules regarding the stay of foreign citizens.

Article 14

The import into and export from the territory of the host state of goods by workers, including personal belongings, shall be carried out in accordance with the legislation of the host state, unless otherwise provided by treaties between the Russian Federation and the Democratic People's Republic of Korea.

Article 15

1. The worker must leave the host state upon the expiration of the visa, if no extension has been obtained at the time of expiration.

In the event of objective circumstances preventing the worker from leaving the host state in a timely manner after the expiration of the authorized period of stay (for example, serious illness of the worker, death of a close relative in the host state), the worker must leave the host state immediately after taking measures appropriate to the circumstances.

2. If a worker evades departure from the host state after the expiration of the authorized period of stay and in the absence of objective reasons, he or she shall be held accountable in accordance with the legislation of the host state.

Article 16

Disputes regarding the interpretation and application of the provisions of this Agreement shall be resolved through consultations between the competent authorities.

Article 17

Issues related to the implementation of this Agreement shall be governed by a separate agreement (protocol) concluded between the competent authorities.

Article 18

1. This Agreement shall enter into force on the date of receipt of the last written notification from the Parties confirming the completion of their respective domestic procedures necessary for its entry into force and shall remain in force for a period of five (5) years. Upon the expiration of this period, it shall be automatically extended for successive one-year periods unless one of the Parties notifies the other in writing

through diplomatic channels of its intention to terminate the Agreement at least six (6) months before the expiration of the current one-year period.

2. Amendments to this Agreement, agreed upon by the mutual consent of the Parties, shall be formalized by protocols, which shall enter into force in accordance with the procedure specified in paragraph 1 of this Article.

3. In the event of termination of this Agreement, work permits issued during its validity shall remain effective until their respective expiration dates. The termination of this Agreement shall not affect the implementation of contracts for the performance of work or the provision of services concluded prior to its termination.

Done in Moscow on August 31, 2007 (Juche Year 96), in two copies, each in the Russian and Korean languages, both texts being equally authentic.

For the Government of the Russian Federation

For the Government of the Democratic People's Republic of Korea

Source: Translated from Appendix 2a, original text in Russian from ConsultantPlus, https://www.consultant.ru/document/cons_doc_LAW_94253/

APPENDIX 3A. AGREEMENT ON THE TRANSFER AND RECEIPT OF ILLEGAL ENTRANTS AND RESIDENTS (RUSSIAN ORIGINAL)

Контрагент: КНДР

Дата подписания: 02.02.2016

Дата вступления в силу: 07.08.2017

Действие: Действует

СОГЛАШЕНИЕ
между Правительством Российской Федерации
и Правительством Корейской Народно-Демократической Республики
о передаче и приеме лиц, незаконно въехавших и незаконно пребывающих на территории Российской Федерации
и Корейской Народно-Демократической Республики

Правительство Российской Федерации и Правительство Корейской Народно-Демократической Республики, именуемые в дальнейшем Сторонами,

руководствуясь стремлением к развитию добрососедских и дружественных отношений между двумя государствами, а также сотрудничества между ними в различных областях, в том числе в вопросах борьбы с незаконной миграцией,

будучи убеждены, что введение в действие согласованных Сторонами принципов и норм, определяющих порядок передачи и приема лиц, находящихся на территории их государств в нарушение действующего порядка въезда и пребывания иностранных граждан и лиц без гражданства, является важной частью регулирования процессов миграции и вкладом в борьбу с незаконной миграцией,

уважая суверенное право государства каждой из Сторон в соответствии с его законодательством устанавливать ответственность за незаконную миграцию на его территорию или через нее иностранных граждан и лиц без гражданства,

согласились о нижеследующем:

Статья 1
Определения

В настоящем Соглашении приводимые ниже определения имеют следующее значение:

«незаконный въезд и незаконное пребывание» — въезд или пребывание в нарушение законодательства государства одной из Сторон по вопросам въезда, выезда и пребывания иностранных граждан и лиц без гражданства;

«передача и прием» — передача компетентными органами государства запрашивающей Стороны и прием компетентными органами государства запрашиваемой Стороны в порядке, на условиях и в целях, которые предусмотрены настоящим Соглашением, лиц, въехавших на территорию государства запрашивающей Стороны или находящихся на ней в нарушение законодательства этого государства по вопросам въезда, выезда и пребывания иностранных граждан и лиц без гражданства;

«государство запрашивающей Стороны» — государство одной из Сторон, центральный компетентный орган которого направляет запрос о передаче и приеме или транзите лица в соответствии с настоящим Соглашением;

«государство запрашиваемой Стороны» — государство одной из Сторон, в адрес центрального компетентного органа которого направлен запрос о передаче и приеме или транзите лица в соответствии с настоящим Соглашением;

«граждане третьих государств» – лица, не имеющие гражданства ни одного из государств Сторон и принадлежащие к гражданству государства, не являющегося участником настоящего Соглашения;

«лица без гражданства» – лица, не являющиеся гражданами государств Сторон и не имеющие доказательств принадлежности к гражданству третьего государства;

«компетентные органы» – органы государств Сторон, участвующие в реализации настоящего Соглашения;

«центральные компетентные органы» – компетентные органы государств Сторон, на которые возложены основные задачи по реализации настоящего Соглашения;

«Исполнительный протокол» – Исполнительный протокол о порядке реализации настоящего Соглашения.

Статья 2
Передача и прием граждан государств Сторон

1. Компетентные органы государства запрашиваемой Стороны принимают по запросу центрального компетентного органа государства запрашивающей Стороны лиц, которые въехали на территорию государства запрашивающей Стороны или находятся на ней с нарушением законодательства этого государства по вопросам въезда, выезда и пребывания иностранных граждан и лиц без гражданства, если установлено, что они являются

гражданами государства запрашиваемой Стороны, в том числе граждан государства запрашиваемой Стороны.

2. В случае необходимости компетентные органы государства запрашиваемой Стороны выдают передаваемым лицам документы, необходимые для их въезда на территорию этого государства.

3. Перечень документов, на основании которых определяется наличие у лица гражданства государства одной из Сторон, приводится в Исполнительном протоколе.

Стороны в течение 30 календарных дней с даты вступления в силу настоящего Соглашения обмениваются по дипломатическим каналам образцами таких документов. В последующем каждая Сторона уведомляет другую Сторону по дипломатическим каналам о любых изменениях в образцах указанных документов.

4. Если ни один из документов, указанных в пункте 3 настоящей статьи, не может быть представлен, компетентные органы государств Сторон договариваются о проведении на территории государства запрашивающей Стороны собеседования с лицом, подлежащим передаче и приему, с целью получения сведений о его гражданстве.

5. Компетентные органы государства запрашиваемой Стороны принимают обратно переданное лицо в течение 30 календарных дней с даты его передачи, если полученные компетентными органами государства одной из Сторон после передачи лица результаты проверки будут свидетельствовать об отсутствии необходимых для его передачи и приема условий.

В этом случае центральный компетентный орган государства запрашиваемой Стороны передает центральному компетентному органу государства запрашивающей Стороны имеющиеся в его распоряжении материалы, касающиеся данного лица.

6. В случае если лицо, указанное в пункте 1 настоящей статьи, имеет действительный документ, удостоверяющий личность гражданина государства запрашиваемой Стороны, направление

запроса о передаче и приеме не требуется. Передача таких лиц осуществляется в соответствии со статьей 9 Исполнительного протокола.

Статья 3
Передача и прием граждан третьих государств или лиц без гражданства

1. Компетентные органы государства запрашиваемой Стороны принимают по запросу центрального компетентного органа государства запрашивающей Стороны граждан третьих государств и лиц без гражданства, которые прибыли на территорию государства запрашивающей Стороны непосредственно с территории государства запрашиваемой Стороны с нарушением законодательства государства запрашивающей Стороны по вопросам въезда, выезда и пребывания иностранных граждан и лиц без гражданства.

2. Обязательство по передаче и приему, предусмотренное пунктом 1 настоящей статьи, не применяется, если граждане третьих государств или лица без гражданства:

2.1. непосредственно перед прибытием на территорию государства запрашивающей Стороны находились исключительно в транзитной зоне международного аэропорта на территории государства запрашиваемой Стороны;

2.2. прибыли на законных основаниях на территорию государства запрашиваемой Стороны в безвизовом порядке в соответствии с международным договором.

3. В случае если граждане третьих государств или лица без гражданства, указанные в пункте 1 настоящей статьи, не имеют документа, удостоверяющего личность, и отсутствует возможность выдачи такого документа компетентным органом государства гражданства или постоянного проживания данного лица, то после получения положительного ответа на запрос о передаче и приеме компетентный орган государства запрашивающей Стороны

выдает такому лицу проездной документ, признаваемый государством запрашиваемой Стороны, необходимый для въезда на территорию государства запрашиваемой Стороны.

Стороны в течение 30 календарных дней с даты вступления в силу настоящего Соглашения обмениваются по дипломатическим каналам образцами указанного проездного документа. В последующем Стороны незамедлительно уведомляют друг друга по дипломатическим каналам о любых изменениях в таком документе.

4. Документы, указывающие на наличие оснований для передачи и приема граждан третьих государств и лиц без гражданства, приводятся в Исполнительном протоколе. Стороны в течение 30 календарных дней с даты вступления в силу настоящего Соглашения обмениваются по дипломатическим каналам образцами таких документов. В последующем каждая из Сторон уведомляет другую Сторону по дипломатическим каналам о любых изменениях в таких документах.

5. Компетентные органы государства запрашивающей Стороны принимают обратно переданное лицо в течение 30 календарных дней с даты его передачи, если полученные компетентными органами государства одной из Сторон после передачи лица результаты проверки будут свидетельствовать об отсутствии необходимых для его передачи и приема условий, предусмотренных в пункте 1 настоящей статьи.

В этом случае центральный компетентный орган государства запрашиваемой Стороны передает центральному компетентному органу государства запрашивающей Стороны имеющиеся в его распоряжении материалы, касающиеся данного лица.

6. В случае если гражданин третьего государства или лицо без гражданства имеет действительное разрешение на проживание, выданное полномочными органами государства запрашиваемой Стороны, направление запроса о передаче и приеме не требуется. Передача таких лиц осуществляется в соответствии со статьей 9 Исполнительного протокола.

Статья 4
Сроки направления и рассмотрения запросов о передаче и приеме

1. Запрос о передаче и приеме в отношении граждан государств Сторон может направляться компетентным органом государства запрашивающей Стороны с даты установления факта незаконного въезда на территорию государства запрашивающей Стороны или незаконного пребывания граждан государства запрашиваемой Стороны на территории государства запрашивающей Стороны.

2. Запрос о передаче и приеме в отношении граждан третьих государств и лиц без гражданства направляется центральному компетентному органу государства запрашиваемой Стороны в срок, не превышающий 180 календарных дней с даты установления факта незаконного въезда на территорию государства запрашивающей Стороны или пребывания на ней гражданина третьего государства или лица без гражданства.

3. Центральный компетентный орган государства запрашиваемой
* Стороны в течение 30 календарных дней с даты получения запроса о передаче и приеме лица дает согласие на прием или мотивированный отказ

в его приеме, если компетентными органами государства запрашиваемой Стороны установлено отсутствие необходимых для передачи лица условий, предусмотренных пунктом 1 статьи 2 и пунктом 1 статьи 3 настоящего Соглашения.При наличии обстоятельств юридического или фактического характера, препятствующих своевременному ответу на запрос о передаче и приеме лица, срок ответа на основании соответствующего обращения центрального компетентного органа государства запрашиваемой Стороны продлевается до 60 календарных дней.

Статья 5
Сроки передачи

1. Передача лиц, в отношении которых центральным компетентным органом государства запрашиваемой Стороны дано согласие на передачу и прием, осуществляется в течение 30 календарных дней с даты получения такого согласия центральным компетентным органом государства запрашивающей Стороны, если центральные компетентные органы государств Сторон в каждом конкретном случае не договорятся об ином.

2. По запросу центрального компетентного органа государства одной из Сторон срок, указанный в пункте 1 настоящей статьи, может быть продлен, в частности, ввиду возникновения обстоятельств, препятствующих или значительно затрудняющих передачу и прием лица. В этом случае центральный компетентный орган государства Стороны, ходатайствующий о продлении срока, должен информировать центральный компетентный орган государства другой Стороны о причинах отсрочки. При прекращении существования таких обстоятельств центральные компетентные органы государств Сторон принимают меры по передаче и приему лица в возможно короткие сроки.

3. При невозможности передачи лица центральный компетентный орган государства запрашивающей Стороны направляет центральному компетентному органу государства запрашиваемой Стороны соответствующее письменное уведомление.

Статья 6
Транзит

1. Центральный компетентный орган государства запрашиваемой Стороны по запросу центрального компетентного органа государства запрашивающей Стороны разрешает транзит через территорию государства запрашиваемой Стороны граждан третьих государств и лиц без гражданства, передаваемых в порядке передачи и приема в третьи государства, если государство

запрашивающей Стороны гарантирует, что указанным лицам будет предоставлен беспрепятственный въезд на территорию третьего государства независимо от того, является ли оно государством транзита или государством назначения.

2. Транзит лиц, указанных в пункте 1 настоящей статьи, может осуществляться в сопровождении сотрудников компетентных органов государства запрашивающей Стороны.

3. Запрос о транзите лица в соответствии с настоящей статьей направляется центральным компетентным органом государства запрашивающей Стороны заблаговременно, однако не позднее чем за 15 календарных дней до предполагаемой даты въезда лица на территорию государства запрашиваемой Стороны с целью транзита, если центральные компетентные органы государств Сторон в каждом конкретном случае не договорятся об ином.

4. Центральный компетентный орган государства запрашиваемой Стороны в течение 7 календарных дней с даты получения запроса о транзите лица дает согласие на транзит или мотивированный отказ в осуществлении транзита.

5. При осуществлении транзита лица, указанных в пункте 1 настоящей статьи, компетентные органы государства запрашиваемой Стороны по запросу компетентных органов государства запрашивающей Стороны оказывают им возможное содействие.

6. Компетентный орган государства запрашиваемой Стороны может отказать в транзите лица в следующих случаях:

6.1. существует угроза того, что в государстве назначения или в другом государстве транзита гражданин третьего государства или лицо без гражданства подвергнется пыткам, бесчеловечному или унижающему достоинство обращению или наказанию, смертной казни или преследованию по признаку расовой, религиозной, национальной принадлежности, а также принадлежности к определенной социальной группе или по признаку политических убеждений;

6.2. в государстве назначения или в другом государстве транзита, гражданин третьего государства или лицо без гражданства подвергнется уголовному преследованию или наказанию;

6.3. нахождение таких лиц на территории государства запрашиваемой Стороны является нежелательным, в частности, по соображениям национальной безопасности, охраны общественного порядка или здоровья населения.

7. Компетентные органы государства запрашиваемой Стороны, несмотря на выданное разрешение на транзитный проезд, могут возвратить лиц, указанных в пункте 1 настоящей статьи, компетентным органам государства запрашивающей Стороны, если после их въезда на территорию государства запрашиваемой Стороны в отношении них будут установлены обстоятельства, предусмотренные пунктом 6 настоящей статьи, а также если беспрепятственный въезд на территорию другого государства транзита или государства назначения более нельзя считать гарантированным.

8. Стороны на основе взаимности стремятся ограничивать случаи транзита граждан третьих государств и лиц без гражданства, которые могут быть возвращены непосредственно в государства их гражданства или государства их постоянного проживания.

9. Стороны осуществляют транзит граждан третьих государств и лиц без гражданства воздушным транспортом.

Статья 7
Защита персональных данных

1. Персональные данные, которыми компетентные органы государств Сторон обмениваются или передают друг другу в связи с реализацией положений настоящего Соглашения, подлежат защите в государстве каждой из Сторон в соответствии с его законодательством и международными договорами, участниками которых являются государства Сторон.

2. Компетентные органы государств Сторон обмениваются персональными данными в следующем порядке:

2.1. персональные данные могут использоваться только для целей настоящего Соглашения;

2.2. компетентные органы государств Сторон обеспечивают конфиденциальность персональных данных, получаемых в соответствии с настоящим Соглашением, и не предоставляют их третьей стороне, кроме как с разрешения компетентного органа государства Стороны, передавшего персональные данные, и уведомляют компетентные органы государства Стороны, передавшего такие данные, о том, как они были использованы;

2.3. компетентные органы государств Сторон обеспечивают защиту персональных данных от случайной утери, несанкционированного доступа, изменения или придания гласности.

Статья 8
Расходы, связанные с передачей и приемом и транзитом

1. Расходы, связанные с передачей и приемом лиц, упомянутых в пункте 1 статьи 2 и пункте 1 статьи 3 настоящего Соглашения, и их сопровождением до пункта пропуска через государственную границу государства запрашиваемой Стороны несет государство запрашивающей Стороны, в случае если расходы не могут быть оплачены такими лицами самостоятельно или третьими сторонами.

2. Расходы, связанные с транзитом и сопровождением лиц, указанных в пункте 1 статьи 6 настоящего Соглашения, и их возможным возвращением, несет государство запрашивающей Стороны, в случае если расходы не могут быть оплачены такими лицами самостоятельно или третьими сторонами.

3. Расходы, связанные с передачей лиц, указанных в пункте 5 статьи 2 и пункте 5 статьи 3 настоящего Соглашения, и их возможным

сопровождением до пункта пропуска через государственную границу государства запрашивающей Стороны, несет Сторона, действия или бездействие которой привели к передаче лица, основания для передачи и приема которого отсутствовали.

Статья 9
Исполнительный протокол

Стороны заключают Исполнительный протокол, который в том числе содержит правила, касающиеся:

1. компетентных органов и распределения полномочий между ними;
2. содержания и порядка направления запроса о передаче и приеме или транзите;
3. проведения собеседований;
4. процедуры передачи и приема или транзита;
5. передачи лиц с сопровождением, в том числе в случае транзита граждан третьих государств и лиц без гражданства;
6. порядка возмещения расходов, связанных с выполнением настоящего Соглашения.

Статья 10
Приостановление и возобновление применения Соглашения

1. Каждая Сторона может по причинам, связанным с защитой национальной безопасности, обеспечением общественного порядка или охраной здоровья населения, приостановить применение настоящего Соглашения.

дипломатическим каналам не позднее 72 часов до начала реализации такого решения.

Статья 11
Принципы сотрудничества

1. Все вопросы, возникающие между Сторонами и связанные с выполнением или толкованием настоящего Соглашения, решаются путем консультаций и переговоров между ними.

2. Порядок осуществления консультаций и переговоров определяется по договоренности Сторон.

Статья 12
Отношение к другим международным договорам

1. Настоящее Соглашение не затрагивает прав и обязательств каждой из Сторон, вытекающих из других международных договоров, участником которых является ее государство.

2. Ничто в настоящем Соглашении не препятствует возвращению того или иного лица на основании других международных договоров, заключенных каждым из государств Сторон.

Статья 13
Заключительные положения

1. Настоящее Соглашение вступает в силу по истечении 30 календарных дней с даты получения по дипломатическим каналам последнего письменного уведомления о выполнении Сторонами внутригосударственных процедур, необходимых для его вступления в силу.

2. Стороны по взаимному согласию могут вносить изменения в настоящее Соглашение, которые вступают в силу в порядке, предусмотренном для вступления в силу настоящего Соглашения.

3. Настоящее Соглашение заключается на неопределенный срок и его действие прекращается по истечении 60 календарных дней с даты получения одной Стороной по дипломатическим каналам

письменного уведомления другой Стороны о её намерении прекратить его действие.

4. В случае прекращения действия настоящего Соглашения Стороны урегулируют обязательства, возникшие в период его действия.

Совершено в г. Москве "2" февраля 2016 г. в двух экземплярах, каждый на русском и корейском языках, причем оба текста имеют одинаковую силу.

За Правительство Российской Федерации

За Правительство Корейской Народно-Демократической Республики

Source: Ministry of Foreign Affairs of the Russian Federation, https://www.mid.ru/ru/foreign_policy/international_contracts/international_contracts/2_contract/43686/#sel=8:1:77t,11:7:yww

APPENDIX 3B. AGREEMENT ON THE TRANSFER AND RECEIPT OF ILLEGAL ENTRANTS AND RESIDENTS (ENGLISH TRANSLATION)

Counterparty: DPRK

Date of signature: 02.02.2016

Date of entry into force: 07.08.2017

Status: In force

Agreement
between the Government of the Russian Federation and the
Government of the Democratic People's Republic of Korea
on the transfer and admission of persons who have illegally entered
and are illegally staying on the territory of the Russian Federation
and the Democratic People's Republic of Korea

The Government of the Russian Federation and the Government of the Democratic People's Republic of Korea, hereinafter referred to as the Parties,

Guided by the desire to develop good-neighborly and friendly relations between the two States, as well as cooperation between them in various fields, including issues related to combating illegal migration,

Convinced that the implementation of the principles and norms agreed upon by the Parties, defining the procedures for the transfer and admission of persons located in the territory of their States in violation of the existing rules for entry and stay of foreign citizens and stateless persons, constitutes an important part of the regulation of migration processes and a contribution to the fight against illegal migration,

Respecting the sovereign right of each Party's State to establish, in accordance with its legislation, liability for illegal migration into or through its territory by foreign citizens and stateless persons,

Have agreed as follows:

Article 1
Definitions

For the purposes of this Agreement, the terms below shall have the following meanings:

- **"Illegal entry and illegal stay"** - entry into or stay in violation of the laws of one of the Parties' States governing the entry, exit, and stay of foreign citizens and stateless persons;
- **"Transfer and admission"** - the transfer by the competent authorities of the requesting Party's State and the admission by the competent authorities of the requested Party's State, under the procedures, conditions, and for the purposes specified in this Agreement, of persons who have entered or are staying in the territory of the requesting Party's State in violation of the laws of that State regarding the entry, exit, and stay of foreign citizens and stateless persons;
- **"State of the requesting Party"** - the State of one of the Parties whose central competent authority submits a request for the transfer and admission or transit of a person in accordance with this Agreement;

- **"State of the requested Party"** - the State of one of the Parties whose central competent authority receives a request for the transfer and admission or transit of a person in accordance with this Agreement;
- **"Citizens of third States"** - persons who are not nationals of either Party's State and who hold the nationality of a State that is not a party to this Agreement;
- **"Stateless persons"** — persons who are not nationals of either Party's State and who do not have proof of nationality of a third State;
- **"Competent authorities"** — the authorities of the Parties' States involved in the implementation of this Agreement;
- **"Central competent authorities"** — the competent authorities of the Parties' States charged with the principal tasks of implementing this Agreement;
- **"Implementing Protocol"** — the Implementing Protocol on the procedures for carrying out this Agreement.

Article 2
Transfer and Admission of Nationals of the Parties' States

1. The competent authorities of the requested Party's State shall, upon request from the central competent authority of the requesting Party's State, admit persons who have entered or are staying in the territory of the requesting Party's State in violation of the laws of that State concerning the entry, exit, and stay of foreign citizens and stateless persons, if it has been established that such persons are nationals of the requested Party's State, including nationals of the requested Party's State.

2. If necessary, the competent authorities of the requested Party's State shall issue to the transferred persons the documents required for their entry into the territory of that State.

3. The list of documents used to determine whether a person holds the nationality of either Party's State shall be included in the Implementing Protocol.

The Parties shall exchange, through diplomatic channels, samples of such documents within 30 calendar days from the date this Agreement enters into force. Thereafter, each Party shall notify the other Party through diplomatic channels of any changes to the samples of the aforementioned documents.

4. If none of the documents referred to in paragraph 3 of this Article can be provided, the competent authorities of the Parties' States shall agree to conduct an interview on the territory of the requesting Party's State with the person to be transferred and admitted, for the purpose of obtaining information regarding their nationality.

5. The competent authorities of the requested Party's State shall readmit the transferred person within 30 calendar days from the date of transfer if, following the transfer, the competent authorities of either Party's State obtain verification results indicating that the conditions required for the person's transfer and admission were not met.

In such a case, the central competent authority of the requested Party's State shall transmit to the central competent authority of the requesting Party's State all materials in its possession relating to the person concerned.

6. If a person referred to in paragraph 1 of this Article holds a valid identity document proving their status as a citizen of the requested Party's State, no request for transfer and admission is required. The transfer of such persons shall be carried out in accordance with Article 9 of the Implementing Protocol.

Article 3
Transfer and Admission of Third-Country Nationals or Stateless Persons

1. The competent authorities of the State of the Requested Party shall, upon request from the central competent authority of the State of the Requesting Party, admit third-country nationals and stateless persons who arrived in the territory of the Requesting Party directly from the territory of the Requested Party in violation of the laws of the

Requesting Party concerning the entry, exit, and stay of foreign nationals and stateless persons.

2. The obligation of transfer and admission referred to in paragraph 1 of this Article shall not apply if the third-country nationals or stateless persons:

2.1. immediately prior to arrival in the territory of the Requesting Party, remained solely in the international transit zone of an airport located in the territory of the Requested Party;

2.2. entered the territory of the Requested Party lawfully and visa-free in accordance with an international treaty.

3. In cases where the third-country nationals or stateless persons referred to in paragraph 1 of this Article do not possess identity documents, and the competent authority of the country of nationality or permanent residence of the individual is unable to issue such a document, then—after receiving a positive response to the transfer and admission request—the competent authority of the Requesting Party shall issue to such individuals a travel document recognized by the Requested Party, which is required for entry into the territory of the Requested Party.

The Parties shall, within 30 calendar days from the date of entry into force of this Agreement, exchange through diplomatic channels samples of said travel document. Thereafter, the Parties shall promptly notify each other through diplomatic channels of any changes to this document.

4. Documents indicating the grounds for the transfer and admission of third-country nationals and stateless persons shall be specified in the Implementing Protocol. The Parties shall, within 30 calendar days from the date of entry into force of this Agreement, exchange through diplomatic channels samples of such documents. Thereafter, each Party shall notify the other through diplomatic channels of any changes to such documents.

5. The competent authorities of the Requesting Party shall take back the transferred person within 30 calendar days from the date of

transfer, if the results of post-transfer verification by the competent authorities of either Party indicate that the conditions required for their transfer and admission, as specified in paragraph 1 of this Article, are not met.

In such case, the central competent authority of the Requested Party shall transmit to the central competent authority of the Requesting Party all available materials concerning the person in question.

6. If the third-country national or stateless person holds a valid residence permit issued by the authorized bodies of the Requested Party, no transfer and admission request shall be required. The transfer of such individuals shall be carried out in accordance with Article 9 of the Implementing Protocol.

Article 4
Deadlines for Submission and Review of Transfer and Admission Requests

1. A request for transfer and admission of nationals of the Parties may be submitted by the competent authority of the Requesting Party from the date of establishing the fact of unlawful entry into the territory of the Requesting Party or unlawful stay of the national of the Requested Party in the territory of the Requesting Party.

2. A request for transfer and admission of third-country nationals and stateless persons shall be submitted to the central competent authority of the Requested Party within a period not exceeding 180 calendar days from the date of establishing the fact of unlawful entry into the territory of the Requesting Party or stay therein of a third-country national or stateless person.

3. The central competent authority of the Requested Party shall, within 30 calendar days from the date of receipt of the transfer and admission request, provide consent for admission or a reasoned refusal thereof,

if the competent authorities of the Requested Party determine that the necessary conditions for the transfer of the person, as provided for in paragraph 1 of Article 2 and paragraph 1 of Article 3 of this Agreement, are not met.

If legal or factual circumstances prevent a timely response to the transfer and admission request, the response period may be extended to 60 calendar days based on an appropriate request by the central competent authority of the Requested Party.

Article 5
Time Limits for Transfer

1. The transfer of persons for whom consent for transfer and admission has been given by the central competent authority of the State of the Requested Party shall be carried out within 30 calendar days from the date the central competent authority of the Requesting Party receives such consent, unless the central competent authorities of the Parties agree otherwise in each specific case.

2. At the request of the central competent authority of one of the Parties, the period specified in paragraph 1 of this Article may be extended, particularly in the event of circumstances that hinder or significantly complicate the transfer and admission of the person. In such case, the central competent authority of the Party requesting the extension shall inform the central competent authority of the other Party of the reasons for the delay. Upon the termination of such circumstances, the central competent authorities of the Parties shall take measures to carry out the transfer and admission of the person as soon as possible.

3. If the transfer of a person is not possible, the central competent authority of the Requesting Party shall send a corresponding written notification to the central competent authority of the Requested Party.

Article 6
Transit

1. The central competent authority of the Requested Party shall, upon request from the central competent authority of the Requesting Party,

authorize the transit through the territory of the Requested Party of third-country nationals and stateless persons who are being transferred to third countries in accordance with the procedure of transfer and admission, provided that the Requesting Party guarantees that such persons will be granted unhindered entry into the territory of the third country, regardless of whether that country is a transit state or the country of destination.

2. The transit of the persons specified in paragraph 1 of this Article may be carried out under escort by officials of the competent authorities of the Requesting Party.

3. A request for transit of a person pursuant to this Article shall be submitted by the central competent authority of the Requesting Party in advance, but no later than 15 calendar days before the expected date of entry into the territory of the Requested Party for the purpose of transit, unless the central competent authorities of the Parties agree otherwise in each specific case.

4. The central competent authority of the Requested Party shall, within 7 calendar days from the date of receipt of the request for transit, grant consent for transit or provide a reasoned refusal to permit the transit.

5. During the transit of persons specified in paragraph 1 of this Article, the competent authorities of the Requested Party shall, upon request of the competent authorities of the Requesting Party, provide appropriate assistance.

6. The competent authority of the Requested Party may refuse the transit of a person in the following cases:

6.1. There is a threat that in the country of destination or in another transit country, the third-country national or stateless person will be subjected to torture, inhuman or degrading treatment or punishment, the death penalty, or persecution based on race, religion, nationality, membership in a particular social group, or political opinion;

6.2. The third-country national or stateless person would face criminal prosecution or punishment in the country of destination or in another transit country;

6.3. The presence of such persons in the territory of the Requested Party is deemed undesirable, particularly for reasons of national security, public order, or public health.

7. The competent authorities of the Requested Party may, despite having issued prior authorization for transit, return the persons specified in paragraph 1 of this Article to the competent authorities of the Requesting Party if, after their entry into the territory of the Requested Party, circumstances as provided in paragraph 6 of this Article are established, or if unhindered entry into another transit country or the country of destination can no longer be considered guaranteed.

8. The Parties shall, on the basis of reciprocity, endeavor to limit cases of transit of third-country nationals and stateless persons who can be returned directly to their countries of citizenship or countries of permanent residence.

9. The Parties shall carry out the transit of third-country nationals and stateless persons by air transport.

Article 7
Protection of Personal Data

1. Personal data exchanged or transferred by the competent authorities of the States of the Parties in connection with the implementation of the provisions of this Agreement shall be protected in each Party's State in accordance with its national legislation and the international treaties to which the Party is a signatory.

2. The competent authorities of the States of the Parties shall exchange personal data under the following conditions:

2.1. Personal data may be used only for the purposes of this Agreement;

2.2. The competent authorities of the States of the Parties shall ensure the confidentiality of personal data received in accordance with this Agreement and shall not provide such data to a third party, except with the permission of the competent authority of the Party that provided the data. They shall also inform the competent authority of the providing Party about how the data was used;

2.3. The competent authorities of the States of the Parties shall ensure the protection of personal data from accidental loss, unauthorized access, modification, or disclosure.

Article 8
Expenses Related to Transfer, Admission, and Transit

1. Expenses related to the transfer and admission of persons mentioned in paragraph 1 of Article 2 and paragraph 1 of Article 3 of this Agreement, as well as their escort to the border crossing point of the Requested Party's territory, shall be borne by the Requesting Party if such expenses cannot be covered by the persons themselves or by third parties.

2. Expenses related to the transit and escort of persons referred to in paragraph 1 of Article 6 of this Agreement, and their possible return, shall be borne by the Requesting Party if such expenses cannot be covered by the persons themselves or by third parties.

3. Expenses related to the transfer and possible escort to the border crossing point of the Requesting Party's territory of persons referred to in paragraph 5 of Article 2 and paragraph 5 of Article 3 of this Agreement shall be borne by the Party whose actions or inactions led to the transfer of a person for whom the grounds for transfer and admission were absent.

Article 9
Implementing Protocol

The Parties shall conclude an Implementing Protocol, which shall include provisions concerning:

1. the competent authorities and the distribution of powers among them;

2. the content and procedure for submitting requests for transfer, admission, or transit;
3. the conduct of interviews;
4. the procedure for transfer, admission, or transit;
5. the transfer of persons under escort, including in the case of transit of third-country nationals and stateless persons;
6. the procedure for reimbursement of expenses related to the implementation of this Agreement.

Article 10
Suspension and Resumption of the Application of the Agreement

1. Each Party may suspend the application of this Agreement for reasons related to the protection of national security, public order, or the protection of public health.

2. The Parties shall notify each other in writing via diplomatic channels of the suspension or resumption of the application of this Agreement no later than 72 hours prior to the implementation of such decision.

Article 11
Principles of Cooperation

1. All issues arising between the Parties in connection with the implementation or interpretation of this Agreement shall be resolved through consultations and negotiations between them.

2. The procedure for conducting consultations and negotiations shall be determined by mutual agreement of the Parties.

Article 12
Relation to Other International Treaties

1. This Agreement shall not affect the rights and obligations of each Party arising from other international treaties to which its State is a party.

2. Nothing in this Agreement shall prevent the return of any person on the basis of other international treaties concluded by either Party's State.

Article 13
Final Provisions

1 .This Agreement shall enter into force 30 calendar days after the date of receipt, via diplomatic channels, of the last written notification confirming the completion by both Parties of the domestic procedures necessary for its entry into force.

2. The Parties may, by mutual consent, make amendments to this Agreement. Such amendments shall enter into force following the procedure established for the entry into force of this Agreement.

3. This Agreement is concluded for an indefinite period. Its validity shall terminate 60 calendar days after the date of receipt, via diplomatic channels, of a written notification from one Party to the other of its intention to terminate the Agreement.

4. In the event of termination of this Agreement, the Parties shall settle obligations that arose during its period of validity.

Done in Moscow on February 2, 2016, in two originals, each in the Russian and Korean languages, both texts being equally authentic.

For the Government of the Russian Federation

For the Government of the Democratic People's Republic of Korea

---

Source: Translated from Appendix 3a, original text in Russian from the Ministry of Foreign Affairs of the Russian Federation, https://www.mid.ru/ru/foreign_policy/international_contracts/international_contracts/2_contract/43686/#sel=8:1:77t,11:7:yww

APPENDIX 4A. REGULATIONS ON EXTERNAL ECONOMIC PROJECTS (KOREAN ORIGINAL)

경제무역참사부와 경제협조단,
경제실무대표단의 대외경제사업규정

주체109(2020)년 7월 1일 내각결정 제49호로 채택됨

경애하는 김정은동지께서는 다음과 같이 말씀하시였다.

《대외경제부문에서는 자립적민족경제건설로선에 철저히 립각하여 나라의 경제토대를 강화하는데 실질적 도움이 되는 부분과 교류를 보충하는 방향에서 대외경제협조와 기술교류, 무역활동을 다각적으로, 주동적으로 전개해나가야 합니다.》

제1장 총칙

제1조. 이 규정은 경제무역참사부와 경제협조단, 경제실무대표단이 대외경제사업에서 엄격한 제도와 질서를 세워 대외경제협조와 기술교류, 무역활동을 다각적으로, 주동적으로 전개하게 함으로써 여러 나라들과의 경제협조와 교류를 확대발전시키는데 이바지하기 위하여 제정한다.

제2조. 이 규정에서 용어의 정의는 다음과 같다.

1. 경제무역참사부는 우리 나라와 주재국(겸임국 포함)의 경제무역사업에서 교류와 협력이 적극 추진되도록 경제외교사업을 하며, 주재국 안에서 경제협조단, 경제실무대표단의 대외경제사업을 장악·지도하는 국가외교대표부의 경제외교부서이다.
2. 경제협조단은 무역회사(총회사 포함)의 지사, 대표부, 국외투자기업, 해외기술협조기구, 대외건설회사 같은 경제적 리익을 얻을 목적으로 다른 나라에 상주하여 경제사업을 하는 조직체이다.
3. 경제실무대표단은 대외경제계약체결, 전람회, 감수, 실습, 관관 같은 대외경제사업을 목적으로 다른 나라에 파견되는 대표단이다.

제3조. 경제무역참사부와 경제협조단, 경제실무대표단은 다음과 같은 원칙과 요구에 맞게 대외경제사업을 진행하여야 한다.

1. 위대한 수령님과 위대한 장군님, 경애하는 김정은동지의 경제적 권위를 철저히 옹호하고 그에 의거하여 대외경제사업을 힘있게 진행하여야 한다.
2. 위대한 수령님과 위대한 장군님, 경애하는 김정은동지의 위대성을 널리 소개·선전하여야 한다.
3. 경애하는 김정은동지의 유일적 령도체계를 튼튼히 세워야 한다.
4. 대외경제사업에서 자주성의 원칙을 철저히 지키며 국가와 인민의 리익을 견결히 옹호·고수하여야 한다.
5. 국가외교대표부 책임자의 통일적인 지휘 밑에 부여된 권한과 기능, 승인된 사업계획에 따라 대외경제사업을 하며, 직능과 권한 밖에 제기되는 문제를 자의대로 처리하지 말아야 한다.
6. 대외경제사업에서 혁명적 경각성을 높이고 국가의 비밀을 엄격히 지켜야 한다.
7. 주재국의 법절차와 국제법을 준수하며, 다른 나라의 내부문제에 간섭하지 말아야 한다.

제4조. 이 규정은 경제무역참사부와 경제협조단, 경제실무대표단이 대외경제사업과 관련있는 기관, 기업소, 단체의 일군에게 적용한다.

제5조. 이 규정은 다른 나라에 나가 활동하는 경제무역참사부와 경제협조단, 경제실무대표단의 대외경제사업절차를 규제한다.

제2장. 경제무역 참사부

제6조. 경제무역참사부는 국가외교대표부 책임자의 통일적인 지휘 밑에 자기의 공인과 명판을 가지고 주재국 정부 또는 비정부기구와 대외경제계약을 진행하여야 한다.

경제무역참사부에는 경제무역참사와 경제무역대표부가 포함된다.

제7조. 경제무역참사부는 정령의 위임에 따라 그를 대표하여 주재국과의 경제무역협정, 의정 같은 경제조약을 맺기 위한 교섭과 교제 및 리행을 추진하는 사업을 하여야 한다.

제8조. 경제무역참사부는 주재국의 정부, 비정부기구, 민간단체로부터 자금 및 대부자금, 협조물자를 들여오는 사업을 바로하여야 한다.

제9조. 경제무역참사부는 주재국의 경제정책과 법, 국제경제협정 및 국제경제기구 가입, 환차제 및 시장경제변동 같은 경제무역자료를 정상적으로 조사하여 대외경제성(이 아래에 놓은 중앙대외경제지도기관과 함께)에 보고하여야 한다.

제10조. 경제무역참사부는 대외 홈페이지(조선의 무역)를 통하여 주재국에 우리 나라의 경제법률과 정책과 규정에서 정한 회사, 수출품을 비롯한 무역자료, 경제무역분야에서 이룩한 성과를 소개·선전하여야 한다.

제11조. 경제무역참사부는 주재국에서 우리 나라의 기관, 기업소, 단체가 상품전람회, 무역 및 투자상담회 같은 각종 협의조치에 참가하도록 하여 인민경제 발전에 필요한 무역통로를 더 많이 개척하여야 한다.

제12조. 경제무역참사부는 나라의 경제발전과 인민생활향상에 절실히 필요한 통상자료를 들여오기 위한 사업을 장악하여야 한다.

가치있는 통상자료를 들여온 경제무역참사부의 일군은 통상자료의 실험 및 도입결과에 따라 해당한 상금을 받을 수 있다.

룽성자료의 심의, 평가절차와 방법은 중앙과학기술행정지도관리기관이 정한 데 따른다.

제13조. 경제무역참사부는 주재국에서 가공무역품, 기술무역, 봉사무역, 되거래무역, 중계무역 같은 무역방식으로 무역을 진행하여 학술, 학과, 대외건설, 기술교류 같은 경제협조의 방식으로도 경제계를 하려는 대상을 찾아 우리 나라 기관, 기업소, 단체와 련계를 맺어줄 수 있다.

제14조. 경제무역참사부는 우리 나라의 기관, 기업소, 단체와 주재국의 회사 사이에 경제무역거래를 실현시켜주고 받은 료금(사례금 포함)을 경비예산자금으로 적립하고 써야 한다.

제15조. 경제무역참사부는 경제무역거래를 실현시켰을 경우, 우리 나라의 기관, 기업소, 단체로부터 다음과 같이 료금을 받을 수 있다.

1. 수출품의 판로를 개척하여 실현시켜주었을 경우 : 건당 수출품판매액의 규모에 따라 2~5%
2. 대외건설, 합영, 합작, 기술협조와 같은 대상을 실현시켜주었을 경우 : 대상건당 우리측 리윤몫 규모에 따라 배율 2~5%
3. 공장, 기업소에 원료, 자재를 대주고 가공무역을 실현시켰을 경우 : 건당 락득금의 규모에 따라 1~3%

제16조. 경제무역참사부는 경제협조단 및 경제실무대표단의 파견 및 대표단초청과 관련한 의뢰서가 제기되는 경우 목적과 실용성을 따져본 다음 국가외교대표부 책임자의 승인을 받아 국가외교대표부 명의로 중앙대외사업지도기관에 보내주어야 한다.

제17조. 경제무역참사부는 비밀보장체계를 엄격히 세워 대외경제사업과정에 비밀이 류설되지 않도록 하여야 한다.

제18조. 경제무역참사부는 주재국에 있는 경제협조단, 경제실무대표단의 대외경제사업을 장악·지도하여야 한다.

제19조. 경제무역참사부는 경제협조단, 경제실무대표단의 사업평가보고서와 대외경제사업경형을 제때에 중앙대외경제지도기관에 보고하여야 한다.

제3장. 경제협조단, 경제실무대표단

제20조. 경제협조단, 경제실무대표단은 경제무역참사부의 지도 밑에 대외경제사업을 하여야 한다.

제21조. 경제협조단은 해당 기관, 기업소, 단체에서 받은 과업과 대외경제사업과정에 제기되는 문제를 국가외교대표부 책임자와 경제무역참사부에 보고하고 그 집행대책과 방도를 협의하여 처리하여야 한다.

제22조. 경제협조단은 국가관계에 영향을 미칠 수 있는 문제가 제기되었을 경우 국가외교대표부 책임자, 경제무역참사부와 협의하고 국가외교대표부를 통하여 중앙대외사업지도기관에 보고하여야 한다.

제23조. 경제협조단은 경제무역거래를 실현하기 위하여 지방출장을 조직하려 할 경우 경제무역참사부의 협의와 국가외교대표부 책임자의 승인을 받으며, 제3국·조국출장을 조직하려는 경우에는 경제무역참사부와 협의하고 국가외교대표부를 통하여 중앙대외사업지도기관에 제기하고 승인을 받아야 한다.

제24조. 경제협조단은 주재국의 회사와 무역거래, 합영, 합작, 경제기술협조를 위한 계약의 체결, 상품전람회조직 같은 문제가 제기되었을 경우 국가외교대표부 책임자, 경제무역참사부와 협의한 다음 처리하여야 한다.

제25조. 우리 나라의 기관, 기업소, 단체는 대외경제계약의 체결, 전람회 참가, 강습, 실습, 관관 같은 대외경제사업을 목적으로 다른 나라에 경제실무대표단을 파견할 수 있다.

제26조. 경제실무대표단은 주재국에서 대외경제사업을 다음과 같이 하여야 한다.

1. 해당 나라에 도착하는 즉시 대표단사업계획을 국가외교대표부 책임자와 경제무역참사부에 보고하여야 한다.
2. 대외경제사업과정에 제기되는 문제와 대책안을 조국에 보고하려 할 경우 경제무역참사부와 협의하고 국가외교대표부를 통하여 보고하며 결론을 받아 처리하여야 한다.
3. 대표단사업계획에 없는 대외면담, 참관, 관람 같은 의례사업, 지방출장이 예정되었을 경우 경제무역참사부를 통하여 국가외교대표부 책임자의 승인을 받아야 한다.
4. 대외경제계약은 국가의 대외경제정책과 법규범의 요구에 맞게 체결하여야 한다.
5. 주재국의 경제실태 및 상품가격조사, 판르개척을 위한 사업을 책임적으로 하여야 한다.
6. 대표단사업이 끝났을 경우 대표단사업 총화보고서를 경제무역참사부를 통하여 국가외교대표부에 제기하며 대표부사업평가서를 받아야 한다.

제4장. 지도통제

제27조. 경제무역참사부와 경제협조단, 경제실무대표단의 대외경제사업에 대한 내각의 통일적 지도 밑에 중앙대외경제지도기관이 한다.

제28조. 중앙대외경제지도기관은 경제무역참사부와 경제협조단, 경제실무대표단의 대외경제사업을 정상적으로 장악하고 해당한 대책을 세워야 한다.

제29조. 이 규정을 위반하였을 경우 엄중성 정도에 따라 기관, 기업소, 단체의 책임있는 일군은 해당한 행정적 책임을 진다.

(주): 주체110(2021)년 10월 19일 내각결정 123호로 수정보충됨

Source: Daily NK, https://www.dailynk.com/20250502-1/

APPENDIX 4B. REGULATIONS ON EXTERNAL ECONOMIC PROJECTS (ENGLISH TRANSLATION)

Regulations on Foreign Economic Activities of the Economic and Trade Counselor's Office, Economic Cooperation Units, and Economic Delegation

Adopted by Cabinet Decision No. 49 on July 1, Juche 109 (2020)

Respected Comrade Kim Jong Un stated the following:

"In the foreign economic sector, we must firmly base ourselves on the principle of building an independent national economy and actively promote diverse and proactive foreign economic cooperation, technology exchange, and trade activities in ways that strengthen our economic foundation and supplement areas where exchange is truly beneficial."

Chapter 1
General Provisions

Article 1. These regulations are enacted to establish strict systems and order in the foreign economic activities of the Economic and Trade Counselor's Office, Economic Cooperation Units, and Economic

Delegations, and to develop and expand foreign economic cooperation, technology exchange, and trade in a diverse and proactive manner, thereby contributing to the strengthening of economic ties and exchanges with other countries.

Article 2. The definitions of terms used in these regulations are as follows:

1. Economic and Trade Counselor's Office refers to the foreign economic affairs department within our country's overseas diplomatic missions (including concurrent posts), which carries out economic diplomacy to actively promote exchange and cooperation in foreign economic activities. It oversees and directs the foreign economic work of Economic Cooperation Units and Economic Delegations in the host country.
2. Economic Cooperation Unit refers to an entity stationed abroad for economic activities with the goal of generating economic benefit. These include branches or representative offices of trading companies (including general trading companies), foreign-invested enterprises, overseas technical cooperation organizations, and foreign construction companies.
3. Economic Delegation refers to a delegation dispatched to another country to engage in foreign economic contracts, participate in exhibitions, conduct inspections, training, technical exchanges, and similar foreign economic activities.

Article 3. The Economic and Trade Counselor's Office, Economic Cooperation Units, and Economic Delegations shall carry out foreign economic activities in accordance with the following principles and requirements:

1. They must resolutely defend the economic authority of the Great Leader, the Great General, and the Respected Comrade Kim Jong Un, and actively pursue foreign economic activities based on that authority.
2. They must widely publicize and promote the greatness of the

Great Leader, the Great General, and the Respected Comrade Kim Jong Un.
3. They must firmly establish the unified leadership system of the Respected Comrade Kim Jong Un.
4. They must strictly uphold the principle of self-reliance in foreign economic activities and resolutely defend and protect the interests of the state and the people.
5. They must carry out foreign economic activities under the unified direction of the head of the state's diplomatic mission, and not arbitrarily handle issues that fall outside of their assigned authority and functions.
6. They must heighten revolutionary vigilance in foreign economic activities and strictly safeguard state secrets.
7. They must abide by the laws and procedures of the host country and international law, and not interfere in the internal affairs of other countries.

Article 4. These regulations apply to the personnel of institutions, enterprises, and organizations related to foreign economic activities conducted by the Economic and Trade Counselor's Office, Economic Cooperation Units, and Economic Delegations.

Article 5. These regulations govern the procedures for foreign economic activities carried out abroad by the Economic and Trade Counselor's Office, Economic Cooperation Units, and Economic Delegations.

Chapter 2
Economic and Trade Counselor's Office

Article 6. The Economic and Trade Counselor's Office shall conduct foreign economic agreements with the government or non-governmental organizations of the host country under the unified guidance of the head of the state's diplomatic mission, bearing official recognition and credentials.

The Economic and Trade Counselor's Office includes both Economic and Trade Counselors and Economic and Trade Representative Offices.

Article 7. The Economic and Trade Counselor's Office shall, under the mandate of the state, represent the country in negotiating, communicating, and implementing economic treaties such as trade and economic cooperation agreements and protocols with the host country.

Article 8. The Economic and Trade Counselor's Office shall be responsible for the work of securing funds, loans, and cooperative materials from the host country's government, non-governmental organizations, and private entities.

Article 9. The Economic and Trade Counselor's Office shall regularly investigate economic and trade data such as the host country's economic policies and laws, international economic agreements, accession to international economic organizations, foreign exchange systems, and market economy fluctuations, and report the findings to the Ministry of External Economic Relations (including the Central External Economic Guidance Body under its authority).

Article 10. The Economic and Trade Counselor's Office shall, through the foreign trade website (*DPRK Foreign Trade*), publicize in the host country the companies, export products, and achievements in the field of economic and trade activities that are stipulated under the laws, policies, and regulations of the DPRK.

Article 11. The Economic and Trade Counselor's Office shall encourage institutions, enterprises, and organizations from the DPRK to participate in exhibitions, trade and investment consultations, and other coordination events in the host country, thereby opening up more trade channels essential for the development of the people's economy.

Article 12. The Economic and Trade Counselor's Office shall be responsible for managing activities aimed at importing trade-related resources and materials essential to the country's economic development and the improvement of people's livelihoods.

Personnel of the Counselor's Office who successfully bring in valuable trade materials may receive awards based on the results of testing and implementation.

The review, evaluation procedures, and methods regarding *rungseong* materials (룽성자료) shall follow the standards set by the Central Scientific and Technological Administration and Management Agency.

Article 13. The Economic and Trade Counselor's Office may facilitate trade using various methods such as processing trade, technology trade, service trade, counter-trade, and intermediary trade in the host country. It may also identify parties interested in economic cooperation through academic exchange, joint research, overseas construction, or technology transfer, and link them with relevant institutions, enterprises, and organizations in the DPRK.

Article 14. The Economic and Trade Counselor's Office shall manage fees (including honoraria) received for facilitating economic and trade transactions between DPRK institutions, enterprises, or organizations and companies in the host country, by properly depositing and using them as part of the official budget.

Article 15. When the Economic and Trade Counselor's Office facilitates a trade transaction, it may receive the following fees from the involved DPRK institutions, enterprises, or organizations:

1. For facilitating the sale of export products: 2–5% based on the transaction amount.
2. For facilitating contracts related to overseas construction, joint ventures, or technology cooperation: 2–5% based on the DPRK's profit share.
3. For supplying raw materials to factories and enterprises for processing trade: 1–3% based on the revenue earned per transaction.

Article 16. When a request is submitted for the dispatch or invitation of Economic Cooperation Units or Economic Delegations, the Counselor's Office shall review the purpose and practical viability of the request, obtain approval from the Head of the DPRK Diplomatic Mission, and submit the request to the Central External Affairs Guidance Body in the name of the diplomatic mission.

Article 17. The Economic and Trade Counselor's Office shall establish a strict confidentiality system to ensure that state secrets are not leaked during the course of foreign economic activities.

Article 18. The Economic and Trade Counselor's Office shall oversee and guide the foreign economic activities of Economic Cooperation Units and Economic Delegations operating in the host country.

Article 19. The Economic and Trade Counselor's Office shall report business evaluation reports from Economic Cooperation Units and Economic Delegations, as well as foreign economic activity updates, to the Central External Economic Guidance Body in a timely manner.

Chapter 3
Economic Cooperation Units and Economic Delegations

Article 20. Economic Cooperation Units and Economic Delegations shall carry out foreign economic activities under the guidance of the Economic and Trade Counselor's Office.

Article 21. Economic Cooperation Units must report tasks received from relevant institutions, enterprises, or organizations, as well as any issues arising in the course of foreign economic activities, to the Head of the DPRK Diplomatic Mission and the Economic and Trade Counselor's Office. They must consult on countermeasures and implementation plans accordingly.

Article 22. If issues arise that may affect state relations, the Economic Cooperation Unit must consult with the Head of the Diplomatic Mission and the Economic and Trade Counselor's Office and report the matter to the Central External Affairs Guidance Body via the Diplomatic Mission.

Article 23. If the Economic Cooperation Unit intends to arrange domestic travel for the purpose of executing trade transactions, it must obtain approval from the Head of the Diplomatic Mission through consultation with the Counselor's Office.

For third-country or return visits to the DPRK, consultation must take place with the Counselor's Office and approval must be obtained through the diplomatic mission and submitted to the Central External Affairs Guidance Body.

Article 24. If a company in the host country proposes trade transactions, joint ventures, partnerships, or economic-technical cooperation contracts, or requests organization of trade exhibitions, the Economic Cooperation Unit must consult with the Counselor's Office and the Head of the Diplomatic Mission and process the matter accordingly.

Article 25. DPRK institutions, enterprises, and organizations may dispatch Economic Delegations to other countries for purposes such as foreign economic contract signing, participation in exhibitions, training, technical internships, or field inspections.

Article 26. Economic Delegations shall carry out the following duties in the host country:

1. Upon arrival, they must immediately report their delegation activity plan to the Head of the Diplomatic Mission and the Economic and Trade Counselor's Office.
2. If issues arise during foreign economic activities that require reporting and proposing countermeasures to the home country, they must consult with the Counselor's Office and report through the Diplomatic Mission and act based on conclusions received.
3. If any unplanned events such as diplomatic meetings, site visits, or ceremonies arise, or domestic travel is proposed outside the delegation plan, approval must be obtained through the Counselor's Office from the Head of the Diplomatic Mission.
4. Foreign economic contracts must be signed in accordance with the country's foreign economic policies and legal norms.

5. Economic Delegations must responsibly carry out investigations into the host country's economic situation, product price surveys, and market development.
6. Upon completion of the delegation's activities, they must submit a final activity report to the Economic and Trade Counselor's Office, which will forward it to the Diplomatic Mission. A formal activity evaluation must also be received.

Chapter 4
Guidance and Control

Article 27. The Central External Economic Guidance Body shall be responsible for overseeing the foreign economic activities of the Economic and Trade Counselor's Office, Economic Cooperation Units, and Economic Delegations under the unified guidance of the Cabinet.

Article 28. The Central External Economic Guidance Body shall monitor the foreign economic activities of the Economic and Trade Counselor's Office, Economic Cooperation Units, and Economic Delegations in a regular and systematic manner and shall establish appropriate countermeasures as needed.

Article 29. In cases of violation of these regulations, responsible officials from the relevant institutions, enterprises, or organizations shall bear administrative responsibility in proportion to the severity of the infraction.

(Note): Revised and supplemented by Cabinet Decision No. 123 on October 19, Juche 110 (2021)

Source: Translated from Appendix 4a, original text in Korean from Daily NK, https://www.dailynk.com/20250502-1/

LIST OF PUBLICATIONS BY NKDB

Title	Author(s)	Year of Publication	Price
▶ **Annual Publications**			
White Paper on North Korean Human Rights (Korean)			
2007 북한인권통계백서	윤여상 외	2007	₩20,000
2008 북한인권백서	북한인권기록보존소 윤여상 외	2008	₩20,000
2009 북한인권백서	북한인권기록보존소 윤여상 외	2009	₩20,000
2010 북한인권백서	북한인권기록보존소 윤여상 외	2010	₩20,000
2011 북한인권백서	북한인권기록보존소 윤여상 외	2011	₩30,000
2012 북한인권백서	북한인권기록보존소 윤여상 외	2012	₩30,000
2013 북한인권백서	북한인권기록보존소 윤여상 외	2013	₩30,000
2014 북한인권백서	북한인권기록보존소 윤여상 외	2014	₩30,000

	2015 북한인권백서	북한인권기록보존소 윤여상 외	2015	₩30,000
	2016 북한인권백서	북한인권기록보존소 안현민 외	2016	₩30,000
	2017 북한인권백서	북한인권기록보존소 최선영 외	2017	₩30,000
	2018 북한인권백서	북한인권기록보존소 임순희 외	2018	₩30,000
	2019 북한인권백서	북한인권기록보존소 임순희 외	2019	₩30,000
	2020 북한인권백서	북한인권기록보존소 안현민 외	2020	₩30,000
	2024 북한인권백서	북한인권기록보존소 윤여상 외	2024	₩30,000

White Paper on North Korean Human Rights (English)

	White Paper on North Korean Human Rights Statistics 2007	북한인권기록보존소 윤여상 외	2008	₩20,000
	White Paper on North Korean Human Rights 2008	북한인권기록보존소 윤여상 외	2008	₩20,000
	White Paper on North Korean Human Rights 2009	북한인권기록보존소 윤여상 외	2009	₩20,000
	White Paper on North Korean Human Rights 2010	북한인권기록보존소 윤여상 외	2010	₩20,000
	White Paper on North Korean Human Rights 2011	북한인권기록보존소 윤여상 외	2011	₩30,000
	White Paper on North Korean Human Rights 2012	북한인권기록보존소 윤여상 외	2012	₩30,000
	White Paper on North Korean Human Rights 2013	북한인권기록보존소 윤여상 외	2013	₩30,000
	White Paper on North Korean Human Rights 2014	북한인권기록보존소 윤여상 외	2014	₩30,000
	White Paper on North Korean Human Rights 2015	북한인권기록보존소 윤여상 외	2015	₩30,000

	White Paper on North Korean Human Rights 2016	북한인권기록보존소 윤여상 외	2016	₩30,000
	White Paper on North Korean Human Rights 2017	북한인권기록보존소 최선영 외	2018	₩30,000
	White Paper on North Korean Human Rights 2018	북한인권기록보존소 임순희 외	2019	₩30,000
	White Paper on North Korean Human Rights 2019	북한인권기록보존소 임순희 외	2019	₩30,000
	White Paper on North Korean Human Rights 2020	북한인권기록보존소 안현민 외	2020	₩30,000

White Paper on Religious Freedom in North Korea (Korean)

	2008 북한종교자유백서	윤여상, 한선영	2008	₩10,000
	2009 북한종교자유백서	윤여상, 한선영	2009	₩10,000
	2010 북한종교자유백서	윤여상, 한선영	2010	₩10,000

	2011 북한종교자유백서	윤여상, 한선영, 윤중근	2012	₩10,000
	2012 북한종교자유백서	윤여상, 한선영, 장은실	2013	₩20,000
	2013 북한종교자유백서	윤여상, 정재호, 안현민	2013	₩20,000
	2014 북한종교자유백서	윤여상, 정재호, 안현민	2014	₩20,000
	2015 북한종교자유백서	윤여상, 정재호, 안현민	2015	₩20,000
	2016 북한종교자유백서	정재호, 안현민, 윤여상	2016	₩20,000
	2017 북한종교자유백서	안현민, 윤여상, 정재호	2017	₩20,000
	2018 북한종교자유백서	안현민, 윤여상, 정재호	2018	₩20,000
	2019 북한종교자유백서	안현민, 윤여상, 정재호	2019	₩20,000

	2020 북한종교자유백서	안현민, 윤여상, 정재호	2020	₩20,000
	2024 북한종교자유백서	양수영, 김유니크	2025	₩20,000

White Paper on Religious Freedom in North Korea (English)

	White Paper on Religious Freedom in North Korea 2009	윤여상, 한선영, 장은실	2009	₩10,000
	Religious Freedom in North Korea 2012	윤여상, 한선영, 장은실, 최선영	2013	₩10,000
	White Paper on Religious Freedom in North Korea 2013	윤여상, 정재호, 안현민	2013	₩20,000
	White Paper on Religious Freedom in North Korea 2014	윤여상, 정재호, 안현민	2014	₩20,000
	White Paper on Religious Freedom in North Korea 2015	윤여상, 정재호, 안현민	2015	₩20,000
	White Paper on Religious Freedom in North Korea 2016	정재호, 안현민, 윤여상	2016	₩20,000

	White Paper on Religious Freedom in North Korea 2017	안현민, 윤여상, 정재호	2018	₩20,000
	White Paper on Religious Freedom in North Korea 2018	안현민, 윤여상, 정재호	2019	₩20,000

Trends in Economic Activities of North Korean Escapees (Korean)

	2006 북한이탈주민 경제활동 동향 - 취업,실업,소득	엄홍석, 윤여상, 허선행	2007	₩5,000
	2007 북한이탈주민 경제활동 동향 - 취업,실업,소득	윤여상, 허선행	2008	₩5,000
	2008 북한이탈주민 경제활동 동향 - 취업,실업,소득	북한인권정보센터	2009	₩5,000
	2009 북한이탈주민 경제활동 동향 - 취업,실업,소득	허선행, 임순희	2010	₩5,000
	2010 북한이탈주민 경제활동 동향 - 취업,실업,소득	서윤환, 이용화	2011	₩10,000
	2011 북한이탈주민 경제활동 동향 - 취업,실업,소득	서윤환, 이용화	2012	₩10,000

	제목	저자	발행년도	가격
	2012 북한이탈주민 경제활동 동향 - 취업,실업,소득	서윤환, 신효선	2013	₩10,000
	2013 북한이탈주민 경제활동 동향 - 취업,실업,소득	서윤환, 신효선, 박성철	2014	₩12,000
	2014 북한이탈주민 경제활동 동향 - 취업,실업,소득	임순희, 안현민	2015	₩12,000
	2015 북한이탈주민 경제사회통합 실태	윤여상, 임순희	2016	₩17,000
	2016 북한이탈주민 경제사회통합 실태	임순희, 윤인진, 양진아	2017	₩17,000
	2017 북한이탈주민 경제사회통합 실태	임순희, 윤인진, 김슬기	2018	₩17,000
	-2018 북한이탈주민 경제사회통합 실태	임순희, 김석창	2019	₩17,000
	2019 북한이탈주민 경제사회통합 실태	안현민, 김성남	2019	₩17,000
	2020 북한이탈주민 경제사회통합 실태	김성남, 김소원	2020	₩17,000

	2021 북한이탈주민 경제사회통합 실태	임순희, 김가영, 성민주	2021	₩17,000
	2022 북한이탈주민 경제사회통합 실태	임순희, 성민주, 이경현	2022	₩17,000
	2023 북한이탈주민 경제사회통합 실태	임순희, 성민주, 이승엽	2023	₩17,000

Trends in Economic Activities of North Korean Esacpees (English)

	2009/2010 Trends in Economic Activities of North Korean Defectors	허선행, 임순희, 서윤환, 이용화	2011	₩15,000
	2018 Social and Economic Integration of North Korean Defectors in South Korea	임순희, 김석창	2019	₩17,000

South Koreans' Perception of North Korean Human Rights (Korean)

	북한인권에 대한 국민 인식 조사	윤여상, 임순희	2014	₩15,000
	2015 북한인권에 대한 국민 인식 조사	윤여상, 임순희	2015	₩15,000
	2016 북한인권에 대한 국민 인식 조사	윤여상, 임순희	2016	₩15,000

	2017 북한인권에 대한 국민 인식 조사	임순희	2018	₩10,000
	2018 북한인권에 대한 국민 인식 조사	윤여상, 임순희	2019	₩10,000
	2019 북한인권에 대한 국민 인식 조사	윤여상, 임순희	2019	₩10,000
	2020 북한인권에 대한 국민 인식 조사	윤여상, 임순희	2020	₩15,000
	2021 북한인권에 대한 국민 인식 조사	윤여상, 임순희, 지성호	2021	Not for sale
	2022 북한인권에 대한 국민 인식 조사	윤여상, 임순희, 윤기웅	2022	Not for sale
	2023 북한인권에 대한 국민 인식 조사	윤여상, 서보배	2023	₩20,000
	2024 북한인권에 대한 국민 인식 조사	임순희, 이승엽	2024	₩20,000

▶ **Special Reports**

	Are They Telling Us the Truth?	Hiroshi Kato, 김상헌, 윤여상, Tim Peters	2003	¥2,500
	북한 정치범수용소 완전통제구역 세상밖으로 나오다	신동혁	2007	₩13,000
	서독 잘쯔기터 인권침해 중앙기록보존소	Heiner Sauer, Hans-Otto Plumeyer(이건호 譯)	2008	₩12,000
	북한 인권 문헌 분석	윤여상 외	2008	₩20,000
	국군포로 문제의 종합적 이해	오경섭, 윤여상, 허선행	2008	₩15,000
	북한의 반인도적 범죄에 대한 국제사회의 긴급대응	세계기독연대 (북한인권정보센터 譯)	2011	₩15,000
	북한 정치범수용소의 운영체계와 인권실태	윤여상, 이자은, 한선영	2011	₩30,000
	북한 구금시설 운영체계와 인권실태	윤여상, 구현자, 김인성, 이지현	2011	₩25,000

	Political Prison Camps in North Korea Today	윤여상, 이자은, 한선영	2011	$20
	Prisoners in North Korea Today	윤여상, 구현자, 김인성, 이지현	2011	$20
	북한인권사건리포트: VICTIMS' VOICES 제1권	북한인권기록보존소	2013	Not for sale
	北韓人權事件レポート: VICTIMS' VOICES 第1卷	북한인권정보센터	2013	Not for sale
	North Korean Human Rights Case Report : VICTIMS' VOICES Volume I	북한인권정보센터	2013	Not for sale
	북한인권사건리포트: VICTIMS' VOICES 제2권	북한인권정보센터	2013	Not for sale
	北韓人權事件レポート: VICTIMS' VOICES 第2卷	북한인권정보센터	2013	Not for sale
	North Korean Human Rights Case Report : VICTIMS'VOICES Volume II	북한인권정보센터	2013	Not for sale
	중국의 탈북자 강제송환과 인권실태	윤여상, 박성철, 임순희	2013	₩20,000

	Title	Author	Year	Price
	North Korean Defectors in China - Forced Repatriation and Human Rights Violations -	윤여상, 박성철, 임순희	2014	$20
	Nordkoreanischer Menschenrechtsfallbericht VICTIMS' VOICES	북한인권정보센터	2014	$20
	Cahiers d'observations des droits de l'Homme en Corée du Nord VICTIMS'VOICES	북한인권정보센터	2014	$20
	북한 해외 노동자 현황과 인권실태	윤여상, 이승주	2015	₩17,000
	Human rights and North Korea's Overseas Laborers: Dilemmas and Policy Challenges	윤여상, 이승주	2015	₩17,000
	북한 구금시설 총서: 북한 구금시설 현황과 개선방안	북한인권정보센터	2016	₩10,000
	북한 구금시설 총서I:개천 1호 교화소	이승주	2016	₩10,000
	북한 구금시설 총서I:강동 4호 교화소	유혜정	2016	₩7,000
	북한 구금시설 총서I:함흥 9호 교화소	안현민	2016	₩10,000

	북한 구금시설 총서I:증산 11호 교화소	임순희	2016	₩10,000
	북한 구금시설 총서I:전거리 12호 교화소	김인성	2016	₩10,000
	북한 구금시설 총서I:오로 22호 교화소	서윤환	2016	₩7,000
	2014 유엔 북한인권조사위원회(COI) 보고서 발간 이후 북한 인권 평가보고서 : 북한인권정보센터의 DB 분석을 중심으로	북한인권정보센터	2016	Not for sale
	An Evaluation Report of the North Korean Human Rights Situation after the 2014 UN Commission on Inquiry Report-Based on an Analysis of NKDB's Database	북한인권정보센터	2016	Not for sale
	북한 밖의 북한	윤여상, 이승주	2016	₩20,000
	북한 정치범수용소 근무자, 수감자 및 실종자 인명사전	북한인권정보센터	2016	Not for sale
	North Korean Political Prison Camps A Catalogue of Political Prison Camp Staff, Detainees, and Victims of Enforced Disappearance	북한인권정보센터	2016	Not for sale

	Title	Author	Year	Price
	北朝鮮政治犯収容所 勤務者、収監者および失踪者 人名事典	북한인권정보센터	2016	Not for sale
	Campos de Concentración para Prisioneros Políticos Norcoreanos	북한인권정보센터	2016	Not for sale
	러시아 지역 북한 노동자의 근로와 인권 실태	박찬홍	2016	₩20,000
	North Korean Overseas Laborers in Russia	박찬홍	2016	₩20,000
	The North Korea outside the North Korean State	Yoon Yeo-sang, Lee Seung Ju	2017	$20
	유엔인권이사회 제1차 보편적 정례검토와 북한	최선영, 양진아, 이나경, 송한나	2017	₩20,000
	The UN Universal Periodic Review and the DPRK	최선영, 양진아, 이나경, 송한나	2017	$20
	군복 입은 수감자 북한군 인권 실태 보고서	김인성, 안현민, 송한나	2018	₩15,000
	북한 여성 생리 관련 실태-이런 것은 부끄러운 것으로 알아요	안현민, 심진아	2018	Not for sale

	The State of Menstrual Health of North Korean Women - "Periods are a shameful thing in North Korea"	안현민, 심진아	2018	Not for sale
	두 번째 기회: 제2차 보편적 정례검토 권고사항의 수용 및 실행에 대한 모니터링	송한나	2019	₩20,000
	UN 지속가능발전목표(SDGs)와 인권의 결합 - SDG 목표3: 건강권을 중심으로	임순희	2019	Not for sale
	UN Sustainable Development Goals and Human Rights - SDG 3: The Right to Health in North Korea	임순희	2019	Not for sale
	스토리북 : 나의 세 번째 집	김동주	2019	Not for sale
	스토리북 : 다시 찾은 인생길	김주희	2019	Not for sale
	스토리북 : 푸르른 삼각산아	박용석	2019	Not for sale
	2020 초기 정착 생활 길라잡이	정착지원본부	2020	Not for sale

	북한 사회주의 대가정의 노동 정책과 세포 가정의 균열: 성역할의 탈가부장적 재구성의 강제와 부부갈등	최선영	2020	Not for sale
	스토리북 : 내 마음의 보물섬	한나라	2020	Not for sale
	스토리북 : 까만 가로등	정 진	2020	Not for sale
	북한의 SDGs와 인권 연계 프로젝트	북한인권정보센터	2021	Not for sale
	The Human Rights Guide to DPRK's SDGs	북한인권정보센터	2021	Not for sale
	Democratic People's Republic of Korea 2021 Progress Report on the Implementation of the Sustainable Development Goals	Chad Miller, Hanna Song	2021	Not for sale
	Prisoners in Military Uniform: Human Rights in the North Korean Military	김인성, 안현민, 송한나, 이승주	2022	$20
	북한의 난제: 인권과 핵안보의 균형	로버트 킹, 신기욱 편집, 북한인권정보센터 옮김	2022	₩30,000

	파놉티콘 사회 속 감시자들: 북한 비사회주의 그루빠 인권침해 실태 및 가해 매커니즘 중심으로	서보배, 성민주, 양수영	2023	Not for sale
	North Korea's Non-Socialist Group: Inspections, Crackdowns and Human Rights Violations in a Panoptic Society	Bobae Su, Minju Sung, Suyoung Yang	2023	Not for sale
	닫힌 문 너머: 보위부와 안전부의 명령체계 중심으로	양수영, 성민주, 송한나	2023	₩15,000
	Behind Closed Doors: Mapping the System of Command in the Ministry of State & Social Security	Suyoung Yang, Minju Sung, Hanna Song	2023	$12
	스토리북 : 마지막 항해	이재근	2023	Not for sale
	스토리북 : 인생의 갈림길	유상혁	2023	Not for sale
	스토리북 : 삶의 굴곡 한가운데	박순실	2023	Not for sale

	도록 : 낯선말_표현의 그림자	북한인권정보센터 북한인권박물관건립 추진위원회	2024	Not for sale
	스토리북 : 어둠속의 불덩어리	이상철	2024	Not for sale
	스토리북 : 압록강 저 너머	이동일	2024	Not for sale
	스토리북 : 잊혀진 70년, 우리는 그곳에 있었다	유영복	2024	Not for sale
	스토리북 : 감나무밭, 작은 집	남상식	2024	Not for sale
	스토리북 : 두승산 밑 골짜기	한민석	2024	Not for sale
	세 번째 기회 : 북한 제3차 보편적 정례검토 실행에 대하여	송한나, 옥주연, 윤여상	2024	₩20,000

	Third Time's a Charm? : North Korea's Implementation of Its Recommendations during its Third Universal Periodic Review	Hanna Song, Juyeon Ok, Yeosang Yoon	2024	$20
	스토리북 : 고향으로 향하는 발자국	노만식	2024	Not for sale
	스토리북 : 흙먼지 길을 지나 별빛 아래로	최상철	2024	Not for sale
	스토리북 : 남북의 끝마을	박명일	2024	Not for sale